*Im Kwon-Taek*

# IM KWON-TAEK
*Photography by Myong-hwa Chung*

# Im Kwon-Taek

## THE MAKING OF A KOREAN NATIONAL CINEMA

EDITED BY DAVID E. JAMES AND KYUNG HYUN KIM

WAYNE STATE UNIVERSITY PRESS   DETROIT

CONTEMPORARY APPROACHES TO FILM AND TELEVISION SERIES

*A complete listing of the books in this series
can be found online at http://wsupress.wayne.edu.*

GENERAL EDITOR
Barry Keith Grant
Brock University

ADVISORY EDITORS

Patricia B. Erens
Dominican University

Lucy Fischer
University of Pittsburgh

Anna McCarthy
New York University

Peter Lehman
Arizona State University

Caren J. Deming
University of Arizona

Robert J. Burgoyne
Wayne State University

Tom Gunning
University of Chicago

Peter X. Feng
University of Delaware

*Designed by Chang Jae Lee*

Manufactured in the
United States of America.

08  07  06  05  04        6  5  4  3  2

**Library of Congress Cataloging-in-Publication Data**

Im Kwon-taek : the making of a Korean national
cinema / edited by David James and Kyung Hyun Kim.
p. cm. — (Contemporary film and television)
Includes bibliographical references and index.
ISBN 0-8143-2868-7 (alk. paper) — ISBN 0-8143-2869-5 (pbk. : alk. paper)
1. Im, Kwæon-t'aek—Criticism and interpretation.   I. James,
David E., date   II. Kim, Kyung Hyun, date   III. Series.
PN1998.3.I42 I47 2002
791.43'0233'092—dc21
2001005380

# Contents

# Acknowledgments

A s detailed in the preface below, this collection of essays originated in a festival of the films of Im Kwon-Taek and a conference about them held concurrently at the University of Southern California in 1996. We would like to thank the many people and agencies who contributed to these events, including the School of Cinema-Television, USC; the East Asian Studies Center, USC; the Korean Studies Institute, USC; the Asian Pacific Media Center, USC; the Korea Foundation; the Korean Cultural Center, Los Angeles, its then director, Mr. Hong Sok Lee, and Consul Jin Young Woo; the Korean National Film Archive; and the Korean Ministry of Culture and Sports. Ms. Hyun-Ock Im did much of the difficult and complicated coordination of these events, and without her vision and industry, the festival would not have been possible. We also thank Ms. In Young Nam for her assistance during the festival.

The Korean Cultural Center very generously supported the preparation of this manuscript, and we are deeply grateful to Director Jong-Moon Park and Consul Kyu Hak Choi. Additional research and manuscript preparation work were supported by the Association for Asian

Studies Northeast Asia Council and the Center for Humanities at the University of California at Irvine. The Korean Film Archive supplied us with many of the illustrations. Mr. Chung Sung-Ill greatly helped us with resources in Korea and advice on many matters. We also thank Chŏng To-hwan of the Hwachon Film Studio, Park Chŏng-ch'an of the Shinhan Film Studio, and Yi Tae-wŏn of the Taehung Film Studio for permission to reproduce stills from the films of Im Kwon-Taek: all rights are reserved.

The actress Ms. Kang Su-yŏn, the cinematographer Mr. Chŏng Il-sŏng, and the actor Mr. An Sŏng-gi gave us very valuable insights into Im Kwon-Taek's films.

We would especially like to thank Jane Hoehner, Jennifer Backer, and Kathryn Wildfong, our editors at the Wayne State University Press, for their guidance and unstinting support for this project. Sandra Williamson's creative and sensitive copyediting considerably improved the manuscript; thanks also to Han Ju Kwak and Kelly Jeong for additional proofreading and for standardizing the romanization of Korean words according to the McCune-Reischauer system. (The Korean government recently certified a different system of romanization, but the McCune-Reischauer one is presently the norm in academic publishing.)

Finally, we would like to thank director Im Kwon-Taek himself for personally delivering preview tapes of his films, for securing permission for us to publish the still photographs in this volume, and for honoring us with his presence during the USC festival. Most of all we thank him for his contributions to cinema.

David E. James and Kyung Hyun Kim

# Preface

This collection of essays on the work of the film director Im Kwon-Taek is the first English-language scholarly book on South Korean cinema published outside Korea. It originated in a retrospective of twelve of Im's most important films and an accompanying conference, organized by the editors of the present collection and held at the University of Southern California in Fall 1996. The retrospective and conference were jointly sponsored by the university's School of Cinema-Television and its Korean Studies Institute, the Korea Foundation, and the Korean Cultural Center of Los Angeles. The festival culminated with Im's visit to Los Angeles and to the university, where he was presented with a lifetime achievement award by Arthur Hiller, the director of *Love Story*, who was at that time president of the Academy of Motion Pictures. *Festival* (*Ch'ukche*), Im's then most recent film, received its international première in the school's showcase theater, which was filled to overflowing with people from both the university and the local Korean American community. The events received extensive coverage in local Korean-language and English-language newspapers, and on Korean and Korean American television; extended reviews also appeared in Korea's two major film journals, *Kino* and *Cine 21*.[1]

I mention these details at the outset to note our gratitude to the people and the institutions who made possible this small step in the dissemination of Korean cinema abroad, but also to underscore their diversity. Even though the line dividing the Korean from the American cinema has never been entirely categorical and has lately been breached in new ways, the Korean cinema been singularly unknown in the West—in effect it was a "hermit cinema," reenacting the isolation that once supplied the myth of the Hermit Kingdom. Whatever viable knowledge of it we might now aspire to may only be constructed within an international exchange of many economies as well as those of desire. In mounting this dialogue, we of course hoped to forestall the construction of an idea of Korean cinema as either a reflection of the Western one or as an exotic, orientalized other; but also, and more fundamentally, we hoped to forestall the construction of any binary that would have Western film theory as its active subject and Korean cinema its passive object. The present collection of essays attempts to understand Im and the portion of Korean cinema for which he is most immediately responsible in their own context; yet it also understands that context to be comprised of both the specificity of Korean culture and history and the international economy of cinema in which his films have been produced. Toward this end, we took care that the conference would include scholars and critics from South Korea as well as American and Korean American ones; together they approached the issues at hand from a spectrum of geographical, institutional, and discursive situations. We were not able to bring all the South Korean presentations to an appropriate maturity, but with other contributions that were subsequently solicited, the present volume contains essays by non-Korean academics from two continents, Korean scholars and critics, Korean American scholars, and Korean graduate students presently studying in the United States—where, it is to be hoped, their schooling in Western film theory will not preclude their critical resistance to and transformation of it.

This being said, we remain all too aware of the presumptions and difficulties in our attempt to read the significance of Im Kwon-Taek's work in the theoretical context of a Korean national cinema. Well before the period of the conference, any concept of a national cinema as the authentic cultural expression of a unified, self-identical political commonality had been challenged, if not discredited, from several perspectives: the critique of the idea of nation-state on the grounds that its apparent naturalness concealed a historical and ideological product of European modernism, integrally linked to the dominance of the bourgeoisie and the era of global colonialism; Marxist and post-structuralist critiques of the repression of internal differences that secures the ostensible unity of any nation; and the analysis of the inescapable hegemony of the American capitalist cinema over all others that precludes the possibility of any national cinematic autonomy. All these issues are fully relevant to the case of South Korea, but they are remarkable in also being inseparable there from a compelling devotion to a national culture—in fact from conditions that give the concept a unique plausibility. In Korea, community and art alike have been caught between an extraordinarily rich array of the preconditions of a national culture and the ruinous negation of them. For Korea, more dramatically than anywhere else, a national cinema has been simultaneously an imperative and an impossibility.

Korea has been self-conscious of its ethnic, geographic, cultural, and linguistic unity for almost fourteen hundred years, during which time, aside from fealty to the Chinese emperor and periodic Japanese invasions, the country was essentially isolated from foreign influences. *Hangŭl,* its unique (and uniquely efficient) script—first promulgated in 1446 in a document called *Hunmin chŏngŭm:* "proper sounds to instruct the people"—is as potent a figure for a vernacular national culture as might be found. But the national wholeness *Hangŭl*'s history emblematized for four hundred years was devastated by late nineteenth-century incursions that culminated with the Japanese annexation in 1910 and a half-century of the most vicious colonialist exploitation and cultural repression, including attempts to exterminate the Korean language itself. Brought to an end by Japan's defeat in World War II, that occupation was followed not by freedom but by the division of the country into Soviet and U.S. spheres of influence. Korea, it has been said, was free for a day. Immediately thereafter the U.S. installed former collaborators with the Japanese to administer what became a military dictatorship in the South, while the North passed into the hands of a military dictatorship sustained variously by the People's Republic of China and the Soviet Union. A devastating, fratricidal civil war followed, and though an armistice ended it, hostilities have never properly ceased, and the two Koreas have been torn apart across the virtually impermeable De-Militarized Zone.

With the fall of the Berlin Wall, the zone stands as the most dangerous and oppressive vestige of the cold war. Since the armistice, the North has struggled in carceral stagnation. The South, where for a quarter-century conditions were hardly any better, has been revitalized after a succession of intense labor struggles and the *minjung* movement—a national popular campaign for democracy that broke the military dictatorship and culminated in the 1992 presidential elections, the first in the nation since 1960. These liberalization movements led to the eventual election of President Kim Dae Jung, an extraordinarily tenacious and courageous leader of the opposition to the dictatorship, and allowed him to develop his "sunshine policy" of reconciliation with the North. Together with complementary initiatives by the North Korean leader Kim Jong-Il, the policy has produced at the time of the present writing a profound series of breaks with the past: the first meetings between the two sides for the fifty years since the war began; the euphoric expectation of visits and of cultural, athletic, medical and environmental exchanges across the border; and the possibility of eventual reunification. But until the events of this new century, the history of the peninsula as a whole had been so catastrophically destructive that Korea, it seemed, could not leave the twentieth century without first suffering all its most extreme traumas.

Given the strength of the Korean literary tradition and the fact that the South Korean cinema has for its entire existence been the subject of government control and censorship, debates about a national culture have inevitably been conducted primarily in terms of literature. Pivoting on the issues of decolonization and unification, as well as the class and gender inequities that in the South are immense, considerations of a national literature have attempted to elucidate a heritage of emancipatory writing that could be both distinguished from an ultra-nationalist, reactionary nostalgia and affiliated with attempts to create a modernized, liberated, and fully autonomous Korea.[2] Essentially the same issues have been raised in the best South Korean films, but the possibility that the literary debate could be recreated in cinema was circumscribed by the military dictatorships' direct administration of the film industry as well as by the intrinsic limits and possibilities of the medium, as it had historically developed in Korea. Officially, a series of Motion Picture laws imposed censorship and regulated the domestic industry, especially its importation of foreign films—an issue that was, of course, subject to very immediate pressure by the United States. At the same time, the development of cinema as a capitalist industry, and the absence of government subsidies of the kind that had supported the postwar national "New Waves" in the West, marginalized cinema's role in Korean national reconstruction—except in the 1960s, when the industry flourished. But during the *minjung* period, an affiliated, illegal, underground, agitational cinema nourished participatory social engagement and also fostered a generation of cinéastes who, in the period of liberalization that followed it in the early 1990s, created the vibrant New Korean Cinema that flourished from the mid-1980s to the early 1990s.

Having made his first film in 1962 and almost 100 since then, Im Kwon-Taek spans the histories of these modern South Korean cinemas. In his prolificness, the range of genres and themes he mastered, the vitality of his formal innovations, and his long road from routine genre quickies to ambitious art films—from purely domestic, even local, Korean consumption to the stage of the most prestigious international festivals—Im navigated the tidal surges and retreats of the medium more completely than any other artist in the nation. But more resonant than his quantitative and qualitative preeminence has been the specific focus of his work in the last quarter-century, in which he investigated key periods in Korean history and motifs in traditional culture—the historical constituents of a contemporary national culture—so as simultaneously to restore them to the Korean people of today and make them known and intelligible to the world outside. In his maturity, he has been able to work with one eye on the local constituency and the other on the international market, negotiating a global presence for his vision of his homeland's historical and geographical uniqueness. *Sopyonje*, Im's 1993 film about the postwar social imperilment of traditional Korean folk opera (and the subject of special attention in the essays below) figures this achievement. It became the highest grossing film in Korean history, occasioning a national debate on the status of traditional culture; it also became an international festival favorite that drew unprecedented attention to the Korean cinema.

Since *Sopyonje*, there have been rapid changes in Korea and in cinema. The international success of the Korean New Wave with Im at its head—coupled with the realization that in the year of its release *Jurassic Park* made more money than Hyundai's annual exports to the U.S.—attracted corporate leaders. In the mid-'90s Daewoo, Samsung, Cheil Jedang, and other conglomerates or *chaebols* not only developed entertainment divisions, they began to imitate Japanese corporate expansion into Hollywood. In 1996, for example, two months before the USC conference, Cheil Jedang became the second largest investor in the DreamWorks studio at a cost of $300 million. But the industrialization of Korean culture was anything but smooth.[3] The economic collapse of 1998—what the Koreans meticulously designated as the "IMF crisis"—caused the *chaelbols* to pull their investments out of cinema, though as the recovery from the crisis has recently accelerated, capital is returning, and Korean cinema is again attracting the world's attention—as well as Hollywood's interest.

The same week that this collection was accepted for publication, the heading "Seoul Train: S. Korea Drives World Cinema" on the front page of the *Hollywood Reporter* announced the country's recent transformation "from an embattled cinematic backwater into the hottest film market in Asia."[4] Yet another new generation of directors had emerged, the article revealed, who modeled their product on American action films and slapstick comedies, spiking them liberally with sex. Working with the international market specifically in mind, they had succeeded in sharply increasing exports: the $5.7 million earned in 1999 marked a twelve-fold increase over the 1991 figure. The *Reporter's* chief exhibit was *Shiri* (1999), the second feature by the young filmmaker Kang Che-gyu. With successful runs in Japan, Taiwan, and Hong Kong, *Shiri* had already scored heavily on the foreign market, and it replaced *Sopyonje* as the highest grossing film in Korea: it took in $25 million at the domestic box office, even more than *Titanic*. Alongside the *Reporter's* account of these accomplishments came news of another form of international recognition for South Korean cinema, the acceptance of Im Kwon-Taek's *Chunhyang* into the Official Competition Section" at the Fifty-fifth Cannes Film Festival, the first time a Korean film had been so honored. These two films, juxtaposed for the West in the *Hollywood Reporter,* frame the terms in which South Korean cinema may in the future assert a national culture and negotiate it internationally.

*Shiri* is a high-tech action film about renegade members of the North Korean special forces who infiltrate the South, murder prominent scientists and government leaders, steal an immensely powerful new weapon, and almost succeed in using it to blow up the soccer stadium where an epochal North versus South reconciliation game is being played. A superbly paced and intricately constructed thriller, it is replete with special effects recruited from Hollywood, especially from MTV and genre films like the *Die Hard* and *Mission Impossible* series that have been the industry's most dependable international blockbusters. Vertiginous in its special effects and thematic contradictions alike, it exploits the hoariest cold war paranoia and yet advances newly generous attitudes to the North; it reasserts a newly empowered South Korean masculinity, even as it shows that masculinity threatened by a glamorous—and virtually omnipotent—female North Korean secret agent.

Im's *Chunhyang,* his version of the beloved and often-filmed folk tale about a virtuous woman who is tortured by a corrupt local governor when she insists on remaining true to her absent betrothed, is very different. Im filmed a *p'ansori,* or folk opera version of the story, interweaving the singers' account of Chunhyang's virtue and endurance with scenes of a modern audience attending the opera and extended dramatic recreations of the tale. Like Shakespeare's late plays, it is a magisterial and self-consciously reflexive reprise of the themes and motifs of his greatest works. Photographed by Im's longtime collaborator Chŏng Il-Sŏng, who surpassed even his previously masterful achievements in creating extraordinarily beautiful images of the Korean countryside, *Chunhyang* recreates a precolonial past where luxurious natural beauty is the setting for vicious class and gender violence. Yet Im's film articulates a militant populism by linking Chunhyang's suffering and final triumph to the lives of the common people.

Though *Shiri* marks a reversal in Korea's cultural subalternization, it does so by creating a pastiche of the culture of transnational corporate capital, raising again the central question about postmodern culture, one that has often been asked in Korea: "If nowadays 'postmodernity' rather than 'modernity' is touted to efface the issue of decolonization, it can only suggest that 'postmodernity' may be yet another variant of 'colonial modernity.'"[5] *Chunhyang*, on the other hand, rooted in premodernity and expressed through a cinematic accommodation of the premodern operatic form's own accommodation of an even more ancient folktale, mobilizes the most affecting images of the past. Yet it addresses the present only in a displaced allegorical form. Where, between the premodern and the postmodern figured in these two films, will the future Korean cinema find itself?

Kim Jong-Il is, of course, himself a film aficionado and the author of a treatise on cinema in the auteur tradition; predictably perhaps, his writing reflects his own political position, privileging the director as "the commander of the creative group. . . . [with] overall responsibility for artistic creation, production organization and ideological education."[6] During the North-South summit, Kim publicly mentioned *Chunhyang*, discussed its fortunes at Cannes with the South's delegates, and proposed that *Festival*—Im's earlier film about premodern cultural forms—could serve as a model of the kind of work on which the two Koreas could collaborate. He also expressed concerns about *Shiri*, raising its depiction of the North as a terrorist state and its overall unfaithfulness to reality as an impediment to mutual understanding. But as he and we too must know, the differences in the visions of Korea the two films promulgate will not be the only cultural, or even cinematic, divisions any viable future will have to reconcile. In the South, these contrasting forms of the resurgent commercial cinema are flanked by what is presently the most vital workers' cinema in the world; and whatever accommodation is made with that and the politics subtending it will have to be renegotiated when and if what was at one time its imaginary ideal—the cinema of North Korea itself—comes into view. If this book's contribution to the international understanding of Korean cinema can also play a role, however small, in cultural exchanges that facilitate these accommodations, then all who have worked on it will be more than sufficiently rewarded. For no less than in the political and social spheres, cultural work of any worth can be inspired and guided only by the hope of the eventual recovery of an integral freedom in Korea.

David E. James
Los Angeles, June 15, 2000

# Notes

1. The first of its kind in the U.S., the USC retrospective followed an eight-film retrospective at the Munich Film Festival in 1990 and the inclusion of four of Im's works in a fifteen-film festival of Korean films, "Seoul Stirring: 5 Korean Directors," held in London in 1995. The USC retrospective was itself followed by other forms of international recognition for the director, including an Award for Excellence in Filmmaking at the Hawaii International Film Festival in 1996 and the Kurosawa Award for Lifetime Achievement in Film Directing at the San Francisco International Film Festival in 1998.

2. For example: "The 'national question' for the current movement thus entails not only the general task of defending national dignity and autonomy from colonial/neocolonial powers, but the specific one of overcoming national division." Paik Nak-chung, "The Idea of a Korean National Literature Then and Now," *Positions* 1, no. 3 (1993): 575.

3. As Bruce Cumings observed, "an industrial economy lauded by every U.S. president since Kennedy . . . mutated overnight into a nightmare of 'crony capitalism' in the twinkling of the I.M.F's eye." "Korea's Other Miracle," *Nation*, March 30, 1998, 16.

4. *The Hollywood Reporter*, April 18, 2000, 1 and 14–16, weekly international edition.

5. Paik, "The Idea of a Korean National Literature," 578.

6. Kim Jong-Il, *The Cinema and Directing* (Pyongyang: Foreign Languages Publishing House, 1987), 2. On North Korean cinema, see Kyung Hyun Kim, "The Fractured Cinema of North Korea: The Discourse of the Nation in *Sea of Blood*," in *In Pursuit of Contemporary East Asian Culture*, ed. Xiaobing Tang and Stephen Snyder (Boulder, Colo.: Westview Press, 1996), 85–106.

*Kyung Hyun Kim*

CHAPTER I

# Korean Cinema and Im Kwon-Taek:
# An Overview

*Lousy films had to come first*
Im Kwon-Taek, "Lousy Films Had to Come First: Interview with Im Kwon-Taek,"
interview by John Lent, *Asian Cinema* 7, no. 2 (winter 1995): 86–92.

Anyone who has tried to locate English-language books, articles, or even encyclopedia entries on Korean cinema must surely have met with great frustration. When I first began my research on Korean cinema in 1992, the lengthiest—and perhaps the only available—treatment of the topic appeared in Roy Armes's *Third World Film Making and the West* (1987), one of the most comprehensive books on non-Western cinemas. Armes gave courteous attention to South Korean cinema, remarking that "[h]ardly any of South Korea's huge output is shown abroad, and there are no internationally known film directors."[1] More than a decade has passed since both the publication of Armes's book and the first showcases of the New Korean Cinema, which changed the reputation of a national cinema that previously was known only for the regressive language of its "violently introspective melodramas."[2] Yet the relative neglect of Korean cinema by Western film scholars continues. For instance, the recent *Oxford History of World Cinema*, which allegedly "covers every aspect of international film-making," makes no reference to Korean cinema.[3]

# Cinema of the Colony and Na Un-gyu

Western ignorance of Korean cinema can largely be attributed to its inaccessibility. No film made before 1943 has been recovered, despite an active industry that produced approximately 240 feature films during the colonial period and a desperate search by South Korean film archivists and scholars for them in recent years. Cinema was the most popular cultural medium of nationalist expression during the Japanese colonial period (1910–45), when Na Un-gyu, a flamboyant director and actor, starred in the "golden era of silent films" of the late 1920s. At the age of twenty-two, with only a couple of years of acting experience behind him, Na wrote, directed, and starred in one of the most popular films Korea has ever produced, *Arirang*, released in 1926 and widely known as Korea's first nationalist film.[4] *Arirang*'s plotline involves a philosophy student who, in the midst of his studies, goes mad. Every effort is made to treat him, but to no avail. Only when his sister is about to be raped by a Korean collaborator, a bureaucrat who works closely with the colonial government, does he regain his senses. Yet his reawakening—not unlike Korea's enlightenment project, which did not begin until after the country had been gobbled up by Japan's colonial machine—comes too late: not until after he has murdered the collaborator. The authorities take him away over the Arirang hills, beyond the point of no return. Figuring visual allegories such as cats and dogs fighting each other and a thirsty young couple hopelessly lost in what is clearly an open field, the film found loopholes in Japanese film censorship.[5] Na was quite possibly Korea's first legitimate pop star. His persona expressed the virtues of national independence, and he exhibited the aura of a rebellious underdog, making him especially suited for peasant roles. He was hardly a muscular, masculine icon: indeed he was a short man with a toad-like look. Na's emaciated and manic image tapped into the fury and frustration that allegorized Korea's grief as a nation deprived of its sovereignty.

The popularity of Korean cinema during the silent film period was short-lived. Film censorship and the general suppression of Korean culture intensified during the 1930s. The Japanese invasion of Manchuria in 1931 and the escalating war efforts gradually transformed the cinemas of both Korea and Japan into propaganda machines. The prohibition of Korean as a civil language in the late 1930s virtually dismantled the national film industry, since Korean "talkies" could no longer be made.[6] By the 1930s, Na Un-gyu himself became engaged in *shinp'a* (*shimpa*) melodramatic moviemaking, betraying the nation with an acting role that paired him with a Japanese woman as his romantic counterpart.[7] In 1937, the year Japan institutionalized repressive film laws in its newly acquired territories in Manchuria, and two years before all filmmakers were required to formally consent to the forced assimilation policy called *naisen ittai* (Korea and Japan collapsed into one body), Na died. Though he was only thirty-two at his death, he had twenty-six films to his credit as an actor and fifteen as a director.

Korea's liberation from colonialism was hardly a done deal on August 15, 1945. As soon as Japan surrendered to the Allied Forces, other foreign troops quickly moved in: Russians above the 38th parallel and Americans below it. As An Chae-hong, a moderate nationalist leader then remarked, "our independence only lasted one day, the 16th [of August 1945]."[8] This scoffing comment reflects the irony that Korea's liberation was immediately undermined by U.S. military occupation and the subsequent division of the country into communist North and capitalist South, which escalated into full-scale military confrontation and permanent partition.[9] The extreme manner with which Japanese colonial administrators imposed their policies left a Korean social structure that was critically deficient in ideological and economic "middle-class" constituencies. The absence of a middle class and of moderate political factions fueled the insecurities of the post-liberation period, and these were reflected in the popular movements that split along the widening gap between rightists and leftists.[10] Global anxiety, heightened by the nascent developments of the cold war and the communist victory in the Chinese Civil War in 1949, further exacerbated the already tense domestic situation. Political assassinations, peasant uprisings, and fraudulent elections became more and more frequent in the South. The chaos and havoc of the "post"-colonial period soon turned into a full-scale military collision: a "virtual holocaust ravaged the country," leaving three million people dead.[11]

# The Golden Age of Korean Cinema in the 1960s and Im Kwon-Taek's Debut

In the Korean War, buildings were destroyed, families fragmented, and industries ruined. Moreover, a national culture that valued humanity and humility was lost, thus opening the door for more than a generation of brutal military dictatorships in South Korea. The suppression of cinema in South Korea during the postwar period was more acute than that of other mediums. Perhaps this was because cinema is more dependent on imported technology and equipment as well as on popular appeal. Though it was too expensive to privately produce films in the war-ravaged and impoverished nation, the people demanded cinema. Responding to this demand, the authorities sought to firmly control the filmmaking industry, initially requiring its political acquiescence and eventually its collaboration. After Korea terminated diplomatic ties with Japan, public performances and screenings in Japanese were banned;[12] the relative difficulty of importing foreign language films during the early years of liberation placed more emphasis on domestic production. Like many other industries in South Korea, cinema migrated to the southern port city of Pusan to avoid the worst effects of the war. It was here—with new personnel, a new location, and a new ideological orientation—that the industry first attracted Im Kwon-Taek, then a teenager wandering the streets looking for work.

The editors of this volume chose to focus on the career of Im Kwon-Taek not because he stands apart from the Korean cinema's historical contradictions but because his films demonstrate any filmmaker's inability to escape the contradictions embodied in the national cinema. Beginning with his first feature film in 1962—one year after Park Chung Hee's coup—and continuing to the present, Im's career spans four decades, during which he has directed more than 100 films. It coincides with Korea's dramatic emergence as a major industrial power under a highly organized, yet repressive and authoritarian, rule. Im is the only director whose life's work includes both the Golden Age of Korean cinema in the 1960s and the New Korean Cinema of the '80s and '90s, covering the entire history of South Korea's military rule (1961–92). Not all of his films consistently display the mark of genius, but he has continuously rediscovered himself in order to both survive and overcome the limitations and contradictions of his medium.

Im's films are as uneven as the postwar history of Korean cinema itself. During the 1960s, he was a formulaic studio director trying to learn the professional trade of directing even as he was practicing it. Initially Im was given genre film projects, most famously action films. In the 1970s, when Korean cinema operated under the ideological auspices of the Yushin system of dictatorship that guaranteed a lifetime executive term to Park Chung Hee, Im was the director of "quality films" (*usu yŏnghwa*), ones that were politically sanctioned and financially rewarded by the government. When new military generals came to power during the 1980s and tested the endurance of the people, Im established himself as a serious director. Im's work explored and visualized the tension between modernity and tradition, becoming staple features at international film festivals. Having received recognition in the '80s from international critics who touted him as the most eminent Korean filmmaker, he focused his appeal on the constituencies that shunned him the most during his career as a "quality film" and "film festival" director: his domestic audiences. During the '90s, his films *The General's Son* (*Changgun ŭi adŭl*, 1990) and *Sopyonje* (1993) broke domestic box office records; along with *The Taebaek Mountains* (*T'aebaek sanmaek*, 1994), these are among the most controversial Korean films ever made.

Lousy films had to come first for Im Kwon-Taek, and not only because of censorship. The government certainly impeded his maturation process as a maker of art films, but his belated arrival on the international film scene—almost twenty years after he made his directorial debut— can also be attributed to the specific correlation between his personal background and the unfortunate social and ideological prejudices of postwar South Korean society. Im's social class, his ideology, and his regional background were all impediments to success; he was an underdog in a society that was intolerant of disadvantaged persons and abusive of private civil liberties. Not unlike the veteran painter who remains reticent about his dissident, imprisoned father in Park Kwang-su's *Chilsu and Mansu* (1988), Im had to cautiously avoid sensitive political subjects in the early stage of his career; given any provocation at all, the authorities would have tagged him with the label "commie sympathizer."

Im was born in 1936, in a small town called Chang-sŏng, located at the southwestern edge of the Sobaek Mountains and only fifteen miles away from Kwangju, the bedrock of modern Korea's democracy. Experiencing the Korean War as a teenager, he—like many around him—was closely tied to the leftists. As Im repeatedly asserts in interviews, the victory of the rightists at least in the southern half of Korea during the Korean War cast him as an outsider for the rest of his life.[13] Once the sanctions on sensitive modern history subjects were lifted in the late 1980s and the early 1990s, Im's leftist family background furnished him with a different perspective for films on historical subjects. On the other hand his background initially inhibited his ability to make the kind of films he wanted. Unlike many directors active and popular during the Golden Age—for example, Shin Sang-ok, Kim Ki-yŏng, and Yu Hyŏn-mok, who had college training in art, theater, and literature respectively—Im did not even finish middle school; the paucity of his education was a severe handicap in a society that is extremely prejudiced against the uneducated. Im's regional ties with Chŏlla Province also placed him at a serious disadvantage. Chŏlla is a region famous for such dissident activities as the Kwangju Student Uprising in 1929, the Yŏsu-Sunch'ŏn Rebellion in 1948, and the Kwangju Massacre in 1980. It is also the home of former activist and now president Kim Dae Jung. Chŏlla was effectively the "land of exile," its inhabitants systematically discriminated against during three decades of military dictatorship. Yet Im was like the durable *chapch'o* (weed)—ironically, the title of his first serious film in 1973.[14] He kept a low profile throughout the 1960s and '70s, and, when the system permitted and even endorsed provincial aesthetics in subsequent decades, he pursued his art by taking advantage of his regional and class experience. His national and international reputations would perhaps have been impossible to attain had he not been equipped with an instinctive capacity to survive—to know when to conceal and when to activate his identity.

It was sheer "hunger" that led Im to take a job in the entertainment industry in 1956 when he was twenty. Pusan, a booming port city that had temporarily assumed the function of the nation's capital during the Korean War, was then the principal city of filmmaking, before the industry returned to Ch'ungmuro, the district in Seoul heavily

KOREAN CINEMA AND IM KWON-TAEK

populated by film production companies. Im's first experience in the film industry was working on a production crew run by the director Chŏng Ch'ang-hwa. In only five years he managed to scale the professional ladder from errand boy to director. This rapid rise was largely because of the surging popularity of cinema in the late 1950s and the early '60s, as well as because of the scarcity of human resources to meet the demand. During the Japanese colonial period, many filmmakers were *Filmmaker* aligned with leftist ideology, and when the war ended in a stalemate *went to* in 1953, they defected to the North; the only notable film directors *N. Korea* who remained in South Korea were Yi Kyu-hwan and Yun Pong-ch'un, both of whom failed to cultivate significant careers after the Korean War.[15] The migration of filmmakers created a significant vacuum in the South Korean film industry, which had no choice but to promote young, inexperienced personnel, thus paving the way for a new, postwar generation of film directors. Shin Sang-ok, Chŏng Ch'ang-hwa, Yi Kang-ch'ŏn, Han Yŏng-mo, and Yu Hyŏn-mok all made their debuts in the 1950s. They would lead the Golden Age of Korean cinema, which grew into a popular industry producing more than 100 films each year.

Films made in Korea during the '60s and '70s were largely unknown in the West, and today they have mostly been forgotten even by domestic audiences. Yet this was Korean cinema's most glorious period, a time when it gained a measure of glamour and fame that have since been unmatched. It was one of the most profitable and active industries in Asia, producing at its peak from 1968 to 1971 over 200 films a year—a figure that dwarfs the production average of approximately sixty films a year in the 1990s. In 1969, for example, the average Korean visited a movie theater five or six times a year, compared to about once a year in the 1990s.[16] Currently only one out of four Koreans chooses a domestic film over a foreign one, and while this is a respectable number in a global era dominated by Hollywood, in 1967 nearly half of the people flocking to the movies chose to watch Korean films.[17] Korean cinema was also profitable overseas; 210 films were exported in one year alone (1971), with many of them sold to Hong Kong entrepreneurs.[18] By contrast, during most of the 1980s and the 1990s, Korea became one of the major markets for the Hong Kong film industry, importing seventy to eighty films a year from the former British colony but exporting none in return.[19]

Im Kwon-Taek participated in this postwar frenzy for the cinema as a young director with little expectation of reward from his job other than a paycheck. Throughout the 1960s, he worked on any picture his producer gave him, shooting war films, martial arts action, romantic melodramas, and period films. Even though his stature then was far below that of Shin Sang-ok or Yu Hyŏn-mok—whose names were immediately recognized by popular audiences—he did manage a few successes. His debut film *Farewell to the Duman River* (*Tumangang a chal ikkŏra,* 1962)—a period piece about the independence movement in Manchuria during the Japanese colonial period, and packed with action sequences—became a blockbuster hit, allowing him to continue filmmaking throughout the decade. Im made films with intent and relentlessness; once the job of director was handed to him, he never wavered from his dedication. From 1962 to 1994 he produced at least one film a year. In many of those years, he directed more than five films a year, and in 1970 alone he directed eight.

## Closed-door Screenings of the '70s and Im's "Quality Films"

The highly profitable industry that for a time had Im and other genre filmmakers shooting two films simultaneously could not weather the wave of political repression. The Golden Age came to a screeching halt when the Park Chung Hee administration demanded that the film industry play by new rules in 1973. That year's new Motion Picture Law amendment (the Fourth Amendment) radically restructured the cinema by centralizing it. This centralization served two purposes: to cut back the number of production companies in an overcrowded film market and to force production companies to support the ideology of the Yushin constitution, implemented in 1972.[20] All film production companies now had to meet strict government guidelines, which required them to make films that were not only "morally correct" but also promoted the state ideology of hard work, frugality, and anticommunism. Films could not be made without permits, and these could only be obtained by companies equipped with substantial studio facilities. Even some of the most productive companies, including Shin Sang-ok's film studio, became casualties of this ludicrous policy, which had the effect of making the South Korean film industry resemble more closely that of North Korea, the country's sworn enemy, rather than that of the U.S., its close ally.[21]

Twenty production companies crumbled in 1973 alone. Before long, one of the most glamorous industries in South Korea, championed by the people for more than a decade, became crippled and decrepit, capable only of churning out quota quickies and propaganda "quality films."[22] Ironically, the new system that sought to curtail the number of low-quality films ended up generating an alarming number of poor ones. Also, the policy of restricting imports to one-third (about twenty-five to thirty) of the total films screened each year—a policy intended to protect the domestic film industry—backfired, for limiting the number of Hollywood products only increased the public's taste for them.

The industry soon found out that the government never really intended to defend its national cinema. Instead the state institutionalized the "quality film" system, in which bureaucrats nominated about fifteen films each year that, in their judgment, most effectively promoted the Yushin ideology and rewarded those films' producers with foreign import licenses. This system accomplished two things, neither of them related to preserving and promoting Korean films. First, it forced the collaboration of the film industry by obliging producers to "voluntarily" make films that best served the interest of the regime. Second, since the state held exclusive distribution rights to all imports, including the most profitable Hollywood films, the system rewarded only those entrepreneurs who were morally corrupt and ideologically loyal. The vague and flexible criteria for judging "quality films" made it easy to funnel slush funds between the bureaucrats who determined the best "quality films" and the producers who wanted lucrative import licenses. Further, by restricting the number of imports and making them scarce to the public, the price of "kickbacks" paid for distribution rights rose sharply, instantly profiting the government and eventually bankrupting the film industry. As long as "quality films" were made and the right to import and distribute foreign films was secured, it didn't matter if the actual award-winning film remained theatrically unreleased. Why risk

spending money on domestic film production, distribution, and pub-
licity if you could guarantee success with a proven Hollywood import
that has limited competition? Designed to provide a safety net for local
Korean films, the quota system instead ravaged the domestic industry
and benefited only the state and its collaborators. As in other Korean
industries, the success rate of your business was much higher if you
were on good terms with the commissioners and the statesmen. Some
of the "quality films" deemed "best" during the Yushin period were
screened behind closed doors, with only the bureaucrats—the judges of
the "quality film" competition—in attendance; they were never made
available to the general public. Only the most effective lobbyists survived
the '70s, and the ones who protested, like Shin Sang-ok, Yi Chang-ho,
and Ha Kil-jong, were literally shown the door.[23]

The most confounding time for many Korean filmmakers became
the most opportune time for Im Kwon-Taek. Ironically, he advanced his
career in the midst of the national cinema's demise. While well-known
names in the business were exiled from cinema, Im was consistently
given the director's helm, shooting these "quality films"—which were
invisible to the public—because he visualized ideologies and moralities
consistent with the state's mores. As he stated in 1986: "Although [the
six-year period between 1975 and 1980] was the worst time [for Korean
cinema], it was the best time for me. Before then, if the box office results
weren't good, the director had to be responsible. Then once the 'quality
film' system was implemented, a new trend settled in that didn't care
for the box office results. In other words, [the financial loss suffered in
a film] was compensated for in other ways."[24] Not only did Im use this
time to refine his trade without the pressure of box office results, he
also re-familiarized himself with Korean history as he made numerous
adaptations of period novels. While the Korean cinema suffered, Im
learned to articulate the language of realist cinema and turn history into
his primary source of themes and settings.

The promise of his cinematic talent took more than a decade to
polish and refine, but once he developed it, Im became the principal
shaper of the Korean national cinema. Most of the films he made in
this era—from the obscure *Who and Why* (*Wae kŭraettŏnga*, 1975) to
the often-discussed *The Genealogy* (*Chokpo*, 1978), *The Hidden Hero*

(*Kippal ŏmnŭn kisu*, 1979), and *The Pursuit of Death* (*Tchakk'o*, 1980)—
engaged sensitive historical issues and investigated the reasons behind
historical crimes and human obsessions. For instance, *Who and Why*,
Im's first "quality film," focuses on characters who are common in
Korean history but often ignored in its historiography: the traitors to
the nation during the colonial period. In *The Genealogy*, adapted from
a Japanese short story by Kajiyama Keiji, the main character is a figure
who is rarely depicted favorably in Korean literature or film: a Japanese
man sympathetic to Korean nationalist causes during the colonial period;
indeed, this character anchors the film's primary perspective. During this
phase of his career Im continued to experiment with a static camera,
restricting movements to highlight the subtlety of human emotions as
he visually engaged with other motifs of the national cultural heritage,
such as traditional tilted tile roofs, exquisite porcelain, and mountainous
landscapes.

Even though they were made to please the producers and the bureaucrats whose only concern was promoting cinema that was compliant
with the regime, Im's nationalist films redefined the conventions of propaganda cinema in Korea. Although safely within the official category
of anticommunist films, *The Hidden Hero* and *The Pursuit of Death*
present themes that are much more subtle than the facile dichotomy
between the destructive evil of communism and the benevolent virtues
of capitalism. *The Hidden Hero* depicts the life of a liberal journalist, Hŏ
Yun, during the tumultuous period of liberation (1945–50). Hŏ's disdain
for communism drives him to abandon his position as a moderate and
ultimately provokes him to commit terrorist acts against an inhuman
labor leader. Although the film's narrative trajectory generates an ending where the protagonist punishes the villainous socialist Yi Ch'ŏl—
who instigates riots and brainwashes the poor—the film critiques the
contemporary political situation. It represents liberal humanism as an
intellectual pursuit that is scarcely maintained or honored during the
Park Chung Hee administration. Moreover, *The Hidden Hero*'s call for
action eerily presages the actual dictator's abrupt demise: In its last scene
the fictional tyrant is gunned down. Park Chung Hee himself was shot
a few months after the film was completed.

The existential question and human obsessions investigated in *The*

FIGURE I.I.
*The Hidden Hero:* Hŏ Yun, a liberal journalist, wages war against a tyrannical socialist leader, Yi Chŏl

*Hidden Hero* are also evident in *The Pursuit of Death.* In this film, the protagonist, a former soldier in the South Korean army, is placed in a mental asylum after a destructive quest for personal revenge against a communist guerilla, Tchakk'o. His lifelong pursuit, spanning three decades, ironically ends in this asylum, when Tchakk'o appears at his bedside. The protagonist's demand that the murderous guerilla be arrested as a criminal against society is incomprehensible to the institution's authorities, and the two men eventually end up escaping from it together. *The Pursuit of Death* is a prelude to Im's work of the 1980s and '90s, which focuses on depicting the ideological fragmentation suffered throughout the nation's modern history. Here the nationalist soldier and the socialist guerilla do not dichotomously oppose each other. Indeed, they are ultimately bound together by the humanist sentiment that reverberates in all of Im's subsequent films. The use of flashbacks in the film as the primary device to reconstruct slices of public history and interweave them into personal memories is likewise ubiquitous in Im's later work. The film's constant shift between the present and the past articulates the tragedy of history that intersects private lives and memories.[25] At this intersection, we locate the libidinal force that drives Im's sense of nationhood, the foundation that so effectively structures some of his most representative narratives, including *Mandala* (1981), *Gilsottum* (1985), *Sopyonje,* and *Festival* (Ch'ukche, 1996).

## The New Korean Cinema and Im's Developing Reputation as Auteur

Im's reputation as a director was at best ambiguous at the beginning of the 1980s. He was already a veteran in his forties, but he had achieved little critical respect or public acclaim as a filmmaker. By the decade's end, however, he had emerged as the only director of his generation to work consistently, and he was by far the most decorated Korean filmmaker on the international scene. The decade of the '80s, a paradoxical period that featured intense political protest as well as tremendous economic growth in Korea, presented Im with both a stumbling block and an opportunity. After the self-indulgent '70s, when films played self-promotional narcissistic tunes for Park Chung Hee, the Korean film industry fell into severe disarray. But the unsettling '80s worked to Im Kwon-Taek's advantage. He could continue to produce films without the pressures of the box office because the new military regime, headed by Chun Doo Hwan (1980–87), encouraged international recognition, and thus Im's version of national history—inculcated rigorously through the "quality film" period of the '70s—finally met the expectations of the Western art film circuit.

During the 1980s, the state initiated programs that subsidized the development of subtitled film prints for festival use, underwrote filmmakers' trips to foreign film festivals, such as Cannes, Venice, and Berlin, and also provided financial rewards for films that won prizes in those festivals.[26] The financial incentive to win the best picture prize was often as lucrative as 50 million Won, equivalent at that time to U.S. $40,000. In the mid-'80s, this figure represented only slightly less than

an average film budget, and thus filmmakers coveted the international
festival awards rather than the "quality film" decorations, which became worthless. But because Korean cinema was wholly unrepresented
in international film competitions during the '70s, it was unprepared to
submit its films abroad. Local competitions—which for many years had
established patriotism, anticommunism, and even fascism (an emphasis
on greatness, the cult of personality, and self-sacrifice rather than equality
and humanism) as thematic and ideological standards—had bankrupted
the cinema financially and aesthetically. This made Korean filmmaking
insular and noncommunicative with the outside world, where cinematic
experimentations with form and theme were taking place. Cinematic
language that was once as stylish as any in the world, including the West,
began to regress, with excessive use of zooms, rejection of long-takes,
and predictable plotlines.

None of the celebrated Golden Age filmmakers had survived the
absurdity of the '70s. Shin Sang-ok, Yu Hyŏn-mok, and Yi Man-hŭi,
whose works were most promising during the 1960s, had all faded away.
Shin, probably the most influential director of his time, clashed with the
Park Chung Hee administration and was banned from film activity in
1976. After he mysteriously disappeared and could not be located for a
couple of years, he was found in North Korea with his wife and muse
Ch'oe ŭn-hŭi. He directed renowned socialist films there for about a
decade, then made a dramatic return to the South in 1988. Yu Hyŏn-
mok, whose filmmaking activities were sporadic after frequent run-ins
with the law, gave up filmmaking after *The Son of Man* (*Saram ŭi adŭl*,
1980), and he would not make another feature until 1995.[27] Yi Man-
hŭi, one of the most accomplished stylists, died prematurely in 1976. In
contrast to these "big-name" directors—who were either dead, banned,
or active in another regime during the 1980s—Im, a filmmaker never
known for artistic craft during the 1960s and 1970s, was a rare veteran,
and he emerged relatively unscathed.

The overnight change of emphasis from "quality films" to international festival films steered by the state was not based on a decision
made independently by the new Chun regime. Korea's phenomenal economic growth during the '60s and '70s and the dwindling importance
of the global cold war confrontation in the '80s led the U.S. to strip

Korea of the benefits of "favored trading partner" status. Throughout the mid- to late 1980s, U.S. pressure on Korea to lower its tariffs and eliminate its import quotas heavily impacted the Korean film industry: the Korean government squandered its monopolistic grip on foreign imports and had to write new film laws that better suited the interest of Hollywood. The government's lucrative relations with the film industry, monopolizing the distribution channel of all imports, was terminated not because of local business demand but because of American pressure. The protest of the Motion Picture Export Association of America (MPEAA)—which hollers "unfair trade" whenever its president Jack Valenti wants to push the nation's button—was extremely vocal in respect to Korea. The indigenous film industry, previously insulated from market competition, was suddenly exposed to the rude reality of the recharged and remasculinized giant, Hollywood, which broke the door wide open with innumerable *Rambo*'s and *Rocky*'s. In 1986, the Korean National Assembly passed a new amendment clause to the Motion Picture Law that included the most contentious legislation in the history of Korean cinema, for it allowed foreign film companies to run their own distribution branches in Korea. The floodgates that had been held fast by the government were instantaneously flung open, without a national debate. To filmmakers' dismay, they were forced to play the crude and cruel game of "fair competition," a game in which Hollywood excelled and in which it has continued to prevail over the rest of the globe since the 1980s. The old import quota was replaced by a new screen quota, a regulatory guideline that was both unobserved by theater owners and unmonitored by the Korean government.[28]

When both quotas—the production quota and the foreign film one—were removed in order to allow foreign distribution companies to freely operate their businesses, Korean filmmakers mobilized protests against the state's senseless and imprudent decision, which virtually gave the market away without a fight. Anti-Americanism heightened when *Fatal Attraction* (Adrian Lyne), the first film distributed by an American company (UIP), was released in Korea in 1988. Ch'ungmuro, the commercial industry, and *pi-chedokwŏn yŏnghwa*, the underground cinema—previously bitter rivals—now had an issue with appeal for both of them: the protection of the national cinema against Hollywood.[29]

Daily demonstrations in front of theaters by movie celebrities attracted the media spotlight, but the Korean government would not reinstall the foreign film quota because it feared trade retribution by the U.S.[30] The Korean film marketplace was effectively "liberalized" without consulting filmmakers themselves, and the national cinema—still with no public clamor for increased government funding—now had to fight a battle to protect its own backyard, with the home team advantage removed. In other words, in order to survive, Korean cinema had no choice but to play David to the Goliath of Hollywood, unsupported by its government and its national banking system.[31] Ironically, the only people who could influence the distribution of Korean cinema's meager public funding were the foreign film festival juries who knew scarcely anything about Korea.

The paradoxical state of the national cinema was further accentuated by the divergent interests of the Korean government and the international critics. Many foreign critics anticipated that social critique films—like the work of the Chinese Fifth Generation directors—would emerge out of Korea, but though the local government lusted for a national cinema of international fame, it was reluctant to permit protest films or films critical of recent history. Unlike the Chinese government, which eventually issued an official declaration describing the Cultural Revolution as a disastrous experience, the Korean government has never explicitly denounced the Park Chung Hee reign of terror between 1961 and 1979.[32] The state, which continued to give executive powers to former military generals throughout the 1980s, acceded to the demands of domestic filmmakers and relaxed the censorship codes, but only those governing the representation of erotic images; censorship of political themes remained firm. Depictions of sexual activity became ever more explicit, diverting the public's attention away from politics by permitting the sex industry and quasi-pornographic images to proliferate.[33] To counter the masculine killing bodies of Arnold Schwartzenegger and Sylvester Stallone pictured in Hollywood films, Korean cinema highlighted the naked bodies of women and other erotic images to lure its audiences back. Most films released at this time tested the government's forbearance, offering obligatory and formulaic sex scenes, each more lewd than the one before. Even a Buddhist film like *Mandala* includes sex scenes not always necessitated either by thematic concerns or narrative structure.[34]

The situation presented by the military government's desire to market its culture globally and the Korean cinema's survival tactics after the Hollywood onslaught allowed only a few filmmakers to actually test the competition standards of the West. Im, who had cultivated his talent through local aesthetics and national history yet was disinterested in the direct political protest the young filmmakers generated, was a perfect fit for the Chun regime that lusted after international recognition. With all the other talents of Korean cinema summarily retired, banned from activity, or exiled to mediocrity, Im was the only director who stood up to the challenge of international art film standards. *Mandala,* which won the grand prix at the 1981 Hawaii Film Festival, ended the drought of Korean films in Europe when it was invited to compete in Berlin that same year, and Im's visibility on the European film festival circuit grew. His later '80s films all won awards in international film festivals: *Gilsottum* at Berlin in 1986, *Surrogate Mother* (*Ssibaji*) at Venice in 1987, and *Come, Come, Come Upward* (*Ajeaje paraaje*) at Moscow in 1989. Each of these films redefined the cinematic repositories of "Korean-ness." The communal village, victimized female subjects, and the historical violence of the nation's past patented and enfranchised Im's imagination—and subsequently that of the Korean national cinema.

*Mandala* drew universal accolades and announced to the world a new auteur from a nation which was at that point still obscure at international art cinema competitions. A film about the agonies and temptations of a faithful Buddhist monk, *Mandala* is a classic, even when measured by postmodern standards. If Im's *Sopyonje,* a later film that blends localized sentimental codes of melodrama with long-takes and long shots was responsible for spoiling the New Korean Cinema because of its tremendous box-office success, *Mandala* itself was responsible for initiating the movement. The gritty scenes on the road and the representation of the wandering and tested souls of the Buddhist monks evince both the potential of an auteur and the failure of a national cinema that has not allowed Im to develop it more consistently and regularly. The depth generated by the long shots in *Mandala* hardly pales even when compared to some of the most classic scenes in the films of his great contemporaries such as Andrei Tarkovsky, Theo Angelopoulos, and Abbas Kiarostami, who are all well known for their intense long-takes. Desperately realistic, many of the shots rendered in *Mandala* transgress to the realms of the fantastic and the imaginary. Yet the rendering of these images indigenously reaffirmed—more so than any other films—Korea's painful reality. *Mandala* does not elicit merely aesthetic pleasures, it actuates the pain realized by a Buddhist monk who abandons his orthodox faith. It unleashes energy, perhaps the most fiery in Im's catalogue and certainly rare in the films produced at that time, demanding changes and realizing the potential for political resistance and social critique that the realist convention so often neglects.

During the late '80s, a new form of Korean cinema appeared on the international art film circuit with more frequency and intensity than even the Golden Age could muster at its peak. Im Kwon-Taek presaged and later led a movement that throughout the '80s and '90s best represented the New Korean Cinema. Along with the films of Park Kwang-su and Chang Sŏn-u (Jang Sun-woo), which figured a genre of protest film for the first time in Korean cinema history since Na Un-gyu's era, Im's work began to enter the European marketplace of art cinema with regularity. Suddenly the world began to take notice of the assemblage of a young cinema that acrobatically strutted to the new tempos of post-dictatorship vibration while cautiously testing the boundaries enforced by vigilant censorship.

Although Im's films continued to flourish in the international art film circuit—*Gilsottum, Surrogate Mother, Adada* (1988), and *Come, Come, Come Upward* garnered many awards at film festivals—they did not break new ground in international film language. Like Korea itself, belonging neither to the First World nor the Third, Im's name was not mentioned when critics spoke and wrote of Ousmane Sembene, Lino Brocka, and Glauber Rocha, directors who rewrote Third World film aesthetics. Im was not included in the "pantheon" that listed these monumental names because his aesthetics did not comply with the political codes of Third World aesthetics that sought to revolutionize not only cinema but society itself. There were reasons other than local censorship that discouraged Im from further engaging in revolutionary art. Once he began to seriously tour the world with his films in the mid-

*(handwritten margin note: "Im not a revolutionary director (naturally)")*

and late 1980s, the cinematic languages of Sembene and Rocha had already become outdated, as the dismantling of the Soviet Union and the Eastern Bloc redefined the meaning of the Third World. Not only was Im's cinematic world limited; his vision depended on nostalgic forms of aesthetics, and he refused to completely set aside the cinematic language  of melodrama. After all, he was a commercial filmmaker working in an industry that had not yet come to understand cinema as a "public" enterprise or a "political" weapon.[35] While many Third World filmmakers sought to construct a new cinematic language, Im continued to stylize his realism, invariably depicting the sorrow of familial disintegration. Im's field of dreams was not the future but the nostalgic past, a premodern universe where the values of tradition, nation, and family remained intact and united—however illusory and fictitious this universe might be. As *Ticket* (*T'ik'et*, 1986), *Sopyonje*, *The Taebaek Mountains*, and *Festival* (*Ch'ukche*, 1996) continued to reassert, nothing was more important for Im than harmonious families. Instead of fighting against the Confucian virtues, he refined and sentimentalized them, conjuring up exhaustive images of contaminated women to symbolize a victimized nation in the midst of the ongoing process of modernization and globalization.[36]

Having been a B-grade hit filmmaker in the '60s, a "quality film" director in the '70s, and an international film festival director in the '80s, Im's next move was to weld all three elements together. If Im Kwon-Taek became a household name in the 1980s, in the 1990s he became a national hero. Following the success of *Sopyonje*, which produced one of the most powerful nationalist discourses in Korea, *Tong-a Ilbo*, one of Korea's premier dailies, nominated him as the "man of the year" in 1993. *Sopyonje* dramatically emblematizes and grieves the dying national aesthetics, to a point where masculinist sacrifice of the female body is thematically legitimated.[37] The eight films Im made in the 1990s ranged from moderate to phenomenal successes—if not with the critics, then with the public. The years of living through compromise had taken their toll, however, and even the greatest success did not change him significantly. Despite the sensations he generated, he continued to work within the conventions of popular genres, and too often he compromised his vision. For instance, one of his most recent films, *Chang, the Prostitute* (*Nonŭn kyejip, Ch'ang*, 1997), is a regressive melodrama; it failed to

**FIGURE 1.2.**
Im Kwon-Taek on the set of *The Taebaek Mountains*. With him is his
longtime collaborator and cinematographer Chŏng Il-song

please any of its local critics and was shunned by international film festivals. As evidenced by *Chang, the Prostitute*, the aesthetic conventions
of nation-making represented by a woman's dirtied body—so popularly
embraced by the country until the early '90s—became a trite formula
even for Im himself. Yet the vagaries of his career were further affirmed
by the phenomenally successful *The General's Son*, which spurred two
sequels, effectively countering the Hollywood action and Hong Kong
martial arts films that dominated Korean cinema at that time. This series
reinstated Im in a familiar role—action genre director—and visualized
his themes in the ultra-masculine bodies of young gangsters, a contradictory stance for a man who had once been recognized for his sensibilities
toward women's issues.

If there has ever been a director who could not be interpreted
through the prism of auteurship, it is Im Kwon-Taek. The inconsis-
tencies, the transformations, and the contradictions produced by four
decades of work and over 100 feature films illustrate what it was and

FIGURE I.3.
The sleek, masculine heroes of *The General's Son*

continues to be like working in a nation that historically features even more tumultuous contours than Im's career. He has exuded a spirit of endurance and tolerance, if not resistance, that far outweighs the complicity and compromises involved in the shaping of his career. Through the mediations Im made between expectations of his domestic audience, the demands of producers, and the standards of the art film marketplace, the dilemmas and the history of Korean national cinema become pronounced. His career mirrors the paradox of trying to locate one's national identity in the face of challenges from both Western artistic expectations and domestic audiences' desires, for each of these anticipates indulgences and excesses of different kinds. Im has surely been versatile, but this versatility is inseparable from his understanding of the needs of a desperate national cinema. When Korean cinema required "quality films," he refined his skills; when it reeled from the threats of "Hollywood action" and "Hong Kong gangsters," he offered the local version of cinematic masculinity; and when it needed an auteur who understood the realist film language in terms of international standards, he refitted local aesthetics for international consumption. Most importantly, when Korea needed to be reminded of the culture of humanity and humility lost during the long period of military violence, he was there to represent it. Im was never Korea's Mizoguchi. Rather he was Korea's Spielberg—but more versatile, radical, and profound than Spielberg ever dreamed of being.

## Notes

I would like to acknowledge the following people who have read this essay and made helpful suggestions: David E. James, Henry Em, Chris Berry, and Yi Hyoin.

1. Roy Armes, *Third World Film Making and the West* (Berkeley: University of California Press, 1987), 156. This statement haunted me for years and provided me with a reason to pursue my research on Korean cinema.

2. Ibid.

3. Quoted inside the back cover of Geoffry Nowell-Smith, ed., *The Oxford History of World Cinema* (Oxford: Oxford University Press, 1996).

4. Cho Hŭi-mun, a Korean film historian, has recently argued that *Arirang* was directed not by Na Un-gyu but by a Japanese. Cho's assertion has

infuriated many Korean film historians for, despite official records that support Cho's argument, many oral histories by filmmakers from the early period have confirmed Na as the de facto director of *Arirang;* these filmmakers contended that a Japanese name was attached to it to evade the Japanese colonial government's censorship. Whether Cho's claim is correct or not, the controversy reflects a colonial history where claims of truth and national purity often become contentious and muddled. The situation is additionally complicated by the fact that no Na Un-gyu film including *Arirang* has ever been found. "*Arirang* 1-pyŏn ilbon'in yi kamdok haetta" (The First *Arirang* was directed by a Japanese), *Chugan Chungang* (Weekly Central Daily), May 6, 1995: 4.

5. In 1926 the Japanese Governor-General's Office enacted a law related to film production and dissemination. Called the Motion Picture Censorship Guideline, this law required that all films—domestic and foreign—be reviewed by censors.

6. The first Korean talkie, *Ch'unhyang chŏn* (The Story of Chunhyang), was produced in 1935 by Yi Myŏng-u.

7. Produced hastily by a Japanese *shinp'a* (*shimpa*) actor, *Kŭmgang han* (The Grief of Kŭmgang) featured a formulaic, melodramatic story line, with Na Un-gyu as its star. According to the Korean film historian Yu Hyŏn-mok, the film had a devastating impact on Na Un-gyu's career. Korean cinema began to spiral downward in 1931, both in terms of popularity and critical reception. Na's treachery accelerated its decline.

8. Though it was proclaimed by the Japanese emperor on August 15, 1945, via radio, Korea's liberation was not celebrated openly, both because many people were skeptical of the news and because most of them still feared police brutality and suppression. Photos of crowds of people rejoicing in Japan's defeat and Korea's liberation were mostly taken on August 16, 1945.

9. Even though the U.S. military subsequently withdrew from the Korean peninsula one year after the Republic of Korea was proclaimed in 1948—well after Russia had pulled its troops from the North—they returned in 1950, providing the most decisive factor in determining the outcome of the civil war that began that year. Today, about 37,000 troops still remain in Korea, a number the U.S. has consistently maintained following a mutual defense treaty signed between the U.S. and South Korea in October 1953. So far the only American president who has publicly expressed interest in phasing out the presence of the American soldiers stationed in Korea was Jimmy Carter, who announced in 1977 that all U.S. ground troops in Korea would be withdrawn over a period of four or five years. Of course, this plan met with opposition in both the U.S. Senate and the Republic of Korea, and it never materialized. See Han Sung-joo ed., *U.S.-Korea Security Cooperation: Retrospects and Prospects* (Seoul: Korea University Press, 1983), 20.

10. Nowhere is this better represented than in Im's film *The Taebaek Mountains* (1994). See my essay in this volume, "Is This How the War Is Remembered?," for an analysis of this film.

11. Bruce Cumings, *Korea's Place in the Sun* (New York: W. W. Norton, 1997), 298.

12. Korea's total ban on Japanese movies, popular music, and public performances continued from 1945 until 1998.

13. See "An Interview with Im Kwon-Taek" in this volume.

14. Titled in English *The Deserted Widow*.

15. Young-il Lee, *The History of Korean Cinema*, Korean ed.(Seoul: Motion Picture Promotion Corporation, 1988), 412.

16. During the four-year period between 1968 and 1971, more than 200 films were produced each year. In the peak year, 1969, 229 films were made, a record that still holds today and that stands in marked contrast to the less than fifty films made in 1999. The statistics presented here are compiled from several sources, including Ch'oe Chin-yong et al., *Hanguk yŏnghwa chŏngch'aek ŭi hŭrŭm gwa saeroun chŏnmang* (The tendency and the new perspective of the Korean film policies) (Seoul: Chipmundang, 1994); *Hangyŏre 21*, no. 222, August 27, 1998; and *Hanguk yŏnghwa yŏngam* (Korean Film Annals) (Seoul: Korean Motion Picture Promotion Corporation, published annually).

17. A notable exception occurred in 1999, when the domestic market share rose to 36%, largely due to the popularity of *Shiri* (Kang Che-gyu), a spy thriller blockbuster that broke the all-time box office record.

18. The figures given here from the Korean Motion Picture Promotion Corporation during the '60s and the '70s may be exaggerated. Yet during this period, annual revenues generated from the sale of these films reached nearly U.S. $1,000,000; this is a significant sum—particularly in light of the state of the Korean economy at the time—and it remained unmatched until the late 1990s.

19. In the early '90s, only fifteen films per year were exported to the foreign market, most of them low-budget films that targeted Japan's soft-porn video market. On average, the annual net profit realized from the export business was around U.S. $200,000. In the last three years of the 1990s, however, the export trend changed radically. Since 1997, the Korean film industry's export business has been extraordinarily vibrant, yielding over U.S. $5,000,000 in 1999. For the year 2000, because of the huge success of *Shiri* in Japan—which grossed U.S. $16,000,000 alone, the figure is expected to be even higher. Meanwhile, the decline of Hong Kong's cinema throughout the '90s has led to its dwindling popularity in Korea. The last Hong Kong films to be ranked among the year's top ten box-office foreign films were Tsui Hark's *Once Upon a Time in China* (1991) and *Asia the Invincible* (1992).

20. Park Chung Hee, who last ran for the presidency in 1971 when he defeated Kim Dae-jung, decided to implement a system that would strengthen his authoritarian rule; he ran the country by emergency decrees and simply declared himself president for life. The Yushin system was the brainchild of a man with a loose hold on his sanity, and it terrorized the nation until Park Chung Hee's's death in 1979. For an insightful analysis of the Yushin system, see Cumings, *Korea's Place in the Sun*, 356–63.

21. The government had in mind the Japanese film industry and its major studio system as the model for the Korean industry's restructuring. However, as all filmmakers agree, the government's experiment was a disaster.

22. Misguided governmental policies were not the only reason for the decline of the film industry. The '70s global recession caused film attendance to drop all around the world. And, as in many other nations, the explosive popularity of television was a primary reason for the downturn in Korean cinema. But the severity of the recession was especially dire in Korea, where the domestic film industry, despite its enormous popularity, did not regain its form until the late 1990s.

23. Ha Kil-jong, Yi Chang-ho, and Kim Ho-sŏn were among the group euphemistically called "yŏngsang sedae" (image generation) directors. Making their debuts in the mid-'70s, they facilitated a young film movement and culture influenced by European art film aesthetics, social criticism, and contemporary urbanism. Their popularity was short-lived, however. Yi Chang-ho was banned from filmmaking from 1976 to 1979, Ha Kil-jong was found dead in 1979, and Kim Ho-sŏn retreated to sexploitation films. The official explanation given for Yi Chang-ho's retirement during the latter part of the 1970s—after he emerged as a "hitmaker" in Korean cinema with his debut film *Home of the Stars ( Pyŏldŭl ŭi kohyang)*—tied it to his arrest in 1976 on charges of marijuana use. A misdemeanor charge, this should have led to no more than a small fine or a warning by the court; but Yi Chang-ho was banned from participating in any public work, including filmmaking. This "marijuana incident" gave the government a convenient excuse to force Yi, a prominent director of "social problem" films, into retirement. During the Park Chung Hee regime, hundreds of other entertainers were also banned from performing in public, on the basis of dubious charges.

24. "Im Kwŏn-t'aek ŭn malhanda" (Im Kwon-Taek Speaks), in Chŏng Sŏng-il, ed., *Im Kwon-Taek* (Seoul: Onŭl, 1987), 143.

25. In Young Nam, "Narrating History: Flashback as Collective Memory in Im Kwon-Taek's Films" (paper presented at "Im Kwon-Taek: Heart of Korean Cinema," an academic conference held on November 2, 1996, at the University of Southern California).

26. The international film festivals recognized by the government as "prestigious" included Cannes, Venice, Berlin, Moscow, Montreal, Tokyo, and the American Academy Awards. As early as 1984 the state financially rewarded films that received awards at these festivals and other "minor" ones.

27. Yu Hyŏn-mok may be the only person ever to have been charged with violating both decency laws and anticommunist laws. In 1965, a scene featuring a nude actress, shot from behind, that Yu excised from the final version of his *Ch'un-mong* was the basis of a claim against him; the prosecutor argued that nudity even in front of a film crew was a crime. And two years later, Yu's speech defending the *Seven Female Prisoners* (7 in *ŭi yŏp'oro*)—directed by Yi Man-hŭi—at an international academic conference was deemed to be a threat to the state. *A Stray Bullet* (*Obalt'an*, 1961), directed by Yu himself and one of the greatest masterpieces of Korean cinema, was of course heavily censored; it remained unreleased until the 1980s. See "Kaja, Kaja: Yu Hyŏn-mok kamdok ŭi *Obalt'an*, ttonŭn namhan yŏnghwa ŭi *Shimin K'ein*" (*Let's Go, Let's Go: Director Yu Hyŏn-mok's The Stray Bullet or South Korea's Citizen Kane*), *Kino* no. 43 (August 1998): 129.

28. No theater owner has ever been prosecuted for violating the screen quota. Yi Chŏng-ha, who in 1993 served as secretary of the nonprofit surveillance organization that monitors 155 major Korean theaters, reported that while Korean films ostensibly must be screened 146 days a year, they were actually shown, on average, on only fifty-nine days. See Yi Chŏng-ha, "Sŭk'ŭrin k'wŏt'ŏje, sal-rilsunŭn ŏpnŭnga?" (Can the screen quota policy be revived?), *Mal* (Speech) no. 111 (September 1995): 182–85.

29. The first alliance mobilized between Ch'ungmuro filmmakers, independent filmmakers, and film activists was announced in a statement issued to protest the government's decision not to democratically reform the constitution in 1987. Again in 1989, filmmakers from both Ch'ungmuro and the independent cinema united to collectively fight against the direct distribution of the Hollywood films.

30. During the late 1990s, the U.S. threatened even the screen quota that obliges theaters to play Korean films at least 146 days a year. Movie stars and film directors again marched in the streets, receiving more media spotlight. The Korean government responded this time, fighting U.S. pressure to reduce the number of days the Korean films must be screened in theaters.

31. It was virtually impossible to receive a bank loan to produce a Korean film because of the unlikelihood that the film would even recover its production costs, let alone make a profit.

32. The legacy of Park Chung Hee still lives. Long after his death, he still has an impact on Korean politics because of his protegés who remain in power. Kim

Chong-p'il, Park's nephew-in-law and most recently a prime minister, and Park Kŭn-hye, Park's daughter and an important assemblywoman, are two among many who continue to exercise indisputable power in South Korean politics.

33. Although the state relaxed its censorship in other sectors of culture, cinema did not benefit much from the more liberal political atmosphere of the late '80s and the early '90s. Between 1989 and 1992, virtually all feature films produced by filmmakers unaffiliated with Chungmuro had to battle riot police, who blocked screenings, forcibly dispersed the crowds gathered to watch the films, arrested the filmmakers, and confiscated the film prints. Many screenings held on university campuses outside the commercial circuit produced unlooked-for spectacles, featuring students scrambling to safeguard the film prints and the projector from the riot police. Sometimes the struggles outside the theaters were far more spectacular than the ones projected onto the silver screen. The screening of *Oh! Dreamland* (*O kkum ŭi nara*, 1989)—the first 16mm feature film released by independent filmmakers (Changsan'gonmae) and also the first film to depict the Kwangju Uprising—was declared illegal. This led to the arrests of Hong Ki-sŏn, Changsangotmae's representative, and Yu In-t'aek, the owner of the small theater used as its screening venue, Yu In-t'aek. Official reaction reached a manic level when another 16mm narrative film by Changsangotmae, *A Night Before the Strike* (*P'aŏp chonya*), was screened in eleven cities in April 1990, mostly on university campuses. To block the screening of the film on April 13 at Chŏnnam University in Kwangju, 1,800 military police and several police helicopters were deployed. A virtual war was declared against the audience, mostly comprising students. Political reaction to Changsangotmae's third and final narrative production, *Opening the Closed School Gate* (*Tatch'in kyomun ŭl yŏlmyŏ*, 1992), made in alliance with the schoolteachers' union, was less severe. Yet screening the film was declared illegal, provoking another set of battles between the students and the riot police. Finally, in October 1996, charges filed against Changsangotmae—when *Opening the Closed School Gate* was exhibited three years earlier and declared illegal—were ruled unconstitutional. The Supreme Court of Korea found that the 12th Article of the Motion Picture Promotion Law, which places all films screened in Korea under the subject of censorship, was inconsistent with the constitutional prohibition of preproduction censorship of any art or publication.

34. See David E. James's essay on this subject, "Im Kwon-Taek: Korean National Cinema and Buddhism," in this volume.

35. A number of film books were published in the mid- to late 1980s that included translated essays of the famous Third Cinema proclamation written by Fernando Solanas and Octavio Getino. The Third World cinemas of Glauber Rocha, Miguel Littin, and Tomas Gutierrez Alea were also introduced in these

books, influencing many young filmmakers and students. Yet opportunities to actually see the films made by these directors were extremely limited, and Im was already a veteran director in his fifties.

36. See Eunsun Cho's essay on this topic, "The Female Body and Enunci-ation in *Adada* and *Surrogate Mother*," in this volume.

37. See the essays on *Sopyonje* in this volume, particularly Chungmoo Choi's "The Politics of Gender, Aestheticism, and Cultural Nationalism in *Sopyonje* and *The Genealogy*."

*David E. James*

CHAPTER 2

# Im Kwon-Taek:
# Korean National Cinema and Buddhism

In 1926 Han Yong-un, an eminent Buddhist master and leader in the movement to free Korea from Japanese occupation, published a collection of poems, *Silence of Love* (*Nimŭi ch'immuk*) in which he assumed the persona of a woman abandoned by her lover.[1] In the title poem, she looks out across the mountains and the path through them by which he left her; but, with the dialectical logic of Buddhism, she finds in her loss the implication of its opposite, and so she concludes by affirming her anticipation of reunion with him. *Silence of Love* is usually read allegorically simultaneously in religious and political terms, with the absent lover figuring both the void at the heart of Buddhist ontology and the Korean national homeland abducted by the Japanese invaders.

Twenty years later, a similar scene occurs in Yun Yong-gyu's film *Home is Where the Heart Is* (*Maŭmŭi kohyang*, 1948), made during the period of political turmoil that led to the division of the nation, and one of only two Korean films from before the civil war that survive to us. In this film the erotic metaphor is oedipalized. To-song, a young boy being raised by the monks at Chongnam temple, desperately awaits the return of his mother, who abandoned him and who now lives in Seoul. He asks an old woodcutter if his mother is beautiful, and when he hears that she is, he raises his eyes to the mountains that surround him, to the peaks and the forests, which we see from his point of view. As these figure both his mother's beauty and her absence, To-song's scopophilic gaze, like Han's lyric voice, makes palpable and present that which is missing—a function that has been proposed as fundamental to the cinematic signifier and its Oedipal operation, and one that the film's narrative will confirm by bringing him a surrogate mother who is nevertheless invested with all the erotic intensity of a lover.

Thirty years later, the same motifs of loss and restoration begin to pass obsessively through the films of Im Kwon-Taek. In his mature work, Im explored precolonial cultural forms in order to engage the question of Korean national identity, especially as it has been alienated and thrown into crisis by the multiple forms of colonization to which the country has been subjected. Of the traditional cultural vocabularies Im interrogated, Buddhism will be the one considered in detail below; like Han and Yun, he mobilized the resonant metaphors of eroticism and landscape Buddhism contains, though the quite different historical conditions of the three artists ensured that those metaphors would be differently inflected. But before turning to Im's use of Buddhism, we must consider his confrontation with what, for a filmmaker, is an especially immediate form of alienation, that is, a national cinema subject to neocolonial political control and censorship, and marginalized by the global hegemony of the American capitalist film industry. We begin, then, with Im's attempt to turn the colonized Korean film industry into the vehicle of a national culture.

## Korean National Cinema: Im Kwon-Taek as Auteur

Although the theoretical status of the concepts of the art film, national cinema, and the director-as-author has been largely undermined, practically they continue to organize scholarship. Even so, to approach a Korean auteur and a Korean art cinema committed to national reconstruction in the general terms they demarcate demands at the outset

some justification in an account of the material conditions of film production in South Korea.

Designating a number of locally specific variants either within or on
the edges of studio production, the concept of the art film mediates between the division of labor of the industrial feature film and the personal
expressivity associated with authorship in avant garde or independent
films. Although the South Korean film industry, centered in Seoul's
Ch'ungmuro district, has been consistently market-driven (rather than
government subsidized in the manner of, for example, the German or
Taiwanese New Waves), its structure has been unstable, oscillating between the proliferation of small, more or less independent studios and
government attempts to control these by forcing them into conglomerates. The absence of a stable infrastructure is commonly bemoaned
by Korean critics, in terms such as "over the course of its 70-year history . . . the Korean film industry has not established a systematic or
organized industrial structure for itself"[2]—especially since government
censorship inhibited whatever ideological flexibility or variety the dis-
persion of production might otherwise have allowed. The first break
in this control occurred in the mid-1980s, during the *minjung* period,
when a populist alliance of workers, peasants, and factions of the middle
class joined to oppose the authoritarian state, leading to a liberalization
of the political climate and eventually to a democratically elected government.[3] The cultural component of *minjung* included a generation of
young filmmakers who emerged from the university cine clubs to create
an underground, agitational cinema, known as the "small-film movement" (*chagǔn yǒnghwa undong*). Some of these activists subsequently
founded their own small companies, allowing them to explore political
themes in the often very illustrious features that have gained international recognition as the Korean New Wave: Park Kwang-Su's *To the
Starry Island* (*Kǔ sǒm e gago sipta,* 1993) and *A Single Spark* (*Arǔmdaun
ch'ǒng'nyǒn Chǒn T'ae-il,* 1995) are outstanding examples.[4] The authorial
expressiveness allowed by this mode of production emerged, however,
in the shadow, and often within the stylistic vocabularies, of Im Kwon-
Taek's earlier auteurist attempt to fashion a Korean art cinema capable
of addressing national issues, one that was made under entirely different,
fundamentally circumscribed, industrial conditions.

Im has only occasionally had anything like the autonomy of the New Wave directors. During the 1960s and 1970s, he worked for small, usually short-lived studios that were dependent on immediate market returns, and generally not able to sustain long-term commitments of the kind that allowed an innovative directorial style to mature.[5] But still, they had more in common with the director-driven period of the silent American cinema than with the producer- or package-driven systems that replaced it. In the productive system where Im learned his craft, once topics were approved by the studio, directors generally had immediate and more or less complete responsibility for all stages of production: writing, photography, and editing, as well as directing. In this situation, where industrial genre production itself to some degree resembled western art cinema, Im was able to develop the range of skills that makes the idea of authorship credible later in his career when he was able to choose his own topics.

Other specifically Korean conditions shaped his development. A revision to the Motion Picture Law in 1973 giving producers of "quality films" more privileges in importing Hollywood moneymakers coincided with Im's desire to shift the direction of his work, and he quickly became known as a director of "quality films." The relaxation of censorship in the 1980s allowed him to raise, if not deeply to probe, previously proscribed political issues, though typically in historically distanced, allegorical form. The story of the nineteenth-century Tonghak nativist uprising, *Fly High, Run Far* (*Kaebyŏk*, 1991), for example, was read as referring to the contemporary student movement. But undoubtedly behind Im's emergence as a singularly prolific and distinctive director was the length and success of his studio work—ninety-five films in thirty-four years—and the unusual range of responsibilities it centralized in one person. He had already made fifty features in this system when, in 1973, a crisis of conscience set him on the path to the art film. "One day I suddenly felt as though I'd been lying to the people for the past 12 years. I decided to compensate for my wrongdoings by making more honest films."[6]

After this crisis, which Im has described in several interviews, he envisaged his subsequent career in two streams. As long as he continued to make genre works for mass consumption, his producers would allow these works to subsidize his "honest films," without expecting them all necessarily to make a profit. The distinction between the two streams turned out to be anything but categorical. The very profitable genre action film *The General's Son* (*Chang'gunŭi adŭl,* 1990) and its sequels contain many motifs in common with the art films considered here, while Im's "honest films" still mobilize the hoariest melodramatic effects. And *Sopyonje* (*Sŏp'yŏnje,* 1993), Im's masterpiece and the most fully realized of his personal undertakings—which he never expected to be a commercial success—turned out to be the most profitable domestic film in Korean history until the blockbuster *Shiri* (*Swiri,* Kang Je-gyu, 1999). But the arrangement did allow Im to clarify for himself a specific project: In the "honest" films he would confront the manifold traumas of Korean history, and in doing so he would create a specifically Korean art film style.

Since World War II, national art film styles have been conceived in the interplay between deconstructions of the languages of the classic Hollywood cinema and some combination of primarily two other frames of reference: first, the languages of cinemas constructed against capitalism, notably the socialist realisms adopted from the Soviet models in the People's Republic of China, Vietnam, and North Korea or the socialist modernisms developed especially in Latin America; second, the languages of precolonial domestic cultural practices as adapted to the medium of film. The first alternative was categorically unavailable in South Korea during the Park Chung Hee regime in the 1960s and '70s when Im was coming to maturity. During the consolidation of his stylistic strategies and indeed of his fundamental conception of what a film could be, domestic repression, militant anticommunism, and the demonization of North Korea anathematized any gestures toward socialist realism or the revolutionary Third Cinemas. By the *minjung* era, when loosening censorship allowed both directions to be explored in the short-film underground, Im was already fifty years old, successfully entrenched in his own project that had perforce been organized in quite different terms. Of necessity, those terms had been developed out of the other possibility. With no access to a direct critique of capitalist culture per se, Im's address to Korean modernity was negotiated in respect to precolonial national culture.

For East Asian cinemas generally, traditional theater has been the most important of such resources. The very first film made in China, for example, *Dingjun Mountain* (1905), was an adaptation of scenes from a Beijing opera. More recent Chinese films—otherwise as disparate and made in as radically different political conditions as *Two Stage Sisters, The Red Detachment of Women, Woman Demon Human, Peking Opera Blues, Stage Door, Good Men Good Women,* and *Farewell My Concubine*— attest to theater's ability to supply stylistic alternatives to American capitalist cinema. Though *Sopyonje* concerns a traditional operatic form and though precolonial dramatic and ritual forms were refurbished during the *minjung* cultural movement, theater has not supplied such a fundamental resource for Korean cinema. Im's oeuvre as a whole is, then, notable for his search through nontheatrical, pre-modern cultural forms to ground the language of a modern Korean cinema, and in several of his best films traditional cultural practices supply metaphors and models for his own aspirations.

Of Im's films about art, *Sopyonje* is the most comprehensive. The *p'ansori* singer Yu-bong and especially his adopted daughter Song-hwa are proposed as exemplary Korean artists, who attempt to sustain a specifically Korean culture against its debasement and neglect, as well as against the encroachments of foreign media. In *Mandala* (1981), the protagonist expresses his dissatisfaction with the indifference to worldly suffering that he perceives in traditional Buddha images by carving his own primitive, agonized figure. And in *Festival* (*Ch'ukje*, 1996), Im's negotiation between Confucian tradition and contemporary culture is explicitly inscribed in the two roles of the protagonist, Chun-sŏp: He is both a novelist who has made his career by writing about his family and a dutiful son who, on his mother's death, presides over the rituals of a traditional funeral, which the film presents in elaborate ethnographic detail. Bringing together the several narrators who recount the widowed mother's heroic story of raising her seven children, these rituals restage the national question in the form of an allegory of the family, one that explores the terms by which its black sheep may be reintegrated into it. The funeral ceremonies are interwoven with further dramatizations of the family in other mediums: Chun-sŏp composes a children's story of his mother's aging that is presented in a highly artificial film style

utilizing digital technology; and his exploitation of his family in his own
art is explored in critical reviews by a young journalist from a literary
magazine.[7]

Such use of multiple narrators subtends Im's distinctive formal innovations. Omniscient linear narration is replaced by extended, sometimes multiply nested, subjective flashbacks to produce a structural so-
phistication matched only by Hou Hsiao-hsien of contemporary fiction filmmakers. In Im's best films, especially *Mandala, Sopyonje,* and
*Festival,* the subjective narrators do not contradict each other and so
mobilize some humanist ontological uncertainty in the manner of, say
*Rashomon,* the locus classicus of this technique. Rather they fragment
the narrative into tesserae that, as he edits, the filmmaker recombines
to make thematic arguments, turning narrative into argument, *histoire*
into *discourse.* Im's use of the figure of the artist to investigate questions of national identity was first developed in a formally simpler film,
one made at a low point in South Korean cinema midway between
the Golden Age of the sixties and the mid-eighties renaissance. In *The
Genealogy* (*Chokpp'o,* 1978)—the work in which he himself believed he
first successfully "reflected a personal style"[8]—he turned to ceramics,
one of the mediums of Korea's greatest cultural achievement, to limn
the terms of a postcolonial cinema.

*The Genealogy* is set in the late 1930s during the most oppressive
phase of the occupation, when attempts to extirpate cultural difference
included forcing all Koreans to take Japanese names. Believing in the
sanctity of his family line, Sŏl Chin-yŏng, a Confucian clan patriarch,
refuses to dishonor his ancestors by denying his Korean name. The
negotiations between him and the colonial administration are carried
out by a young Japanese, Dani, who is also a gifted artist. Recognizing
the accomplishment of Dani's genre painting in classical styles, Sŏl
welcomes him into his home, more as a son than as an invader, and the
signs of a romance between Dani and Ok-sun, one of Sŏl's daughters,
begin to appear. Dani also experiments in modern idioms; he makes a
pencil sketch of Ok-sun, and she accompanies him as he tries to paint
the Korean countryside in oils (see figure 2.1). Meanwhile Sŏl attempts
to solve his predicament by a linguistic sleight; he simply takes the name
that is the Japanese pronunciation of the Chinese characters that form

FIGURE 2.1.
*The Genealogy:* Dani with Ok-sun, painting the landscape

his Korean name. But the Japanese see through his stratagem. Increasing the stakes, they torture his prospective son-in-law, thereby ruining his other daughter's marriage opportunity; then they draft Ok-sun into the Japanese army support unit, and Dani only narrowly manages to save her from becoming a comfort woman.

Sŏl's realization that he must choose between compromising his lineage and committing suicide comes to a crisis when his grandchildren demand Japanese names. After hearing their request, he turns to his collection of ceramics, and the film cuts to a non-diegetic interlude in which the camera scrutinizes a series of exquisite vases, while in a voice-over Sŏl quotes a Japanese theorist of Korean aesthetics, Yanaki Muneyoshi:

> Whoever reads the history of Chosŏn cannot but feel gloomy at its
> dark, miserable, and sometimes frightful history. This is the reason

why they discuss the quality of solitude in aesthetics, and the aesthetic
quality of solitude. That is, its suppressed destiny sought consolation
in unspeakable loneliness and longing. The aesthetic of Chosŏn is . . .
delicately imbued with the people's indescribable rancor, sorrow, or
longing. Where else in the world could you find such beauty with so
much sorrow? . . . Chosŏn is a country that might be weak outside,
but is strong inside in its art.

"So Yanaki Muneyoshi has written," Sŏl concludes, "but I wonder what
he would think about the suffering of Chosŏn that even forces people
to change their names?" And as the camera passes over the elaborately
wrought ceramic tiles of a Korean roof, the diegesis is restored, and we
see Sŏl walking to his final confrontation with the Japanese—and his
suicide. The film concludes with Dani and Ok-sun together watching
his funeral procession move through the countryside.

As well as experimenting with nonlinear narrative forms (for example, after Dani learns of Sŏl's death there follows a series of subjective interludes in which he imagines himself attacking his superiors in
the occupying forces), *The Genealogy* assembles the terms of Im's mature project. Traditional Korean ceramics supply a referential aesthetic
model; they embody an essential form of Korean culture. Their rounded,
hollowed forms make them readily apposite for female-gendered con-
ceptualizations of the nation, and in them is inscribed the trauma of Korean history. The central concept expressing this trauma is *han*.[9] Taken
by Koreans to be the essential national experience, *han* is constituted
from sentiments of loss and rage at the severance of wholeness and continuity between self and history. The accumulated emotions of sufferers
(and, inevitably in a strict Confucian patriarchy, especially of women),
*han* may be projected onto any political ordeal, but in this century it
has been especially the lived response to devastating colonization and
political division. The *han* sedimented in Sŏl's ceramics thus refers to
the present, but the artworks themselves do not hold practical answers
to present political problems. Any art that aspires to address Korea's
modern traumas has to be rooted in tradition, like ceramics, but also
adapted to modern, colonial mediums, like film. In *The Genealogy*, such
an art is suggested in Dani's turn away from classical ink painting to

experiments in Western art forms; his oil painting of the countryside and his pencil drawing of Ok-sun exemplify the confrontation with modern mediums that can allow the modern story to be told. But Dani's artworks also announce what in his subsequent films Im will mobilize as the two privileged symbols on which the historical trauma of the nation is reenacted: the body of the Korean landscape, especially its spectacular mountains, and the bodies of Korean women, especially those of the working class.

Both tropes are constructed from the position of patriarchal specularity, but beyond that the relationships between them are multiple, reconstructed within the narrative possibilities of each film. Generally they oscillate between parallel and complementary functions. On the one hand, beautiful images of women and landscape signify a precolonial and so prelapsarian Korea. As such they are mutually equivalent and interchangeable. In films about the modern period they both typically appear in violated or degraded forms, with the metaphoric equivalent of the desecrated woman's body being the antithesis of the natural landscape—that is, the metropolis, Seoul. On the other hand, the two tropes can also displace each other, with the natural landscape used to represent the nation in its pristine precolonial state and the woman's ravaged body its recent historical fate. Ubiquitous in Im's work, these two motifs probably reflect his own unconscious, unresolved oedipal drives, and the personal resonances they carry must be rich and complex. But both are also deeply traditional.

Landscape is the core of precolonial Korean painting, and the parallel literary traditions are informed by the rigid sexual codes of Confucian patriarchy. One of the master-myths of Korean culture is the all but sadomasochistic *Story of Ch'unhyang* (*Ch'unhyang'ga*), a fable about the daughter of a *kisaeng* (courtesan)—and so a member of the lowest class (*ch'ŏnmin*) in Chosŏn society—who is cruelly tortured during the prolonged absence of her *yangban* (aristocrat) husband. The story was the subject of the first Korean talkie in 1935, and it has been filmed a dozen times since then, with spectacular success by Lee Kyu-hwan in 1955, and most recently by Im himself.[10] One of the most famous and often-reproduced of Korean paintings, *Women on Tano Day* by Sin Yun-bok (1758–?) (figure 2.2)—itself an innovation against classical Chinese painting, combines the motifs of both the female body and the landscape, while its depiction of furtive male spectators also foregrounds the voyeuristic transactions of patriarchal specularity.[11]

Given this genealogy, any contemporary use of the two motifs must be deeply ideological, inhabited by all the cultural structures of precolonial feudalism as well as by their adaptation to the requirements of colonial and neocolonial capitalist development. However traditional it might be, the idealization of the Korean landscape is for the domestic spectator overdetermined by the industrialization and urbanization that (as at the inception of industrialization and modern landscape art in England at the end of the eighteenth century) cause the rural world to appear as the location not of agrarian labor or deprivation but of recreation and spiritual renewal. For the foreign spectator, an equivalent attraction is fueled by the imbrication of the cultural tourism of cinema with the global politics of the tourist industry, a prostitution of its

FIGURE 2.2.
*Women on Tano Day,* by Sin Yun-bok (1758–?)

spectacular natural landscape in which South Korea has conspicuously
engaged in its attempt to attract international attention.

Korean feminism and film theory have presented fully developed
analyses of the relations between both Confucian patriarchal and contemporary capitalist exploitations of women, and their roles in postcolonial literature and the Ch'ungmuro film industry.[12] The central argument has been that the metaphoric use of women to represent the violation of the nation by Japanese and U.S. aggressors can never be merely
metaphoric, for it also renews the ideological conditions for the ongoing
exploitation of women. The feminist argument is clearly applicable to
the phylum of Im's brutalized heroines: Ok-sun in *Mandala*, Se-yŏng in
*Ticket* (*Tik'et*, 1986), Ok-nyŏ in *Surrogate Mother* (*Ss'ibaji*,1986), Adada
in *Adada* (1988), Song-hwa in *Sopyonje*, Yong-sun in *Festival*, and so
on. In these films, Im represents the historical exploitation of working-
class women through graphic images of sexual victimization that also
provide quasi-pornographic sadistic pleasure for the spectator. *Adada* is
especially problematic in its use of both motifs. The scenes of Adada's
sexual intercourse with her *yangban* husband before he is corrupted
by capital and with her peasant lover before his greed causes her death
are all powerfully erotic, turning her rape into titillating spectacle. And
the sympathetic reflection of her tragedy in images of the countryside
completes the aestheticization of the environment. Whether they represent the fecundity of her youthful purity in spring and harvest time or,
in winter, the devastation to which she is victim, the scenes are always
ravishing.

However the multiple social and cultural pressures that produce
it are understood, the insistent narrative positioning of both women
and nature as objects of a masculinized national subjectivity cannot
be disregarded nor simply ascribed to a self-conscious play with the
expectations of a reifying, self-orientalizing gaze. And neither Im's own
reiterated explanation of the historical grounding of his use of the
trope of the victimized woman nor its ubiquitousness in other cinemas can mitigate its role in reproducing the ideological conditions
that sustain the exploitation of proletarian women in Korea and everywhere else. A progressive cinema will, to be sure, find its own accommodation between (to use Mao's terms) the "raising of standards"

and "popularization." But short of reengaging the utopian gesture of early feminism and jettisoning cinema as a whole with nothing "more than sentimental regret,"[13] any cinema that aspires to a wide social influence will have to work within the terms that constitute national subjectivity.

But in fact, while the two motifs consistently form the basis for Im's symbolic vocabulary, across the oeuvre their positions in the thematic structure of his narratives are not mechanically fixed. Rather, a range of local variations in different films opens out to varying degrees of self-consciousness and critique of the main combinatory. Such indeed has already been instanced in *The Genealogy*, where the invasion is enacted on the *patriarchal* body, and Ok-sun is *saved* by a *Japanese* from being *raped* by the *Japanese*. But even where, as is most common, the nation is gendered as female, the oppression of women is commonly linked not simply to the oppression of Korea by invaders but specifically to the oppression of the working class. This use of women to symbolize the working class is made possible either by virtue of the social status of the women themselves (Ok-nyŏ in *Surrogate Mother*, or Yong-sun in *Festival*) or by allegorical identification—as in the case of *Adada*, where the heroine's expulsion from the *yangban* household allows her intradiegetic affiliation with the landless peasantry and her extradiegetic association with the labor movements of the winter of 1987–88. Im's metaphoric use of gender difference allowed him to imply class issues at times when censorship prohibited any explicit address to labor unrest. It is noteworthy that in none of the cases of the sexual brutalization of women mentioned above is the male a foreign invader. He is always Korean, a "bad" Korean to be sure, who acts as the agent of an internal structural social inequality. Furthermore, in Im's two remarkable films starring actress Kim Chi-mi, the class/gender parallels are extremely complicated. In *Gilsottum* (*Kilsott'ŭm*, 1985), Kim plays an exemplary Im-heroine/victim who has suffered all Korea's trials in the last half-century; yet when she finds the son she lost during the civil war, she rejects him because his lumpen behavior and attitudes manifest a class difference she now finds unacceptable. In *Ticket* Kim's character is a divorced woman who survives by managing a brothel. As a madam, she collaborates with capitalist patriarchy in extracting surplus value from the young women who work for her; but the contradictions between her oppression of them and the oppression she herself experiences as a woman—between her roles as the agent and as the victim of exploitation—finally drive her insane.

Further to illustrate the flexibility and nuance with which Im has mobilized these motifs, I now turn to his two films about the modern existence of one of the most ancient components of Korean culture, Sŏn Buddhism, whose philosophic structures would appear categorically to inhibit the identification of the nation's geographical body and the bodies of its women. One was made before and the other after the *minjung* movement that transformed the possibilities of Korean political and cultural expression.

## Buddhism: Eroticism and Landscape in *Mandala* (1981) and *Come, Come, Come Upward* (*Aje aje para aje*, 1989).[14]

Several schools of Mahayana Buddhism were transmitted from China to Three Kingdoms Korea around the end of the fourth century, and with the Silla unification in 668 the religion became closely associated with the autocratic monarchy. By the end of the seventh century, Sŏn—the Korean form of the Ch'an schools that emphasized individual attainment of enlightenment through meditation rather than through the progressive accumulation of merit by sutra study, ritual acts, or good works—was established as the Nine Mountain Schools (*Kusan Sŏnmun*).[15] Solidifying its relation with state power, Sŏn had by the ninth century become the dominant force in Korean Buddhism, and hence the dominant cultural force in Korea. Despite seminal attempts to syncretize the schools by Ŭich'ŏn and by Chinul in the eleventh and twelfth centuries respectively, tensions between Sŏn and other schools of Buddhism, especially the Kyo schools that emphasized doctrinal study, were continuous, though Sŏn was generally dominant. During the Chosŏn dynasty, Buddhism was persecuted by the Neo-Confucian bureaucracy; monastic lands were confiscated, and most temples, including all those in metropolitan areas, were disbanded. Not until the Japanese occupation did Buddhism begin to reconstruct its former prominence; in 1935 Sŏn and Kyo were merged into a single order called Chogye, and since then both forms have been practiced side by side in all Korean temples. The restoration process has continued in the South since the liberation and partition, with the Buddhist hierarchy also renewing its relations with state power.[16]

Throughout this history, in Sŏn thought the natural world and sexuality have been antithetical. Since the time of Nine Mountain Schools the monasteries have always been built in remote mountain areas, and Sŏn has been so fundamentally associated with the mountains that the Korean vernacular for to become a monk is *ipsan*, "to enter the mountains." Celibacy is similarly fundamental. Following the *Vinaya Pitaka*, the foundational disciplinary text of Buddhism, the third of the ten precepts that the novice monk commits to during the ordination ceremony is the promise not to engage in sexual intercourse; doing so is one of four *parajikas*, offenses that can incur expulsions from the order.[17] In Sŏn thought, then, Im's two dominant tropes—the landscape and erotic relations—are both prominent, but as mutually exclusive terms of a binary: the monastic celibacy of the mountains is the antithesis of sexuality and the city. Im's two Buddhist-themed films force the disjunction between the semiotic structure of Sŏn and that of his own characteristic themes into a productive interaction. Rather than mechanically reproducing either system, they construct their narratives across the tensions between them.[18]

Both *Mandala* and *Come, Come, Come Upward* explore the same question: What is socially at stake in the choice between a pure ascetic life in the mountains and a life of active participation in the world's affairs? The films are structurally parallel, each narratively focused on a pair of Sŏn monks in mountain temples. In both, one monk makes a commitment to meditational retreat but the other leaves to live in the world; and in both, the latter option is followed as a result of expulsion from the monastery for infraction of the prohibition against sexual relations. However, in *Mandala*, both monks are males, and in *Come, Come, Come Upward*, the later film, both are females. The dynamics of sexuality, including the power and scopic relations constructed within it, appear then in antithetical, reversed formulations. *Mandala* exhibits a substantial reconfiguration of Im's usual gender positionings, but in the later film, *Come, Come, Come Upward* where the protagonists are women, they are spectacularly revised. Though the primacy of suffering in Buddhist ontology universalizes *han* in these films, presenting loss as intrinsic to the human situation rather than exclusively a condition of Korean history, nevertheless Buddhism's responsiveness—or lack of it—to the trauma of national social conditions is Im's real concern in both. But since one was made at the beginning of the 1980s and the other at the end, the question is broached from opposite points of the radical transformation of Korean society.

*Mandala,* an adaptation of a best-selling novel,[19] concerns a young monk, Pŏb-un, who meets an older monk, Chi-san, while both are on the road during the free period between winter and summer meditation (see figure 2.3). Chi-san, an obstreperous drunk, tells the story of how he was seduced, not unwillingly to be sure, by Ok-sun, a teenage girl vacationing near his temple. Soon after, her girl friend was raped, and Chi-san was accused; though he was acquitted after a semen test, the scandal of his relations with Ok-sun caused him to be expelled from

FIGURE 2.3.
*Mandala:* Pŏb-un and Chi-san in the world

the temple. Still wearing his robes, he left with Ok-sun for a period of indulgence in Seoul's bars and discos. But, as Chi-san tells Pŏb-un, dealing with sexual desire by confronting it rather than evading it did not bring enduring pleasure; sex temporarily reconciled subject and object, or self and the world, but in the end, "stacking up two bodies was a futile attempt indeed." After a week, Chi-san arrived "at a peak of emptiness" and, realizing that his vocation was still that of a monk, he left Ok-sun and became an itinerant. Later, Pŏb-un encounters Chi-san again and travels with him, eventually back to the red-light district in Seoul, where, now several years later, Ok-sun is a prostitute (see figure 2.4). Pŏb-un returns to meditation in his home temple, where he meets Su-gwan, a monk who tries to gain enlightenment by burning off his fingers. Pŏb-un meets Chi-san yet again, travels with him to the mountains in the winter, and accompanies him when he is called on to consecrate a small temple. But after a night of drunkenness, Chi-san freezes to death in the snow. Pŏb-un builds him a pyre and then returns to Seoul, where

FIGURE 2.4.
*Mandala:* Chi-san and Pŏb-un in the brothel with Ok-sun

he briefly meets his own mother, who had abandoned him as a child. Bidding her farewell, he sets out on the road again.

Chi-san is one of the artist figures who model Im's own project. As mentioned above, on one occasion when Pŏb-un's discipline and absti- nence seem ineffective, he comes across Chi-san carving a Buddha that, unlike traditional images, is crude and grotesque, tortured rather than serene. As the visuals cut to non-diegetic images of traditional smiling Buddhas, Chi-san argues that since Gautama was a human, not a god, he could not have kept smiling when the poor and the weak were "suffering under oppression by the privileged," and so his image should "bear ex- pressions of agony, grief, sorrow, and rage." Against Sŏn's lack of social engagement and the dispassion of conventional Buddhist images, Chi- san's art summarizes the compassion of his socially engaged practice and his concern with the oppression of the lowly by the privileged. These are the issues that Im wants his own art to address. Chi-san's Buddha image and the *han* it expresses figure a socially responsible cinema that can narrate the *han* of Korean history and critique contemporary Ko- rean society while still retaining a dialectical continuity with traditional cultural forms. Conversely, Im's endorsement of Chi-san's humanist re- vision of Sŏn that brings Buddhism closer to social problems also obliges him to reconfigure the deep structures of his own iconography.

The film's most crucial doctrinal issues revolve around Chi-san's sexual indulgence. Initially his doubts and his drunken licentiousness mark him, as he admits, as a degenerate apostate, a *tt'aengch'o,* "an unworthy monk, a disgrace to others." His subsequent rehabilitation demands that these sexual transgressions be not merely absolved but proven to constitute a practice superior to monastic renunciation. The narrative argues such a critique of Sŏn orthodoxy first by demonstrating the limitations of asceticism and second by revealing a soteriological implication in Chi-san's sexuality. The narrative elements that make these points are nowhere to be found in the novel; Im's fabrication of them indicates their importance to his film's argument. The limitation of asceticism are introduced via Su-gwan, a character not present in the novel and implanted in the film's narrative by Im. Su-gwan impugns the insight of his head monk, and, although he has already burned off two of his fingers, he burns off a third, in an act of symbolic castration that Im photographs in excruciating detail.[20] But later, when Su-gwan meets Pŏb-un on the road, he tells him that though his critique of the master still stands, he has realized the futility of self-mortification and indeed of meditation itself. From now on, Su-gwan affirms, he will be guided by the Buddhist precept that there is no distinction between self and others; his route to salvation will be via service to others, and he consigns himself to Kwanseŭm (Avalokitesvara), the Bodhisattva of Compassion. Questioned further by Pŏb-un, he describes how he has been inspired by a heroic monk who, during a plague on Chukto, a remote island off the south coast, devoted himself to the sick without regard for his own safety. The monk's name, he declares, was Chi-san.

The film immediately cuts to Chi-san in meditation. A shot of a flock of birds rising in the air symbolically indicates his enlightenment and prefigures Pŏb-un's,[21] and the narrative returns to the latter as he comes to meet Chi-san for the final movement of the film. From this point on, Chi-san's story unfolds exclusively in the mountains, and here he is finally recognized as a master. Called on to light the eyes of a Buddha in a mountain temple, he delivers his final sermon, emphasizing not doctrinal correctness but the awakening of the heart to Buddha. And here he achieves his fiery apotheosis. In these scenes, Im gives full rein to cinematographer Chŏng Il-sŏng's extravagantly beautiful snow-covered landscapes of Mount Sŏrak, which now read as evidence of Chi-san's enlightenment.[22]

Though in Sŏn meditational practice is absolutely superior to social benevolence, this is not the case in other forms of Mahayana Buddhism. Chi-san's final position and Su-gwan's decision to emulate him have a long genealogy in Mahayana's privileging of the bodhisattva who forgoes personal attainment of nirvana for deliberate rebirth in the cycles of *samsara* in order to save all sentient beings; Avalokitesvara (Kwanseŭm in Korean) and Manjusri are the most celebrated examples of such bodhisattvas. Indeed, Mahayana emerged in antithesis to the self-centered practice of early Buddhism that, in this respect at least, Sŏn reproduces. Similarly, though Sŏn history does record cases of "unconstrained conduct" ( *muae haeng* )—that is, unorthodox practices against the constraints of monastic discipline that resemble Chi-san's—the most important Korean instances are outside Sŏn. The most famous

is the monk, Wŏn-hyo (617–86) who, as well as writing some 240 works
on Buddhism and creating one of the five major schools of early Silla,
named his trousers "No Obstacle" and justified his visits to *kisaeng* on
the grounds that "It's not good for a monk to live in heaven all the time.
He must also visit hell and save the people there, who are wallowing in
their desires."[23] However much it may recall Wŏn-hyo's, Chi-san's sexuality is fundamentally different (as indeed it is different from practices
of ecstatic sexuality in Tantric traditions) in that it is undertaken not in
a state of enlightenment but in one of desperate suffering. In any case,
the narrative claim that Chi-san's sexual promiscuity reflected his correct
recognition of the sterility of meditational isolation and so was necessarily propaedeutic to his enlightenment is constructed across the very
weak bridge of his service to the plague victims of Chukto—an instance
of social responsibility that is not present in the novel, not represented
in the film except in Su-gwan's account, and so not developed as a component within Chi-san's characterization. This benevolent service is an
arbitrary and dramatically unconvincing addition, adduced ex machina
to link Chi-san's "love" for Ok-sun with his "love" for humanity, just as
the cycles of sexual desire and emptiness he experiences with her teach
him the meaning of the parallel cycles of death and rebirth generally. The
strain in the narrative structure reflects the tension between the novel's
vision of Buddhism and the demands of Im's own thematic concerns
and iconographic system.

The final images of Chi-san in the mountains also resolve the discursive use of landscape in the narrative. Where the sexuality/enlightenment
antinomy is resolved by authorial fiat, the parallel mountain/city binary
of the Sŏn tradition is reconfigured through the introduction of a third
spatiality: the intramontane plains of everyday village life and human
labor. The importance of this spatiality is indicated at the very beginning of the film. After the opening scenes of meditation in the mountain temple, a very long stationary shot shows a desolate and empty
winter agricultural landscape, where the only activity is a bus moving
down a primitive road at the edge of the frame. This is clearly one of
the shots that Im has spoken of as his ideal: that is, completely static
shots that articulate the "Korean traditional concept known as 'Chŏng
chung tong' . . . meaning . . . motion (or action) within stillness"—an
ideal with obvious correlatives in Buddhism.[24] But unlike the long-takes

at the beginning of *Gilsottum* and especially the celebrated long-take in *Sopyonje*—which are occupied by human actors and given elaborate thematic depth by the other art forms they each contain (respectively, the plangency of the North/South reunions in the television program and the *p'ansori* recitation)—here the only movement in the frame is the bus that will bring Chi-san and Pŏb-un together. In this liminal space between Seoul and the mountains, Chi-san wanders, performs his ministry, and finds the way to his salvation. Its thematic role is made explicit when, at the nadir of his agony, Chi-san asks where he can go. Pŏb-un tells him to go to the mountains, that is, back to the conventional practice of Buddhism. But Chi-san—whose name means "one who knows mountains"—replies this is not possible for him, setting into play the narrative's task in these everyday places—which is to equip him for precisely his movement across Im's key icons, to return him to his true self by transforming him into "one who knows mountains" from, so to speak, "one who knows women."

Chi-san's odyssey in this liminal space occupies the bulk of the film, sustaining the implication that the work of the true Buddhist is done in the midst of everyday life. The theme is dramatized in Chi-san's own narrative, as well as via his effect on other characters: on Su-gwan, on Ok-sun (who, when she has become a prostitute, devotedly receives him as a holy man), and especially on Pŏb-un. Since generally Pŏb-un's peregrinations follow Chi-san's, the landscape motif is articulated in parallel terms; the world in which Pŏb-un must find his own way between sexuality and asceticism is that of everyday life, between Seoul and the mountains. But certain aspects of the articulation of the two motifs are in Pŏb-un's case even more complex.

Like Chi-san, Pŏb-un is tormented by erotic desires that threaten his practice. Primarily he yearns for his college girlfriend, Yŏng-ju, whom he left to become a monk; the agony of his desire for her makes him a sympathetic interlocutor for Chi-san. But fueling that situation is an unresolved oedipal desire that recalls *Home Is Where the Heart Is*. In fragmentary flashbacks we learn that when he was a child his mother abandoned him to go to Seoul, driven by her own sexual desires after her husband was murdered. Traumatized by the loss of his mother, Pŏb-un continues to have an inordinate amount of affect around her; after he is enlightened by Chi-san, it is she (not Yŏng-ju, who had appeared to reclaim their love) whom he visits before he takes his final leave of human relationships. In the film's concluding scenes, Pŏb-un journeys to Seoul to meet her, and his parting from her supplies the film's most powerful visualization of liberation from earthly attachments.

But though Pŏb-un does not imitate Chi-san's exploration of sexuality, his torment is still illustrated via Im's dominant tropes. During his initiation, for example, when the master reads the precept against sexual intercourse, Im inserts—entirely without diegetic justification—a single shot of a fruit tree in full bloom. Though non-diegetic metaphors are not impossible within the terms of Im's realism, the caprice here suggests that whatever reading we might adduce—that the blossom represents Pŏb-un's realization that religious interdictions fall on life's fairest flowers, perhaps—is as much a function of Im's subjectivity as of Pŏb-un's own. Pŏb-un does not live the tension between the two tropes as fully as Chi-san does, so it surfaces only in fragments like this: cinematic versions of slips of the tongue that voice repressed desire. But in one instance the expression is extraordinary.

During the brothel scene, after Chi-san retires with Ok-sun, Pŏb-un goes to sleep in an unused room. While he is sleeping, a woman who is known to the other prostitutes for liking sex with monks, enters the room and fellates him, a reversal of the violation of women by men so common in Im's oeuvre. Though it does not entail the violent physical penetration and invasion of personhood of a real rape, when Pŏb-un awakens in the middle of it, he experiences the fellation as a horrifying defilement. Before he wakes, however, he dreams: a rapid alternating montage of his face and the back of the prostitute's naked body builds up, cut through by a series of traveling shots across a lush green forest. These are further intercut with a scene that has *no* narrative justification or explanation whatsoever. In this scene, Pŏb-un rapes his old girlfriend, Yŏng-ju. He tears at her clothes, she resists, and, as the act is consummated, Im cuts to a shot of her purse lying in the grass. In this nightmare, the film's unconscious generates a condensed figure for Im's fundamental thematics, reasserting them even at the moment of their most drastic reversal.

Where the novel emphasizes the corruption of the orthodox Buddhist community, Im's rewriting of it as a critique of Sŏn meditative asceticism allows him to reaffirm the humanism of his historically self-conscious art cinema as a whole, and also to foreground the oppression of working-class women and the redemptive power of their sexuality. Like Im's reworking of Buddhist symbolic topography, both themes are incommensurate with Sŏn doctrine. But though the tensions between Sŏn and the structuring combinatory of Im's oeuvre appear as ruptures in the thematic architecture of *Mandala,* they also generate the film's emotive power. By incorporating sexuality and spectacular landscape photography in a complex narrative so profoundly fixed in an integral component of the national culture, Im achieves a film with immense resonances for both domestic and international art film audiences. Its affective force does not come from its critique of Buddhism but from its presentation of Buddhism as a national cultural treasure, the epitome of humanist social responsibility yet also intrinsically exotic and indeed erotic—in a word, "orientalized."[25] *Mandala*'s authority rests on its sublimity, a sublimity in which soaring Buddhist chants hallow sublime Buddhist temple architecture, sublime Buddhist ritual, and even—as in the case of Su-gwan's finger burning and perhaps the "rape" of Pŏb-un—sublime Buddhist anguish.[26]

During the 1980s, the decade after *Mandala,* political liberalization and increased attention to the exploitation of the working class within the Korean economic miracle accompanied a relaxation of censorship laws that allowed filmmakers to address these issues more directly, and also allowed them a new, often exploitative graphicness in the representation of sexuality. In this context, Im made detailed studies of working-class exploitation in *Gilsottum, Ticket, Surrogate Mother,* and *Adada,* all focusing on victimized women. In 1989 he returned to a Buddhist-themed narrative, structurally parallel to *Mandala,* but with the radical difference that its main protagonists are both women. To frame the narrative possibilities that, along with the transformation of the Korean cultural environment between the two films, this change allowed, we may suggest a somewhat more formalized model of the underlying semiotic structure of both films.

Im's turn to Buddhist themes in *Mandala* allowed him to mobilize his personal symbolic system and its underlying oedipal drives within the terms of Korea's richest iconographic traditions, but one that

nevertheless imposed its own regulations on his favored images. Though
certain discrepancies between Im's personal themes and Sŏn's discursive structures generated the local emboli in *Mandala*'s narrative that
we have noted, their general isomorphism allowed him to employ as the
vehicle of his own narrative the primary structures of Buddhist dialectics,
that is, the dualisms of mind/body, self/other, thought/no thought,
and so on. Since these must be the underlying elements of any Buddhist
narrative, in Im's Buddhist-themed films his figures of mountains and
women are coherent signifiers, not simply as themselves the primary
units of narrative meaning (or semes, in structuralist terminology) but
as the form of appearance of the more fundamental structures. These
and hence the narrative grammar of the films they generate may be
represented in the form of a semiotic square[27]:

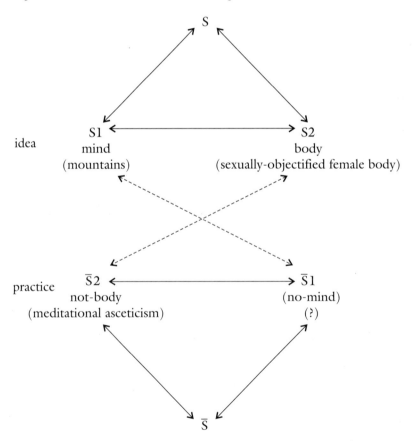

In this, S1 (mind) and S2 (body) are contraries, the fundamental binaries of Buddhist philosophy. S, their dialectical sublation, is a condition of enlightenment itself. As we have seen, in *Mandala* these concepts are mobilized in verbal debates about Buddhist doctrine, but they also appear as semes in the narrative and, in symbolic form, in the geographical environment in which narrative unfolds. When such semes are mobilized in human activity, narrative is generated, but only within the constraints they dictate. S2 produces the contradictory, $\bar{S}2$ or Sŏn meditation, which, though it is a physical practice, aims to transcend the body, as well as any sensuous, social engagement outside the *sangha*, the community of monks. For Im—from a Confucian background, uninterested in Buddhism before the popular success of the novel *Mandala*, and committed to a cinema that would contribute to progressive social reform by representing exemplary responses to the social injustices of neocolonial Korea—$\bar{S}2$ alone is a priori unacceptable. Hence his critique of conventional Sŏn. It appears to entail political disengagement, with debilitating associations with quietism, if not with collaboration in political repression, and so affirmation of it is an unacceptable narrative resolution. In parallel, $\bar{S}1$ will represent its contrary, a "thoughtless" or spontaneous social activity, directed by compassion but in accord with reality as it immediately presents itself. In Buddhist terms this means renouncing the personal attainment of nirvana and sharing all accrued merit with other sentient beings, that is, the activity of a bodhisattva like Kwanseŭm. But beyond this general principle, more concrete terms for $\bar{S}1$ are not given in advance. How should we properly live in this world of suffering is precisely the question that Im's "honest films" confront. The narrative's task is to generate a model of unselfish Buddhist social action compatible with Im's overall humanism and his rejection of ideology. If such could be found, its dialectical reconciliation with $\bar{S}2$ would then produce $\bar{S}$, that is, "enlightenment" as a social condition: a free, peaceful, and non-exploitative commonality.

*Mandala* presents Chi-san as having achieved $\bar{S}1$. But the film's weakness, I have argued, is that the manifestation of his bodhisattva activity in his service to the plague victims of Chukto is dis-articulated from its narrative links with eroticism. The result is a thematic rupture, for the implied association between sexuality and social service is not dramatized or otherwise persuasively presented. While *Come, Come, Come Upward* downplays *Mandala*'s orientalizing spectacularization of Buddhist ritual and architecture—and lacks Chŏng Il-sŏng's ravishing landscape photography—it more fully elaborates the semiotic resources of Im's combinatory. It also vividly demonstrates in both narrative and visual terms the relationship between erotic love and social compassion that is so flimsy in *Mandala*. Moreover, it allows Im to take advantage of the relaxed censorship situation and, since the main protagonists are women, female sexuality becomes to an unprecedented degree proactive. Women appear as both possessed of sexuality *and* as the agents of historical transformation rather than merely the passive objects of male violation and historical trauma. The foregrounding of female sexuality in *Come, Come, Come Upward* allows Im more forcefully to critique Sŏn, to affirm Mahayana Buddhism's compassionate social activity and his own humanism. But now his "non-ideological" humanism appears in contradistinction to the more explicitly "ideological" politics of *minjung* and the more radical New Wave filmmakers who had come to maturity during the decade.

    *Come, Come, Come Upward* is primarily the story of Sun-nyŏ, a young nun who has entered a temple as a novitiate. Despite her fervent desire for a life of meditation, she is several times refused ordination. The head nun Ŭn-sŏn mysteriously tells her that the study she needs is not to be found in the monastery and that rather than joining the *sangha* she should accept herself and the mission that she already knows is hers. The scenes of Sun-nyŏ's early days at the temple are punctuated by a series of extended flashbacks to her life as a schoolgirl, which associate her with a strong sexual energy and also with some of the most traumatic events in Korean history. These range from the defeat of the last king of Paekche by Silla and Chinese forces, through the Tonghak rebellion, to Korea's neocolonial dependency on the United States—represented by the Kwangju massacre and Korean participation in the invasion of Vietnam.[28] These flashbacks, all of which involve some combination of sexual and national politics, preoccupy virtually the first half of the film. Though justified in terms of Sun-nyŏ's characterization, they do not primarily function to reveal her psychological motivation or establish the importance of her subjectivity; in fact, as the narrative unfolds, these are revealed as irrelevant, entirely subordinate to her karma. Instead the flashbacks operate analytically, and, organized by the compositional strategies Im had perfected over the previous decade, they generate a thematic crisis. By the midpoint of the film Sun-nyŏ has become invested with all the *han* of Korean history and contemporary politics, and the film has produced Im's summary theoretical problems: How can traditional culture be used to confront the *han* of present-day Korea, and, here specifically, what part can Buddhism play in that confrontation? The second half of the film answers this question by again contrasting orthodox Sŏn practice—represented by another young nun, Chin-sŏng—with the unconventional, extra-monastic benevolent practice into which Sun-nyŏ is precipitated. Where the first half of the film is an alternating montage of Sun-nyŏ's monastic life and the previous experiences that invest her with Korea's *han,* the second half is an alternating montage of Chin-sŏng's and Sun-nyŏ's contrary practices of Buddhism.

FIGURE 2.5.
*Come, Come, Come Upward:* Sun-nyŏ is ordained

Sun-nyŏ is eventually accepted into the order (see figure 2.5), but no sooner has she taken her vows than the full weight of her karma crashes down on her. A petty criminal whose life she inadvertently saves when he attempts suicide becomes obsessed with her. His attentions are so scandalous that, despite all her appeals, Sun-nyŏ is expelled from the temple. But before she leaves, Ŭn-sŏn implies that one day she might be allowed to return. She gives Sun-nyŏ a *hwadu* or koan that restates the primary dialectics of Sŏn in terms of her own situation: "Between your spirit that stays here and your body rambling around in the world, which one is real?" Sun-nyŏ's experience of her body rambling in the real world leads her to a life of benevolent self-sacrifice among the working class that includes sexual relations with men. Initially she gives herself to the man who caused her to be expelled, and though he rapes her, she reforms him. They are both very happy, especially when she becomes pregnant, but he is killed in a mining accident, and Sun-nyŏ suffers a miscarriage. She continues her practice, becoming a nurse and working heroically through an epidemic on an off-shore island—an event that (unlike its equivalent with Chi-san on Chukto in *Mandala*) is extensively represented and integrated into the narrative. During the epidemic, Sun-nyŏ becomes involved with an ambulance driver named Song, caring for him and his baby son. All the while, her bodhisattva practice of spontaneous benevolence in the real word is counterpointed with the career of Chin-sŏng, who manifests none of Sun-nyŏ's social commitment. Even when she encounters the 1987 democratization riots during a period of university study in Seoul, Chin-sŏng dismisses the activist student who castigates her lack of concern for the struggles of the urban workers and the farmers. But her meditational practice fails to develop, and she too sets out wandering.

The divergent practices reach their crisis in two paired scenes that conclude the film. In the first, a surrealistic sequence parallel to Pŏb-un's nightmare but also recalling Su-gwan, Chin-sŏng's quest has led her to a remote cave. While she is meditating there, she is assaulted by a monk who has castrated himself in a vain attempt to transcend his own sexual desire and so free himself from obsession and anxieties. He seizes her and undoes his clothes as if he would rape her (figure 2.6), yet all he can do is force her to look at his wound. The scene is extraordinary, without

FIGURE 2.6.
*Come, Come, Come Upward:* The attempted rape of Chin-sŏng

parallel in any cinema I know. Beginning as if it will again act out the
violation of a woman by a man, it categorically inverts patriarchal power
and scopic relations. It is the man, not the woman, who is positioned as
the object of the gaze, and when the woman looks, what she sees is the
mark of his castration, his lack of a phallus that figures the impotence
of meditational asceticism and self-mortification. The film then returns
to Sun-nyŏ's ministry. She continues her heroic work, and the epidemic
is eventually contained. After the doctors and nurses have a party to
celebrate their success, she and Song go home together, and, in a very
graphic scene, they make love. But so powerful is her sexuality that
he dies during his orgasm. Again the film cuts, this time back to the
mountain temple: Chin-sŏng has broken the impasse in her practice, but
Ŭn-sŏn is on her deathbed. Sun-nyŏ hurries to Ŭn-sŏn, who welcomes
her and indicates that she—Sun-nyŏ not Chin-sŏng—has fulfilled her
mission. While watching Ŭn-sŏn's cremation, Sun-nyŏ finally realizes
the answer to her *hwadu*. Recognizing the Buddha-nature that was,

as Ŭn-sŏn implied, already hers all along, she collects fragments of the abbess's bones, planning to build a thousand pagodas, each with a bone at its heart. The film ends with her, now fully comprehending the relation between spiritual and material realities, setting out—again—to save the masses from their struggle in illusion.

Together, Sun-nyŏ's and Chin-sŏng's diametrically opposite practices—respectively $\bar{S}1$ and $\bar{S}2$ on the square—catalogue the Im combinatory as it is articulated through contemporary Buddhism and figured in extreme forms of sexuality. The tension between the mountains and the metropolis is again resolved by centering the narrative in small provincial towns, but this time more richly and completely than in *Mandala*. The resultant spatiality appears as the location of industry, ordinary social affairs, human relations, and, of course, epidemic illness (which is a summary figure for the inevitable suffering and transcience of life). It mediates between mountain isolation and the polemically political, Marxist-influenced politics of Seoul—where, by this time, the small-film movement's confrontation with Korean social injustice was more radical, filmically and politically, than Im ever sought to be. Oscillating between the extremes of Seoul and the mountain cave, Chin-sŏng's itinerary links these spaces, denigrating both radical politics and asceticism as opposite sides of the same coin. Sun-nyŏ achieves enlightenment in the liminal geographies between them. Her sexual munificence is metonymic for her general social ministry, and it is the source of her own spiritual development. This allows the film to assert a redemptive humanism, founded in female sexuality and defined in contradistinction to both meditational asceticism in the mountains and the ideological models of violent social change taking place in the *minjung*-dominated metropolis. Sun-nyŏ's sexual self-sacrifice is, of course, on one level a sadomasochistic Confucian male fantasy, and the scene where the intensity of her sexuality kills Song echoes with the motifs of soft-core pornography and exploitation genre films (for example, cult filmmaker Kim Ki-yŏng's sexually voracious "Killer Butterfly" women). But Sun-nyŏ's love is also the benevolence of an enlightened bodhisattva, and we may surmise that if the ecstasy with which she delivers Song from this incarnation does not take him to nirvana, then nothing will.[29] As a conclusion to her work in the epidemic, her act is the fully expressive climax of her overall spiritual itinerary, the peripety of a narrative in which Im negotiates the conventions of both popular melodrama and Korea's richest precolonial heritage to argue a compelling cultural allegory: Rather than merely representing the ravished, colonized nation, a working-class woman becomes both symbol and agent of its redemption.

## Notes

1. For research and other forms of assistance in the preparation of this essay, I am indebted to Jiwon Ahn, Kyung Hyun Kim, and Dale Wright. All translations from the Korean are by Jiwon Ahn and Kyung Hyun Kim. An abbreviated version of this essay appeared in *Film Quarterly* 54, no. 3 (Spring 2001): 14–31.

2. Huh Chang, "Anatomy of the Korean Film Industry," *Koreana* 3, no. 4 (1989): 4.

3. On the *minjung* period, see Hagen Koo, "The State, Minjung, and the Working Class in South Korea," in *State and Society in South Korea,* ed. Hagen Koo (Ithaca: Cornell University Press, 1993), 131–62; and *South Korea's Minjung Movement: The Culture and Politics of Dissidence,* ed. Kenneth M Wells (Honolulu: University of Hawai'i Press, 1995).

4. For an overview of the emergence of this generation of directors, see Isolde Standish, "Korean Cinema and the New Realism: Text and Context," in *Colonialism and Nationalism in Asian Cinema,* ed. Wimal Dissanayake (Bloomington: Indiana University Press, 1994); for a consideration of the authorial role of the director in this period, see Kyung Hyun Kim, "The Emergence of Auteurism in Recent Korean Cinema, " *Korean Culture* 17, no. 3 (1996): 4–11.

5. In the late 1950s, when Im was serving his apprenticeship and the industry was producing about 100 features a year, there were seventy-two companies; in 1973, the Motion Picture Law reduced the number of these companies from seventy-one to sixteen; see Lee Young-Il, "A Thumbnail Sketch of Korean Film History," in *Im Kwon-Taek: Filmemacher aus Korea/A Korean Filmmaker* (Munich: Munich Film Festival, 1990), 72.

6. Quoted in Gina-Yu Gustaveson, "Im Kwon-Taek: Filmmaker and Humanist," in *Im Kwon-Taek: Filmemacher aus Korea,* 30. The film with which Im attempted to move from merely commercial filmmaking was *The Deserted Widow* (*Chapch'o,* 1973). Another account of Im's personal crisis is recorded by Tadao Sato: "It was the fruit of an intense feeling of wanting to throw off the mask that I so fondly wore when entertaining my audiences. I wanted to escape from those blatant lies. . . . [T]he best way to bring out the truth, I thought,

```

DAVID E. JAMES

was to depict the life of my own mother"; see Sato's "Tradition and Transition: Im Kwon-Taek," *Cinemaya* 12 (1991): 63.

7. In this list of artist-protagonists, surrogates for the director himself, one should also note the journalist in *The Hidden Hero* (*Kippal ŏmnŭn kisu*, 1979), and his writer's block; foreshadowing Adada's muteness in *Adada* (1988), it represents Im's narration of the impossibility of telling the Korean story. A parallel complex of issues revolves around language, with the tensions among Chinese, Japanese, and Hangŭl representing the fragmentation of national identity, somewhat in the manner of Hou Hsiao-hsien's use of linguistic dispersal in his films about the colonial period in Taiwan. The name change the Japanese impose on the patriarch in *The Genealogy* is an especially condensed instance; see the discussion below. Adada's imminent degradation is similarly prefigured by her husband's attempts to treat her muteness by teaching her to pronounce Japanese letters. Parallel issues recur with the prostitutes in *The Hidden Hero* who learn English to work the occupying GIs.

8. Quoted in Klaus Eder, "Conversation with Im Kwon-Taek," in *Im Kwon-Taek: Filmemacher aus Korea*, 30.

9. On *han*, see Choi Kil-Sung, *Hankuk-in Ŭi Han* (The Korean's *han*) (Seoul: Yechonsa, 1991). Recently, Korean Americans have superimposed the fact of exile from the homeland on the inherited resonances of *han*; see, for example, Juli Kang, "Stories Behind the Han," *Koream Journal* 9, no. 3 (March 1998): 20. *Sopyonje* contains Im's fullest elaboration of the aesthetics of *han*, articulated in Yu-bong's teaching and dramatized in Song-hwa's performance.

10. Im's *Chunhyang* (2000) was chosen for the Official Competition Section at the Fifty-fifth Cannes Film Festival, the first time ever that a Korean film was so honored.

11. Sin, the first Korean artist to paint *kisaeng*, was eventually expelled from the Bureau of Painting because of his erotic themes. See Marjorie Williams, "Five Hundred Years of Korean Painting." *Orientations* 12, no. 1 (January, 1981): 10–13.

12. For the "violence" of sexualized representations of the nation, see You-me Park, "Against Metaphor: Gender, Violence and Decolonization in Korean Nationalist Literature," in *In Pursuit of Contemporary East Asian Culture*, ed. Xiaobing Tang and Stephen Snyder (Boulder, Colo.: Westview Press, 1996), 33–48. For the ideological function of the Korean "women's film" and for avant-garde feminist critiques of it, see Kim So-young, "Questions of Woman's Film," in *Post-Colonial Classics of Korean Cinema*, ed. Chungmoo Choi (Irvine: University of California Press, 1998). And for the cultural reverberations of the double oppression of postcolonial Korean women, see Chungmoo Choi, "Nationalism and Construction of Gender in Korea," in *Dangerous Women: Gender and Korean Nationalism*, ed. Elaine H. Kim and Chungmoo Choi (New York: Routledge, 1998), 9–30.
```

13. Laura Mulvey, "Visual Pleasure and Narrative Cinema," *Screen* 16, no. 3 (autumn 1975): 18.

14. *Aje aje para aje* are the opening syllables of the Korean form of the Sanskrit mantra *Gate, gate, paragate, parasamgate, bodhi svaha* that concludes the *Heart Sutra*.

15. Deriving from the Chinese *Ch'an*, *Sŏn* is the meditational form of Buddhism known as *Zen* in Japanese. For English language accounts of Korean Buddhism, see especially Robert E. Buswell, "Buddhism in Korea," in *The Encyclopaedia of Religion*, vol. 2, ed. Mircea Eliade (New York: Macmillan, 1987), 421–26; *Tracing Back the Radiance: Chinul's Korean Way of Zen* (Honolulu: University of Hawai'i Press, 1991); and *The Zen Monastic Experience: Buddhist Practice in Contemporary Korea* (Princeton, Princeton University Press, 1991). See also *Dropping Ashes on the Buddha: The Teaching of Zen Master Seung Sahn*, ed. Stephen Mitchell (New York: Grove Press, 1976); *Lives of Eminent Korean Monks*, ed. Peter Lee (Cambridge: Harvard University Press, 1969); Keel Hee-Sung, *Chinul: The Founder of the Korean Son Tradition* (Seoul: Po Chin Chai, 1984); Mu Soeng, Sunim, *Thousand Peaks: Korean Zen—Tradition and Teachers* (Berkeley: Parallax Press, 1987); and *A Buddha from Korea: The Zen Teachings of T'Aego*, ed. J. C. Cleary (Boston: Shambala, 1988).

16. Buddhism was actively supported by both the Syng-man Rhee and Park Chung Hee administrations, and after Roh Tae-woo's government put him on trial for the Kwangju Massacre, Chun Doo-hwan took refuge in a Buddhist temple. Until the mid-1970s neither the Buddhist *sangha* or the Christian church was actively involved in the social and political movements of the time; a "Minjung Buddhism" did not emerge until several years after *Mandala*.

17. In only one period was this celibacy qualified. During the occupation, following the Japanese custom, monks were permitted to marry. Believing that Buddhism had to secularize if it was to regain its contact with the lay population, Han Yong-Un (1878–1944) vigorously proposed this, circumventing the Vinaya prohibition by employing the notion of "the unimpeded interpenetration of all phenomena" (*sasa muae*), a "quintessential doctrine of interfusion" (Buswell, *Zen Monastic Experience*, 27) that he invoked to argue that there was no real difference between celibacy and marriage. The project was initially successful, but in the post-liberation era, hostilities—and sometimes physical conflict—between married and celibate monks for possession of the monasteries flared up. Government intervention eventually secured the dominance of the celibate Chogye Order, which presently retains it.

18. By contrast, the Korean film about Buddhism that is best known in the West, *Why Has Bodhi-Dharma Left for the East?* (*Dalma ga tongtchok kŭro kan kkadakŭn*, Pae Yong-gyun, 1989), simply reproduces them; it is set in the mountains, and women are all but entirely excluded.

19. Kim Song-dong, *Mandala: A Novel*, trans. Ahn Jung-hyo (Seoul: Dong-suh-Munhak-sa, 1990). The two monks have different kinds of relationships and with more women in the novel, and the film makes other substantial changes, some of which are discussed below.

20. On finger burning in Sŏn, see Buswell, *Zen Monastic Experience*, 195–97.

21. A major component of Sŏn meditation revolves around a koan (Korean: *hwadu*) that the master assigns to each novice. Pŏp-un's is the question about how to remove a bird trapped in a bottle without breaking the bottle, and his progress toward solving it is regularly raised in his discussions with the abbot. Placed between scenes involving Chi-san and himself, the unmotivated image of the birds suddenly rising from the ground suggests that Pŏp-un has solved his *hwadu* and links Chi-san's breakthrough to his own.

22. Chŏng Il-sŏng's photography has contributed substantially to Im's overall achievement. As well as *Mandala*, he shot *Gilsottum, The General's Son, Fly High, Run Far, Sopyonje, Adada,* and *The Taebaek Mountains (T'aebaek sanmaek,* 1994)—all of them distinctly alike, distinctly unlike Im's film's with other cinematographers, and also unlike Chŏng's cinematography for other directors (such as Kim Ki-yong). In all cases, the distinctiveness of the landscape photography raises the issue of Im's relation to the language of classical Chinese painting. (Chŏng was in fact trained in classical painting, before he turned to photography.) Korean landscape artists of the early Chosŏn dynasty were strongly influenced by Chinese models, especially of Northern Sung—the same era whose art has been most influential on Chinese cinema since the abandonment of Socialist Realism. But by the eighteenth century, Korean styles and themes were being modified in the direction of greater realism, especially by Chong Son (1676–1759), the first Korean artist to advocate painting directly from nature rather than from other paintings. This movement, called "landscape painting of actual scenes" (*chin'gyong sansu*) also affected genre painting of the same period, including Sin Yun-bok (Williams, "Korean Painting,"10–13). Despite these modifications, it is clear that the multi-perspectival pictorial organization of panoramic views with only the tiniest of human figures, the use of extremely high horizons that flatten visual space, the inclusion of large areas of unpainted surface, and similar properties of Sung landscape inform Im's work, and the result is to affirm an East Asian (if not a specifically Korean) visual language. But in the case of *Mandala,* the formal parallels with Sung painting are less important than the Taoist—and hence Ch'an—epistemological principles they manifest, specifically the lack of a fixed position for the viewer and the limitless extension of space that figure the subjectivity of a consciousness that rejects the distinction between self and object in its embrace of the Void. The transposition of these principles to photography informs the visual composition

of the temple photography (especially the placement of figures in geometrically demarked sections of the frame, otherwise entirely occupied by a monochrome or black "void"), and especially the photography of Sŏrak-san in winter at the climax of *Mandala,* where the snow and mist allow Chŏng to disassemble the mountains into quasi-autonomous fragments that resemble the composition of Sung landscapes.

23. Mitchell, *Dropping Ashes,* 62; see also Mu, *Thousand Peaks.* Buswell notes that the last Sŏn master to practice unconstrained conduct was Ch'unsong *sunim* (1891–1978), a disciple of Han Yong-un whose most notorious act was to make reference to the vagina of Park Chung Hee's wife during the first lady's birthday celebration; see Buswell, *Zen Monastic Experience,* 127–28. More clearly in the novel than in the film, Chi-san invokes Won-hyo, but as a nihilist rather than as justification for his own profligacy; see Kim, *Mandala,* 108.

24. Quoted in Eder, "Conversation," 34. Im continues, "My ideal camera is static. To be honest, my mobile shots, tracking and panning, are only expressions of my fear and insecurity in not having found my ideal static shot." The parallel with Mizoguchi is obvious, though this indicates not his direct influence but their common relationship to a traditional East Asian aesthetic derived ultimately from Chinese Buddhism. Other elements of camera style in *Mandala* and Im's films of this period generally that reflect the same aesthetic include the positioning of figures in a small portion of the screen with the rest occupied by, for example, a flat wall; the effect is to place human subjects in a visual void, again a specifically Buddhist trope.

25. Western fascination with Buddhism, including the current vogue for Tibetan Buddhism in Hollywood, is undoubtedly nourished by the same kind of sliding erotic/aesthetic affectivity that Im develops. Cross-cultural confusions, of course, follow. For example, Cardinal Joseph Ratzinger, designated by the *Los Angeles Times* as "the Vatican's chief guardian of doctrine," recently attacked Buddhism as "'an erotic spirituality' [that] would replace Marxism as the church's greatest challenge by 2000"; see John Dart, "Vesak Festival Celebrates Life of Buddha," *Los Angeles Times,* May 5, 1997, sec. B, p. 3.

26. In this essay I have been careful to avoid the assertion that these are in any categorical sense "Buddhist" films. Rather I propose that in their narratives about Buddhism, the affirmation of certain spiritual and cultural principles pertaining to Buddhism and the use of Buddhist iconography and aesthetics are held in a productive tension with the critical interrogation of Buddhism's contemporary social role. In doing so, I have elided what must surely be the fundamental question for all study of the relationship between Buddhism and cinema: that is, the degree to which Buddhist principles may supply a film's formal properties rather than its thematic concerns. Stated baldly, is it possible for a film to manifest

Buddhist principles and so in some sense to *be* Buddhist or to perform Buddhist functions, irrespective of whether its narrative is *about* Buddhism? Or, can the Buddhism be a function of filmic rather than profilmic or diegetic codes? For a Korean argument that Buddhist teachings are built into the process of making Buddhist art, see Dojin, "Built-in Buddhist Teachings: The Invisible Through the Visible," *Lotus Lantern* (Seoul) 1, no. 1 (spring 1999): 12–13. The possibility that Buddhist meaning may reside in the cultic events a film organizes rather than in its discursiveness is raised by certain Western avant-garde abstract films— James Whitney's *Yantra* and Jordan Belson's *Samhadi,* for example—that may be understood as involving processes correlative to *dhyana.* Presumably parallel issues are raised by other Western media that display meditational functions, either demanding them in the process of their manufacture or inducing them at the point of reception. Ad Reinhardt's all black paintings, together with his admiration for the putatively timeless perfection of Buddhist art, are especially apposite instances; see his essay, "Timeless in Asia," *Art News* 58, no. 9 (January 1960): 33–35. Conversely, given the history of Buddhism's syncretism, it is not likely that any essentially or exclusively Buddhist properties in traditional Buddhist culture will be categorically distinguishable from the more generally Asian aesthetic forms in which they inhere, and presumably the same syncretism allows Buddhism to operate in sympathetic Western culture of entirely different origins. Nevertheless, the question is an important one, for its own sake, and also to allow for the notice of films which may deal in Buddhist iconography without having any real commitment to Buddhist values—though this is not the case with Im, as I take it. Fran Cho's study of *Why Has Bodhi-Dharma Left for the East,* "Imagining Nothing and Imaging Otherness in Buddhist Film," in *Imag(in)ing Otherness: Filmic Visions of Living Together,* ed. S. Brent Plate and David Jasper (Atlanta: Scholars' Press, forthcoming) is an exemplary exploration of the relation between diegetic and filmic expression of Buddhist principles.

27. The following is loosely based on Algirdas Greimas, "The Interaction of Semiotic Constraints," in *On Meaning: Selected Writings in Semiotic Theory* (Minneapolis: University of Minnesota Press, 1987), 48–62.

28. In the first, when questioned by Ŭn-sun, the abbess at her temple, Sun-nyŏ says she comes from Kwangju, the site of the U.S. supported massacre of democratic activists in 1980. In the second, she finds a monk visiting her mother, with whom she lives after her father abandoned them. Conniving to meet the monk, she later travels with him toward his temple, and as they walk together across bleak snowy mountains, he tells her about her father: after serving in Vietnam, he became a monk but, when it was too late, he realized that the most precious things are achieved not by solitary meditation but by suffering with the starving masses. And in the third, still as a school girl, she develops a crush

on her teacher. Although he claims to have a wife and a child, she comes across him one night, alone and drunk on a city street. She connives to travel with him, too, and learns that his wife was killed at the Kwangju massacre, when she was eight months pregnant. The two visit the famous cliff, Nakhwa am, where the teacher recounts the story of the defeat of the last king of Paekche by Silla and Chinese forces, and the suicide of his 3,000 concubines; but he asserts that since history is always written by the victors, the king should be recognized as a patriot and his dissoluteness forgotten. He tells Sun-nyŏ that he promised his wife he would write an epic poem about both the end of Paekche and the Tonghak rebellion. (Sun-nyŏ accidentally comes across this book, just before her final sexual encounter discussed below.) Finally, in an incident that recalls Chi-san's Buddha icon, Sun-nyŏ overhears a tour guide explaining that the large Buddha images in the grounds of her temple are visually ambiguous, resembling traditional images but also ordinary people.

29. Though Sun-nyŏ's sexual benevolence clearly reflects generic requirements and the structures of Korean patriarchy generally, it is not without precedent in the Korean Buddhist tradition. The contemporary Sŏn master Seung Sahn, for example, has made reference to a prostitute called "Pass-a-million," who during the Buddha's time used sex to teach Buddhism; all the men she had sex with became enlightened. See Mitchell, *Dropping Ashes on the Buddha*, 65.

*Eunsun Cho*

CHAPTER 3

# The Female Body and Enunciation in
## *Adada* and *Surrogate Mother*

*Adada,* Im Kwon-Taek's film about a woman who is destroyed by patriarchy, begins with a most unusual scene, a close-up on a hand using sign-language to speak silently on the topic of sick and healthy bodies and minds. As the white hand and its fingers move before a black background, the signifiers they set afloat in the air are simultaneously translated in subtitles: "Although I, a mute, am physically disabled, my mind is healthy. The people who lived around me had healthy bodies, but their minds were disabled." This uncanny scene conjures up many questions and an unsettling curiosity: Is this a voice-over narration of some kind? Who is "I"? Is it male or female? How is the sign-language statement related to the film? And, since the "I" speaks of itself in the present tense and of "the people" in the past, is the living "I" talking about people who are dead?

Though the matter of the life and death of the characters is not resolved until the film's end, answers to the other questions are supplied after the credits, in a sequence where a mute girl breaks a honey pot. We can then identify the "I" with the mute, and understand that in the opening she made comments about herself and the people who troubled her life. But there still remains an eerie impression. For even if we put aside the literal absence of a voice in the voice-over, we are still not able to localize its signifiers. We cannot attach the "voice" to a body from which it issues as in typical voice-over narrations of fiction films for, except for her hand, the narrator's body is outside the frame. Emanating from her "dismembered" body, her partially disembodied narration hovers in cinematic space without being anchored to a source. Further rupturing the typical use of voice-over as an initiator of narrative is the excessive gap between the mute girl's "voice-over" and the film's diegesis. Not only does the credit sequence separate her "voice-over" from the diegesis, her narration does not introduce the diegesis; rather it comments *about* it. Deprived of a determinate location, her "voice" drifts through the border between the inside and the outside of the frame and of the diegesis. The uncomfortable feeling evoked by the unidentifiable enunciator deepens further when the film's conclusion reveals that the dismembered body is already dead, that her signifiers can never return to their corporeal source.

This mysterious posthumous voice-over discloses and illuminates the destiny of the female voice and body in *Adada*. On the one hand it strongly suggests that in the film the female voice is absent, that when she attempts to speak she is cut off and relegated to invisibility. Yet even though her voice is silent, her body speaks nevertheless, by whatever means—even transcending death. The voice-over becomes a "body-over" that goes beyond an otherwise absolute limit.

Women's deaths are a staple in Im Kwon-Taek's films, particularly those that have been successfully received on international film circuits, films like *Surrogate Mother* (*Ssibaji*, 1986), *Adada* (1988), and *Sopyonje* (*Sŏp'yŏnje*, 1993)—which won awards respectively at the Venice, Montreal, and Shanghai festivals—and more recently *Chunhyang* (*Ch'un-hyangdyŏn*, 2000), which was invited to compete in the 2000 Cannes festival. By and large these films are centered on three elements: premodern Korea as a historical setting, beautiful landscapes, and victimized women. Women are abused, humiliated, abandoned, tortured, and sometimes killed in pristine natural settings. Absorbed into the beauty of the mise-en-scène, the suffering women are aestheticized and scarcely allowed to articulate their pain. When they die, they do so in coerced silence, their trouble-ridden bodies effaced.

The aesthetics of Im's films typically suppress women's agency and usurp their voices, disseminating an "imaginary signifier" of Korean-ness: sacrificed but enduring and ever beautiful women. But within this oppressive cinematic space there are intermittent lapses, inconsistent moments when the aesthetic does not completely muffle women's enun-ciation. Sometimes, even when deprived of their voices, women speak through their bodies. And sometimes, when they are killed in filmic space, they appear in the form of a phantasmagoric body to make their suffering heard—as in the opening sequence of *Adada*. Even though female subjects in Im's films are repressed to fabricate images of Kore-anness, the repressed can also return on the surfaces of their bodies.

In this essay I will explore the representation of women in two of Im's films, *Adada* and *Surrogate Mother*. I will demonstrate that the female protagonists' bodies are exploited and erased by patriarchal aes-thetics, yet at the same time the films fail fully to contain them. Women's bodies fracture the order of masculine language, and their energies are never entirely domesticated to it. Through the textual crevices they gen-erate, liminal terrains in the otherwise totalizing discourse of Korean national cinema come into view.

## The Scene of Han and Its Excess in Adada

In an interview, Im Kwon-Taek reflected on the dramatic transformation in his filmmaking:

> Before the mid-1970s, I produced films that pursued only cheap en-tertainment values. Then I became aware that I would not survive as a director if I continued to pursue mere entertainment, like American films do. . . . I began to think, "How can I survive as a film director?" At the time, I was also getting old. Realizing that my life is connected to my films, I had been thinking of myself critically: "How can I spend my whole life so degraded?" "What could I possibly lose from making serious films?"[1]

After he decided to stop making "degraded" films and move to "serious" ones, Im "reached the conclusion that if we could capture the look of Korea as a specific region . . . [and make] films based on our stories that no one else can tell," and if their subject matter were "something that could not be conceived unless you're Korean," then Korean cinema could survive.[2] But what are our stories that no one else can tell, the stories that are inconceivable except by Koreans? The most commercially successful one turns out to be that of sacrificed women set against the landscape of ancient Korea: the stories of Korean women's pent-up sorrow and grief that cannot be expressed, the stories of their *han*.

Based on *Idiot Adada* (*Paekch'i Adada*, 1935), a short story by Kye Yong-muk, *Adada* takes place during the historical convulsions of Korea in the period of Japanese colonization. Adada is a mute woman of a noble family, but in the course of her trouble-ridden life, she is abandoned by every patriarchal figure she meets and is ultimately driven to her death.[3] She marries a man from a noble but impoverished family, who weds her because of her dowry of rice fields. After a short period during which they are both happy, her husband disappears. Drawn by opportunities offered by the Japanese colonialist economy, he becomes a successful capitalist in the Manchurian drug trade. He returns to Korea with a new wife, a former bar-girl. He physically abuses and mentally humiliates Adada, and finally banishes her from his house. She tries to return to her parents' home, but her father's Confucian beliefs prevent him from taking her in. She goes to live with a landless peasant, Su-ryong, who appears genuinely to love her. One day Su-ryong discovers that Adada has some money, given to her by her parents-in-law. He decides to use it to buy a rice-field, but Adada, who knows too well the destructive power of money, throws it into a river. Going berserk, Su-ryong pushes her into the river to retrieve it. As she tries to recover the banknotes from the surging water, Adada drowns.

In her distressed life, Adada encounters three men—a father, a husband, and a lover—who all reject her and who are all complicit in her destruction. Each man reflects a different form of Korean patriarchy. When she returns to her parents after being evicted by her husband, her father abides by the Confucian principle that once a woman is married she can never leave her husband's family; as the Korean proverb says,

"Even after her death a married woman must remain a ghost of her husband's family." Rejecting her at the gate of his house, her father proudly declares that his family has had a *yŏlnyŏ*—a wife who sacrifices herself to serve her husband—and a *hyobu*—a dutiful daughter-in-law— for three generations; her return home would bring disgrace to his family lineage. Traditionally *yŏlnyŏ* and *hyobu* were admired as exemplary women; they enriched the family's reputation and nobility, and the government raised commemorative monuments to them. Through the institutionalized subordination of women to their husbands' families, feudal Korea justified women's repression and sealed them up in their *han.* Having no choice but to be virtuous, they could only bury their pain and sorrow in their minds. Emblematic of the historical shift from the completely Confucian traditional agricultural society to the modern capitalism of the colonial period (1910–45), Adada's husband brings more violence and misery to her. Although his wealth derived from her dowry and labor, when he no longer needs her economic support he claims their marriage is invalid. And finally Su-ryong, the landless peasant, drives her to her death because she destroys his dream of wealth. Whether agrarian or mercantile, feudal or capitalist, bourgeois or proletarian, all the agents of Korean society are patriarchal figures who exile and ravage Adada. In such an inexorably male-centered social structure Adada cannot speak. The severity of patriarchy enforces her silence, locking her up in inaudible *han.*

Though cruelty characterizes the story of *Adada,* in this and Im's other films set in the past, beauty informs the film's images. The stories narrativize a Korean woman's *han,* while the visuals aestheticize it. In the traffic between cruelty and beauty, women's *han* is sublimated into aesthetic images, so that the *han* represented in Im's films indicates something beyond women's suffering. It is always already an index to a certain ethnographic cultural signifier. The process of sublimation thus enacts the function of what Roland Barthes calls "a second-order semiological system."[4] On the sign *han* is imposed the connotation of particular beauty, a beauty that is particular because it always specifically connotes "the Korean." Instead of signifying women's trouble and pain, *han* surreptitiously deploys an additional meaning: a myth of Korean

FIGURE 3.1:
*Adada:* Adada and Su-ryong


cinematic aesthetics. Im's aesthetic thereby conceals women's suffering rather than representing it.

Such a process of sublimation and mythologizing is clearly dramatized in another of Im's films, *Sopyonje*. Its narrative about traditional Korean folk opera, *p'ansori*, portrays aesthetic sublimation's destructiveness for female subjects, especially the protagonist Song-hwa. Aspiring to lead her to the summit of her art, her stepfather teaches her to perfect the expression of *han* in her *p'ansori:* not by articulating it directly but by sublimating it into the beauty of her singing. And though he blinds her, at the end of the film she sings the story of Simch'ŏng, a *p'ansori* about a filial daughter who sacrifices herself to open the eyes of her blind father—as if to affirm that she does not resent the sacrifices her father has imposed on her. Like Song-hwa, Adada is not allowed to speak of her trouble-ridden life. Her function is to produce aesthetic images of Korea; indeed, her life is *trans-mute-ed* into images. Such aestheticization fabricates what I want to designate as "the scene of *han*," a scene in which women wracked with pain are displayed as objects that can be enjoyed on screen—though from a proper aesthetic distance.

In Im's films women's bodies are exploited to fabricate "the scene of *han*" most often by being inserted or transfigured into the scenery of premodern Korea. In the case of *Adada*, the cinematography achieves effects of transparent attenuation, evoking the textures of oriental watercolor painting. The mountains veiled in mist, the green rice fields of spring where people have just scattered seeds, or the golden rice fields of autumn waving in the wind; these natural settings are diffused in light and colors to produce a feeling of natural harmony, nostalgia, and pictorialized sadness. Adada herself is often positioned at the edge of a luminous, pristine landscape, looking like a small, mobile object emanating from its colors and lines. Sometimes a lucent haze produced by soft focus enfolds her body, suggesting a heavenly figure whose suffering cannot be heard on earth. Aestheticized and fetishized, her pain and death are absorbed into a mythic nature.

The sequence of her wedding night shows how Adada's voice is repressed by the aestheticization of the images as well as by the violent patriarchy depicted in the film's narrative. In a sequence romanticized by soft lighting, she attempts to resist her husband's advances, but at the moment he forcibly penetrates her, the camera shifts to a series of close-ups on her body and her contorted face. Though her mouth is wide open as if she is screaming, she cannot scream, for she is a mute. Even the guttural "uh-uh-ah-u" sound she makes is repressed, for the shot cuts away from her face to a sensuous close-up on the shaking *chokturi*, the decorative hair accessory brides wear during traditional wedding ceremonies. Her scream is muffled and dissimulated by an image, a signifier of the Korean. Her humiliation and helplessness during what is a virtual rape are displaced by an exotic sign set up in the "scene of *han*," which doubly afflicts the woman's body and deadens her voice, even as it fabricates the aura of the national.

Im, who at the crisis of his art decided not to make "degraded" images, instead redirected it to capturing "the look of Korea." But played out in that look are a fantasy and ideology associated with women, nature and the ethnography of Korea. Rey Chow has argued

that modernity is structured by what she terms "primitive passions";
it is constructed by intellectuals who "find in the underprivileged a
source of fascination that helps to renew [and] rejuvenate" culture.[5]
Im's "look" of Korea is invested with such "primitive passions." It
seizes upon what is already irretrievable in the present-day, modernized,
even postmodernist nation: a myth of women's *han* imprisoned in the
aesthetics of a historic Koreanness. In the process of (re)constituting the
myth of *han*, women who have been victimized by the male-centered
society become burdened once again with the beauty of the national
cinema. In that sense, what causes Adada to be drowned in the river
is not only the cruelty of the patriarchy depicted in the film's narrative
but the cruelty of a Korean national cinema that fabricates beauty out
of that cruelty.

Pointing out the affinity between the logic of Korea's economic development and that of Song-hwa's stepfather in *Sopyonje*, the postcolo-
nialist/feminist critic Chungmoo Choi argues that the nationalism that
drives the capitalistic development of Korea "destroys a national body
in the name of nationalism, while [in *Sopyonje*] the spiritual essence of
a nation is believed to be maintained only through the destroyed body
[of Song-hwa]. This creates a double-edged, paradoxical allegory of
a postcolonial nation: (anti-colonial) nationalism can be achieved only
through the self-construction of the feminine Other."[6] Adada is similarly
*othered* to create the nation and the national cinema. She is not allowed
to articulate her suffering but she becomes the mythic scenery of Korea.
Her body is effaced into an "eternal fable," deprived of the language to
put her pain into discourse.

Is the "feminine Other," then, quietly submerged in the dissimulated scene of *han* in *Adada*? Is her agonized subjectivity completely
sublimated into the pristine, serene, cultural/natural mise-en-scène? Or
is there any moment of rupture when Adada exceeds the brutal law of
patriarchy, where her body utters her own language different from that
of the masculine aesthetics of the film? To answer these questions, I will
carefully listen to her body and to troublesome sounds attached to it.
Two sorts of sound characteristically adhere to Adada: one is the sound
of breaking dishes, the other is her inarticulate voice.

The sound of breaking dishes is one of the sensory elements clinging

to Adada's character. As the film begins, we hear something being broken, but it is outside the frame of the film. Adada's mother and the
housemaid identify its source as Adada breaking a honey pot in the
kitchen. The sound is repeated when she works in the kitchen of her
husband's house; and a later episode, in which her father-in-law buys
brass ware that even she cannot break, emphasizes her chronic inepti-
tude. Considering that she works obsessively to make up for her physical disability, Adada's habitual mistakes seem profoundly contradictory.
Perhaps they are symptomatic of an inner impulse that impedes her wish
to satisfy the demands of the society she lives in.

At the conscious level she wants to fit into the patriarchal institutions
that define women as exchangeable units of labor; in fact, her work and
the wealth she accumulates endear her to her parents-in-law. Yet on
some deeper level, she resists conforming to those institutions, and her
body refuses to complete the functions society prescribes. The sound
she produces marks the very refusal; it indicates a force within her that
will not be disciplined by the masculine power structure. The fact that
at the beginning of the film she makes herself heard even before being
presented in the frame suggests two things about Adada's stubborn
body. First, by making an involuntary sound her body immediately
weakens the disciplining power enacted by the institutions that surround
her. Second, such an auditory body is out of reach of the frame—the
frame of the apparatuses of patriarchy and of cinema. Thus she signals
that she will not be contained by the apparatuses.

The other sound clinging to Adada comes out of her body: the
unintelligible "uh-uh-ah-u" noise she habitually produces. She voices it
whenever she is not able fully to convey meaning and emotion through
sign language—for example, when she begs her husband's new wife
to help her remain in the house and when the waters of the river
close over her head. Her inarticulate noise is a congealed sonic cluster
that indicates something untransferable into language structured by
difference. It evokes a certain presence within her body, something
which cannot be signified via the network of the language—certain
remnants inside her that are not assimilated to the Symbolic, in Lacan's
sense.[7] If a psychoanalytic subject is constituted as such by accessing
language and entering into the Symbolic, Adada's pre-linguistic sounds

are symptomatic of the presence of a part of her being not totally retrieved into the Symbolic. As vividly illustrated in an episode where her husband tries but fails to teach her Japanese (because she cannot vocalize the sounds of the letters), she is not successfully constituted by the language of "the Father." Her voice, then, marks a site where the "Law" of patriarchy fails. The sounds she does make open up a crucial locus where she denies her full containment by the "Law of the Father."[8]

The incongruity between her voice and her image is striking; the former is so discordant that it collides with her mythic beauty. Such incongruity is antithetical to the cinematic convention that has codified the relation between image track and sound track. Jean Louis Comolli states that sound and speech in cinema together constitute a "decisive supplement, 'the ballast of reality' (Bazin)" which "intervenes straightway . . . as perfectionment and redefinition of the impression of reality."[9] As it is a crucial way to complete the "impression of reality," there has been a strong emphasis on conflation of "proper" body and "proper" voice. Kaja Silverman points out that this emphasis is much more coercive on the female than the male image; a beautiful female body has always been forced to be synchronized with a "voice which seems to belong to the body."[10] In mainstream cinema a sound is thus "married" to an image on a female body, counterfeiting the "illusion of perfect unity." But Adada's voice disturbs the unity of image and sound.

With its disturbing impact, her "ugly" voice obstructs her smooth assimilation into her image, interrupting the harmonious amalgamation of her image and the landscape. Her discordant sound unsettles the visual fetishization attached to her, momentarily suspending the force of aura wrapping her body. The aesthetics of the film are disconcerted; the tranquil beauty enveloping the scenery and Adada is de-sublimated. Such an acoustic de-sublimation provides a pivotal sonic locus that saves Adada from being totally enclosed within the aestheticized landscape. Her jarringly sonorous body refuses to confirm the veracity of the imaged version of her subjectivity. Encroaching upon the scene of *han* that incarcerates her, her voice siphons off her repressed energy into the audible.

The uneasy lingering of her voice thwarts the fulfillment of our expectation of unity of image and sound. Auditorily disillusioned, we are not neatly sutured into the diegesis; rather we are intermittently jolted out of what Stephen Heath calls the "safe place of the story."[11] Resonating outside the safe place, her sound alerts us to what otherwise remains concealed and unknowable about her. Her unintelligible sound is akin to what Mary Ann Doane designates as "interior monologue." Doane writes: "In the interior monologue . . . the voice and body are represented simultaneously, but the voice, far from being an extension of that body, manifests its inner lining. The voice displays what is inaccessible to the image, what exceeds the visible: the 'inner life' of the character. The voice here is the privileged mark of interiority, turning the body 'inside-out.'"[12] Hidden by the aesthetics of the film, Adada's "inner lining" is revealed through the sound she emits; it indicates an interiority that is inexpressible in the sublimated image. While her place in the language of the Father is inevitably absent, her sonorous body is utilized as a vehicle for speech, signifying what is otherwise unsignifiable: her pent-up sorrow and grief. Thus her body talks when her speech is inhibited. By means of her talking body, she produces moments of rupture in the scene of *han*.

As Adada's desire to speak competes with the forces that would silence it, her body becomes a battlefield. The battle staged there between feminine enunciation on one side and patriarchal society and film aesthetics on the other is dramatized one last time in the scene of her drowning. The scene displays the extremity of her victimization and the nadir of her own power, but it also plays out the most powerful image of the female subject defeating the victimizing force. Captured most often in long shots against an oriental painting-like landscape, her body is displayed as a perfect component of nature, and as she disappears into the river, she seems to become part of nature itself. In this involuntary transcendence, she turns into a silent myth, and the violence of patriarchy and its aestheticization are wedded together. The scene also implies that not only is she suppressed by the violent forces that act on her, she simultaneously surpasses them. Such a double movement of meaning is stirred by the striking affinity between the image of Adada and that of the money she throws away. The visual similarity between Adada, dressed in white, and the money, looking like a white paper parcel, draws the two into a common significance. When Adada scatters the money on the cliff, she herself seems to fly away on the air. And as her body and money float together on the water, they seem to indicate a destiny the two share. Her action of throwing away the money allegorizes her unbinding herself from a patriarchy obsessed with money. Although the destruction of the money accompanies her self-destruction, she acts out the unfettering of herself from the chain of fetishization. We cannot just say, then, that Adada is passively victimized; rather, dashing herself against the narrative and aesthetic containment, she enacts her own liberation.

Her moment of liberation is not completely subsumed by her subsequent drowning. When her writhing body moves upward in the water, her upper body rises beyond the frame; it appears that the frame has removed her throat and mouth, the organs of her enunciation. Alternatively, as she finally disappears into the water, she seems to be totally swallowed up by the abyss of nature. But even as she is cut off by the frame, she escapes it, finally transferring her dismembered body somewhere else. In fact, her fragmented body is already found at the border between the inside and the outside of the frame, between the diegesis and the extra-diegesis, perhaps in a space between life and death. Turning cinematic time into reverse, she (re)enters the cinematic space in the opening of the film, this time in phantom signs. Even if the signs are not anchored to their corporeal locus, their message is emphatic enough to manifest Adada as an enunciative subject. In her message she designates herself as "I," identifying herself as a speaking subject. She announces that by overcoming death, she is reborn as a strong enunciator, gaining a privileged status as a narrator. Through her sign language claim that she has a healthy mind and the people who destroy her are mentally "disabled," she judges the characters in the diegesis. Like a "voice-of-God" documentary narrator, she evaluates them with a knowledge superior to theirs. Transcending her death, she exceeds the force of patriarchal institutions and aesthetics. Her final writhing in the water should be understood as a kinetics that registers a double movement: the movement of death and the movement of revival.

*Adada* writes a violent, phallocentric pedagogy. As a woman is deprived of her language, she is abused, exiled, and killed. Her affliction and sadness are coercively transmuted into a trope of the national and national cinema. But her voice leaks from the network of pedagogy, and the signs diffused by her phantasmal body linger. The pedagogy fails to narrativize its rhetoric in a homogeneous vision, leaving its narrative split across the attempt to ease the haunting female and its failure to do so.

## The Female Subject and the Parturition of Language in *Surrogate Mother*

Set in the period of the *Chosŏn* dynasty, *Surrogate Mother* is a film about a seventeen-year-old girl named Ok-nyŏ, who, according to custom, is chosen to give birth to a child for an aristocratic family that lacks a son to continue their family name. But when the child she bears is taken away by the family, Ok-nyŏ kills herself. Featuring a female protagonist whose life is ripped apart by the violence of patriarchy, *Surrogate Mother* presents another story of women's *han*.

The modes of Ok-nyŏ's and Adada's exploitations display a paradigmatic affinity in that both women are trapped in a contradictory use of the three signifiers of women, nature, and culture in masculine discourse. Adada is narrativized as a victim of the institution of patriarchy, but at the same time she is portrayed as an inseparable part of Korean nature. Similarly, Ok-nyŏ is abused by the inhumane custom of surrogate motherhood that equates her with the female biological function. Via such an "ambivalent and co-temporal make-up of 'nature' and 'culture,'" as Chow argues, "woman continues to be the paradigmatic 'primitive' in the phenomenon of primitive passions."[13]

Although the two women undergo the same paradigm of primitivization, the visual techniques by which they are primitivized are different. Unlike Adada's body, which is typically minimized as a small object within an expansive landscape, Ok-nyŏ's is frequently exposed in close-ups and continuously discussed by characters in the diegesis. In both forms Ok-nyŏ is reconstructed as an embodiment of a purely biological function, with other parts of her subjectivity eliminated. The Korean title of the film, which literally means "a receiver of seeds," condenses her into her reproductive function. The metaphorical traffic between nature and a female body takes a different route in each film. In *Adada*

FIGURE 3.2.
*Surrogate Mother:* The violation of Ok-nyŏ

woman is assimilated into the natural landscape, but in *Surrogate Mother*
nature is anthropomorphized into the female body. The film returns
again and again to locations whose distinctively feminine morphology
genders the landscape. In the most prominent of these scenes, a male
fortune-teller guides the uncle of the male protagonist to a valley where
the surrogate women live. Named *okmungol* (Female Cave), the valley
looks like a female sexual organ—a resemblance that invests nature with
the energy of sex and reproduction. Woman and nature are each figured
as a huge womb, the fetish of a society obsessed with phallic authority.
The fortune-teller and the uncle gaze at the green, wrinkled valley for a
while and then walk directly into it. The sequence demonstrates the violation and brutalization of a female body by masculine power, the power
of phallocentric society in the diegesis and also in the cinematography.
When the two men walk into the valley, they are symbolically tramping
on the female sexual organ. Also moving through the valley into the
surrogate women's village, the camera pierces the female body. The

phallic bodies of the male characters and the camera rape the female body. Charged with a masculine desire of pornographic penetration, the cinematography of the sequence visually allegorizes the thematics of the film.

The representation of women in *Surrogate Mother* displays a series of variations on the thematics and stylistics emblematized in the *okmungol* sequence. The accounts of the prospective surrogate women's bodies narrated by the fortune-teller illustrate how a masculine discourse re-constitutes them as fetishistic signs. He classifies them by whether they have a "fertile look" or a "sterile look," and he describes the distinguish-ing features of each. According to him, the "fertile look" has "narrow, slim eyes, a round face, a pointed nose, pink palms, rounded shoulders, a thick back, deep naval, flat butt, and wide hips." The guarantee that a woman with the most fertile "look" will bear a son is the fact that her "face and lips turn purple during sex as her muscles flex." In his classification, the female body is fragmented and transformed into cor-poreal signifiers that indicate degrees of fertility, but no more; masculine discourse disassembles it into appendages of the reproductive organ, eliminating all other forms of subjectivity.

Ok-nyŏ's body is the most focalized image in the film's visual and discursive fetishization. In a ritual where the Chinese character signifying a seed is tattooed on her shoulder, patriarchy marks her body with its language as it identifies her as an organ for nurturing seeds. During her confinement at the aristocrats' house, Ok-nyŏ becomes a reproductive organ, fed and disciplined to be such and nothing else. The film takes specific note of all the things that enter and come out of her body, and it provides detailed explanations of the connection between them and the activities of her womb. We see the esoteric food she eats so that she will bear a son, the blood she bleeds, and close-ups of her contorted, sweating face during sex. In visuals and discourses invested with exotic, ethnographic signs, Ok-nyŏ is spectacularized; at the same time, however, her subjectivity is erased. Her womb is represented in maximum visibility, yet her subjectivity as a human is hidden behind her womb.

In this visual and discursive spectacularization, Ok-nyŏ embodies the process of fetishization, this time in the Marxist sense.[14] As a laborer, she produces what society needs to keep reproducing itself. But the society that appropriates her work deprives her of her rights as a producer and effaces her presence and labor. As a surrogate she is forced to bear a child, but then her child is taken away, and she is banished into an invisibility that mirrors the laborer's status in modern society. Fetishized by the apparatus of cinema as well as by the patriarchal institution of surrogate women, Ok-nyŏ is doubly exploited and alienated. The two fetishizing processes have in common the repression of Ok-nyŏ's enunciation. The family who buys Ok-nyŏ wants to transact the deal "without any family disgrace." In Korean, the phrase is literally "without leaving any blot on the family name." So that she will not leave any blot, they do not let her out of her room in daytime, and they order her not to look at or listen to anything. And when she has delivered the son, they send her away, denying not only her motherhood but also her right to speak the suffering of her stolen motherhood. The visual and discursive devices of the film that reduce her subjectivity into one biological function are complicit in usurping her enunciative voice. Concealed under the fetish of the womb, her subjectivity is buried in invisibility and silence.

How, then, can she break the concealment and refuse to be merely a womb? Does the text allow any space where her affliction and grief can be seen and heard? In brief, how can she utter her *han* and defeat the masculine language of the film? A few tactics of the film do, in fact, imply a critique of the brutal patriarchy it depicts. Through some elements in the characterization of the master whose child Ok-nyŏ bears, the film criticizes the conventions of Confucian patriarchy; although he is bound to those conventions, he admits the absurdity of using a surrogate mother to obtain a son, and of the obsessive ritual worship of ancestral ghosts. Other transgressive possibilities within the narrative are suggested by the genuine affection that Ok-nyŏ and the master feel for each other and in a scene where they have sex on the day set aside for the ancestral rituals. These occasions do not, however, allow Ok-nyŏ herself to articulate her repression and pain. The most emphatic moment when she speaks her suffering comes while she is giving birth to the baby. Her intense emotion and her desperately struggling body in the delivery sequence are portrayed in such vivid detail that the depths of her vulnerability are revealed. Ironically, the moment when she becomes more than merely her reproductive organ is the one when the function of that organ is maximized. How does she exceed the fetishizing force of the film when her womb is most spectacularized and she is most fragile?

Before analyzing this sequence, I want to refer to another delivery scene in *Surrogate Mother*. Immediately before Ok-nyŏ begins her labor, a sequence showing a traditional mask dance (*t'alch'um*) that includes a delivery scene is inserted into the narrative. Originating in a ritual designed to secure a good harvest, this Korean mask dance has various components, including theatrical performance, narrative, song, and dance.[15] In a comic, parodic, or satiric mode, it chiefly represents the conflicts between the *yangban,* the aristocrats of the *Chosŏn* dynasty, and the peasants who attack the *yangban*'s repressive power and the contradictions of their authority.[16] The mask dance does not make a sharp distinction between performers and audience; more often than not, the audience is invited to participate in the performance, and in the denouement performers and audience sing and dance together. Interpreted as a carnivalesque ritual of the lower class,[17] the mask dance emblematizes the power of disenfranchised people. Its counter-hegemonic aesthetics were revived during the *minjung* movement—the popular oppositional movement of the 1970s and 1980s—and were mobilized as a significant cultural force to empower the marginalized people and their culture.[18]

Ok-nyŏ peeps at the performance over the wall of the master's house, insinuating a subversive component in the film in two ways. First, since the mask dance traditionally connotes a cultural power opposed to the ruling class, aristocrats are forbidden to watch it, and, as a housemaid warns Ok-nyŏ, anyone who sees it is not allowed to participate in the ancestral rituals. By watching the performance, Ok-nyŏ transgresses a taboo of the ruling class. Second, the inserted scene marks the site where the film's unfolding narrative is momentarily suspended. The mask dance has nothing to do with the development of the action; indeed, it rather blocks that development. The scene registers a space that is not subordinated to the narrative of the victimized woman, alluding to the possibility of an excess beyond the constraints that organize the film.

Comic devices in the mask dance's delivery segment include the reversal of gender roles. Since all the performers of the mask dance are supposed to be male, men disguised as women play the roles of a woman in labor and a midwife: One character disguised as a woman lies down on the ground, pretending to be in labor, while another character calls a midwife, who appears, dancing cheerfully. The audience, too, becomes involved in this transvestite theatrical event. As the midwife tries to deliver the baby, some of the female spectators shout, "Push more, push more," and when they finally "deliver" a baby—actually, a baby doll—the performers and spectators sing and dance together. The audience, as it were, collaborates and participates in the pleasure of getting the baby.

Even though the comic treatment of parturition in the mask dance is wholly unlike the tragic mode of Ok-nyŏ's own subsequent delivery, the two scenes are closely interwoven, supplementing and referencing each other. In this complementarity, the former lays out multiple meanings that come to fruition in the latter. As well as critically parodying the family's fuss in getting a son, the delivery scene in the mask dance provides key clues to reading the possibility of Ok-nyŏ's enunciation in her own delivery scene. The travestied male characters are analogous to the presence of the master at Ok-nyŏ's delivery, suggesting his deep involvement in her experience and his empathy for her suffering. In her parturition Ok-nyŏ communicates with him through her wriggling, twisting body and her screams and cries. Inflicted with overwhelming pain, her body yields pre-linguistic signs through which she communicates with him. As they converse through the kinetic signs wrested from her body, she identifies herself and is identified as a suffering woman—a human being, not simply a reproductive organ. As the master looks at Ok-nyŏ convulsed with pain, his eyes and his gesture of embracing her express his sympathy with her, as well as his helplessness to aid her. Saturated with sweat and tears, Ok-nyŏ meets his gaze, which is filled with overflowing compassion. At this moment he is not the "bearer of the look," fascinated by the fetishized womb; nor is she the passive object "to be looked at." His gaze signifies not that he is a master of this pathetic body but that he, too, is a victim of a monstrous patriarchy. Identified in their gazes, the two join as human beings crushed by a brutal social order.

As Ok-nyŏ's body speaks to the master in their togetherness, it can also speak to other participants in her labor. This second dialogue is hinted at in the mask dance in the female spectators' laughing collaboration with the travestied male performers in the delivery. Albeit in a tone different from theirs as they shout "Push more," the female viewers of *Surrogate Mother* may similarly collaborate in Ok-nyŏ's parturition. In the excruciating motion of her body as, caught in spasms of extreme pain, she writhes in sweat and tears, her entire being is seized by the bursting energy of her womb; it ceases to be a spectacled fetish, and the accumulated sentiments that have been repressed by the social order become corporeal signs. As she rolls around the room, her hair matted, her teeth clenched, and her limbs contorted, the involuntary kinetics of her convulsion muddled with her bodily liquids are so intense and sensational that they elicit somatic identification from the bodies of female viewers—especially those who have experienced delivery. Women will shudder and perhaps twist their own bodies in spite of themselves, (re)experiencing the labor together with Ok-nyŏ. Overcoming the distance between the film image and its viewers, female audiences participate in a conversation with Ok-nyŏ's body, sharing a particular memory and temporality of motherhood. In their mutual somatography, they join in the "women's time" of maternal anguish, pain, and creation.[19]

The mask dance sequence where performers and audiences enjoy their ritual and the beginning of Ok-nyŏ's parturition scene are interwoven in the crosscutting, knotted in an odd disparity yet also in a potent analogy. They seem disparate, for the celebratory mood of the mask dance is far from that of Ok-nyŏ's desperate situation. Why, then, is it inserted into the scene of her delivery? What are they celebrating? Is it Ok-nyŏ's power to bring her language to the world, her power to position herself as a human being? The analogy suggests the idea that what she bears is not just a child but her own language; that by giving birth to a baby she participates in a ritual that allows her to become a speaking subject. The performers and audiences of the mask dance, we can say, triumphantly display their resistant power, oppressed but ever-resurrected, while at the same time they rejoice in the birth of Ok-nyŏ's language. Tied by significant analogies, the ritual and the actual parturitions reveal the potential significance of the actual delivery. The mask dance illuminates the dialogic moments between Ok-nyŏ and her master, as well as those between her and the film's spectators, and both scenes open up a space for female agency. And so, though she can speak only through her body during the delivery, afterward Ok-nyŏ speaks in verbal language. At last she becomes capable of articulating what she wants to say. When her child is carried away and she is ordered to leave, she howls, "Got to see it before I leave. . . . I'll take baby with me. . . . I'm not an animal bearing babies for others. I'm human."

After this powerful speech, however, Ok-nyŏ hangs herself. Although her death contributes to the narrative closure of her ultimate sacrifice, enforced by the social order, this scene visualizes a complex nexus of signs in which, even in death, the female body is entangled in enunciation. In this final sequence Ok-nyŏ's head is outside our sight, while the rest of her body, dressed in a traditional white outfit, hangs through the frame.[20] A subtitle states that "One year after, Ok-nyŏ killed herself near her son's village. This is a tragedy caused by the obsessive idea that a family name should be continued through a son."[21] The image of her decapitated body epitomizes the violence of patriarchy that punishes women's enunciation. But Ok-nyŏ is not a passive victim of punishment. She chooses her death as the most desperate form of resistance. That she hangs herself "near her son's village" shows that her death is intended as an exhibition of her resistance against the brutal society that disparages her as an animal. As the inserted subtitle appears on the screen, her voice can be heard claiming her humanity. Although she cannot explicitly say, "I am the tragedy of the absurd patriarchal ideology," her howling voice resonates with that message. The spectral image of Ok-nyŏ frozen on the screen after the credits visually echoes her speech. The voice emanating from the dead body hangs in filmic space as if to tell her untold story—and all the other stories never told in the masculine order of meaning.

In *Adada* and *Surrogate Mother* women strive to speak a language different from that of men. Adada and Ok-nyŏ give birth to new significations competing with the language of the Father; in that sense they are the Mothers of female language. A metaphorical tie between Adada and the maternal is not easy to discern; she is never associated with references to motherhood, and the possibility of her having a child is never mentioned. Nevertheless, the maternal within Adada symptomatically surfaces in the text, especially through her "resurrection" in the opening of the film. Julia Kristeva argues that female subjectivity provides maternal "modalities of time" that are essentially distinguished from phallocentric temporality; unlike the linear unfolding of history, the Mother's "cyclical" time is created by her bodily "cycles, gestation, the eternal recurrence of a biological rhythm."[22] Through her revival, Adada lives in such maternal time, challenging the structure of linear narrative that imprisons women in the tale of suffering, sacrifice, and finally death.[23] Just as Ok-nyŏ produces her own language through her parturition, Adada gestates feminine significations in her temporality. Even though the maternal in Adada and Ok-nyŏ is repressed or stolen and killed in the films' respective narratives, it is still a source of energy that allows them to disrupt the Law and the signs of the Father.

*Adada* and *Surrogate Mother* are positioned in "in-between" locations, where the paternal social/linguistic order is ruptured by the power of the maternal. In these liminal sites, masculine power and discourse clash with the implication of female agency and female enunciation. Patriarchal ideology is pushed to its limits, and both films simultaneously show its potency and uncover its weaknesses. As they envision women's strength surpassing even death, *Adada* and *Surrogate Mother* are fraught with tension between the masculine power that *others* women and women's striving not to be *othered*. Through this tension, the pedagogy organizing the films loses its homogenizing force, allowing ruptures and fissures to come into play and creating disjunctive moments. *Adada* and *Surrogate Mother* are in that sense "limit-texts" of the Korean national cinema. In the films of Im Kwon-Taek, who decided not to live a "degraded" life, many female bodies are degraded—but not entirely so.

## Notes

1. See "An Interview with Im Kwon-Taek" in this volume, 247–248.
2. Ibid., 250.

3. As suggested by the film's deletion of the word "idiot" from the title, the elimination of idiocy from Adada's characterization reflects its aestheticized image of her.

4. Roland Barthes, *Mythologies,* selected and trans. Annette Lavers (New York: Hill and Wang, 1972), 111–17.

5. Rey Chow, *Primitive Passions: Visuality, Sexuality, Ethnography, and Contemporary Chinese Cinema* (New York: Columbia University Press, 1995), 19–23.

6. "Nationalism and Construction of Gender in Korea," in *Dangerous Women: Gender and Korean Nationalism,* ed. Elaine H. Kim and Chungmoo Choi (New York: Routledge, 1998), 22–23.

7. On the Lacanian concepts of the Symbolic and the Father (developed below), see *Ecrits: A Selection,* trans. Alan Sheridan, (New York: Norton, 1977), 67, 199, 217, 310, and 314.

8. Adada's sound is akin to what Julia Kristeva designates as the semiotic. While the Symbolic is the language of the Father gained through the oedipal phase, the semiotic is a process of pre-oedipal signification that is "oriented and structured around the Mother's body." Once a subject enters into the Symbolic, the semiotic is repressed, but it is still present in the former as a "rhythmic pulsion," producing disruptive dimensions in the Symbolic language. See Julia Kristeva's *Revolution in Poetic Language,* trans. Margaret Waller (New York: Columbia University Press, 1984), pt. 1, "The Semiotic and the Symbolic." For a helpful explanation of Kristeva's concept of the semiotic, see Toil Moi's introduction to *The Kristeva Reader,* ed. Toil Moi, (New York: Columbia University Press, 1986).

9. "Machines of the Visible," in *The Cinematic Apparatus,* ed. Teresa de Lauretis and Stephen Heath (New York: St. Martins, 1980), 132.

10. Kaja Silverman, *The Acoustic Mirror: The Female Voice in Psychoanalysis and Cinema* (Bloomington: Indiana University Press, 1984), 48.

11. Stephen Heath, *Questions of Cinema* (Bloomington: Indiana University Press, 1981), 55.

12. "The Voice in the Cinema: The Articulation of Body and Space," *Yale French Studies* no. 60 (1980), 41.

13. Chow, *Primitive Passions,* 44.

14. See Karl Marx, *Capital: A Critique of Political Economy,* ed. Frederick Engels, trans. Samuel Moore and Edward Aveling (New York: Modern Library, 1906), bk. 1, 41–96.

15. On the origin and characteristics of the Korean mask dance, see Cho Tong-il, *T'alch'um ui y'oksa wa w'olli* (The History and principle of mask dance) (Seoul: Kirinwon, 1988).

16. Cho, *T'alch'um*, 26–32.

17. On the carnivalesque features of the mask dance, see Kim Uk-tong, *T'alch'um ui mihak* (The Aesthetics of mask dance) (Seoul: Hyŏnamsa, 1994), chs. 3, 4, and 7.

18. For a detailed explanation of the relation between the mask dance and the *minjung* movement, see Chungmoo Choi, "The *Minjung* Culture Movement and Popular Culture," in *South Korea's Minjung Movement: The Culture and Politics of Dissidence*, ed. Kenneth M. Wells (Honolulu: University of Hawai'i Press, 1995).

19. For "women's time" see Julia Kristeva's essay, "Women's Time," in *The Kristeva Reader*, ed. Moi, 187–213.

20. Interestingly enough, the images of both Adada and Ok-nyŏ are strongly associated with the female ghost of the traditional literary and visual imaginations. The death of a woman who suffered from *han* and her traditional, white outfit have been signs inseparably linked to the image of the female ghost in Korea. In the representation of Adada and Ok-nyŏ their repressed *han* seems to return as such ghost-like images.

21. In the English subtitled version, the second sentence of the subtitle is omitted.

22. Kristeva categorizes two types of women's time: "cyclical" and "monumental." The former is linked to the concept of repetition; the latter to eternity. See her "Women's Time," 191–92.

23. The original short story does not have any equivalent to the "voice-over" in the opening sequence of the film version. It seems that the film version, made in 1988, allows much more room for female agency than the short story, written in 1935 during the period of Korea's colonization by Japan. In terms of *Adada* as an allegory of Korea, it might also suggest that the monumental phase of the *minjung* movement, when *minjung*'s power was triumphantly marked by the uprising of 1987, is manifested in the film in the form of the resurrection of the most marginalized as an enunciator.

*Chungmoo Choi*

CHAPTER 4

# The Politics of Gender, Aestheticism, and Cultural Nationalism in *Sopyonje* and *The Genealogy*

In the film *Sopyonje* (*Sŏp'yŏnje*, 1993), there is a scene where Yu-bong, the father, sits on the verandah of an ancient, imposing Korean house. Across from him is an old Confucian gentleman, who plays the traditional string instrument *kŏmungo*. The two men, both swathed in formal white attire, are silent, and *kŏmungo* music spreads over the solemn air. The *kŏmungo* scene follows one in which Yu-bong combs the cascading hair of Song-hwa, his adopted daughter, while the blinded girl wearing a white camisole blouse takes note of the bells tolling through the morning mist from a nearby Buddhist temple. The *kŏmungo* scene quickly cuts to a shot of Song-hwa sitting alone in a room, this time clad in a wine-colored silk blouse over a white camisole and a flowing, full-length, dark blue skirt. In both scenes with Song-hwa, the camera zooms into the room from outside, and the frames are partially taken up with walls and rice-paper doors, thus producing a voyeuristic effect. When we connect this sequence of episodes to the scene that precedes it, we come to a stunning realization: In this scene we learn that the poison Yu-bong stirred into the medicine for the purpose of blinding Song-hwa has begun to take effect. As Yu-bong confirms Song-hwa's blindness, he offers her his arm. As the two walk off arm in arm into the distance—the blinded Song-hwa in a plain black skirt that shows her ankles and a light colored sweater over a white blouse— her braided hair hangs over the woolen scarf around her neck. Two scenes later she appears with her hair up and wearing a full and flowing skirt—the time-honored fashion of a married woman.

These visual images invoke the courtesan culture of precolonial Korea. In that era, when a young courtesan lost her virginity to a male patron, she combed her hair into a bun and fixed it with a phallic ornament, *pinyŏ*. This occasion was euphemistically called "putting up the hair," and it signified that the patron had claimed the courtesan as his mistress. This phrase was never applied to a woman of normative category. Nonetheless, the change of Song-hwa's hairstyle from a braid to a bun is an indication of a change in her status. And the deep hue of her dress, in contrast to a bright bridal color, is also reminiscent of a courtesan.

With these allusions, the film suggests that Yu-bong blinds his adopted daughter, sexually abuses this defenseless girl, and makes her his mistress. The film underscores their sexual relationship with a hint of body contact between the middle-aged man and the girl: walking arm in arm when Song-hwa began to lose her vision might have aroused and encouraged the man's desire for her body. The scene where Yu-bong combs Song-hwa's hair in the depth of the morning mist is even more suggestive of his intimacy with the daughter-turned-mistress. The morning mist here invokes the archaic expression "the passion of mist and rain," which refers to sexual union—the visual image of which Wong Kar-Wai fully mobilized in his film *Happy Together* (1997). All things considered, the four consecutive scenes from Song-hwa's loss of vision to her appearance in the full accouterment of an adult married woman represent a highly allegorized and culturally specific incestuous rape sequence. The last scene in this sequence, the visual invocation of a non-normative woman sitting alone in a room, foretells the predictably harsh future Song-hwa faces—first as her father's mistress and subsequently as a blind entertainer for audiences comprised of countless men.

Though these three scenes explicate the incestuous relationship, the mediating scene with the *kŏmungo* player remains enigmatic. Let me, however, reserve discussion of who this old man may be and why he is inserted in this critical scene for later, and cut to the scene of Yu-bong's deathbed. As he is dying he confesses to Song-hwa that he was responsible for her blindness. But instead of seeking her forgiveness, he justifies his cruelty (and his unspoken violation) as a means of helping her deepen her *han*—the repressed sense of resentment and sorrow. According to Yu-bong, a *p'ansori* singer must embody *han,* for it is a precondition for aesthetic sublimation. In other words, Yu-bong perpetrated visceral violence and sexual violation upon Song-hwa for the perfection of *p'ansori.*

In this essay I will evaluate the ways in which colonized Korean men attempted to respond to the deprivation of national identity and loss of masculinity by inflicting violence on colonized indigenous woman or onto the emasculated self. I will examine this nexus of historical violence by focusing on two kinds of masculinities, represented respectively by Yu-bong in *Sopyonje* and Sŏl in *The Genealogy* (*Ch'okpo,* 1978). I will further explore how these techniques of recuperating masculinities intersect with both the cinematic engagement with aestheticism that is not free from colonial gaze and the masculinist cultural nationalism that justifies greater violence.

*remasculinization through violence (onto women & self)*

## *Han,* Colonial Modernity, and Nostalgia in *Sopyonje*

*Sopyonje* presents a saga of an itinerant family of singers struggling to preserve the disappearing operatic performing art known as *p'ansori.* Yu-bong, the head of the family, is obsessed by the conviction that some day *p'ansori* will once again take pride of place over Japanese *enka* and Western popular song, and he ruthlessly trains his adopted son and daughter to achieve musical perfection. As the film progresses, however, *p'ansori*'s stature declines, and the family's poverty deepens. When Tong-ho and Song-hwa reach adolescence and are awakened to sexuality, a subtle masculine rivalry grows between Tong-ho and Yu-bong over Song-hwa. Either because he fears the outcome of his growing sexual attraction to Song-hwa or because he is tired of abject

poverty, Tong-ho runs away after an altercation with Yu-bong. After
Tong-ho leaves, Song-hwa is heart-broken, and she falls gravely ill.
Under the pretext of curing her, Yu-bong blinds her by introducing
poison into her medicine, and then he rapes her. Though rumors are
rampant in the village that Yu-bong blinded Song-hwa to prevent her
from running away, he is devoted to her musical training. After Yu-
bong's death, Song-hwa wanders from tavern to tavern, eking out a
living as an entertainer, while Tong-ho, now married and the father of
a child, travels the countryside looking for Song-hwa as he carries on
his business of collecting medicinal herbs for a small pharmaceutical
company. When Tong-ho finally tracks her down, Song-hwa is living
with a man who owns a tavern near a remote salt farm. Although the
two have been searching and waiting for each other for years, when
they meet they choose not to acknowledge their relationship. In place
of a melodramatic ending, the film depicts them performing together
the *Tale of Simch'ŏng*, a piece in the *p'ansori* repertory that Song-hwa
has perfected. The two thus sublimate *han*. The next day they set off
in different directions, and we learn that Song-hwa has been raising
a daughter.

*Sopyonje* was a box-office hit and undoubtedly Im Kwon-Taek's
most commercially successful film. One indication of its success is the
degree to which it elicited a collective outpouring of *han*—and an
abundant flow of audiences' tears. At the time, the Korean mass media
explained that this copious collective sentiment stemmed from Koreans'
shared sense of *han*. By contrast, some critics have argued that the film
does not create a sense of sadness; instead, they assert, the *Sopyonje*
phenomenon should be understood as Korean spectators' projection of
their deep-seated historical *han* onto the film. (*Han* is the sentiment
that one develops when one cannot or is not allowed to express feelings
of oppression, alienation, or exploitation because one is trapped in
an unequal power relationship. The feelings of anger, pain, sorrow,
or resentment that find no expression turn into *han*.) This collective
*communitas*[1] to which both the media and the critics refer emerges at
the intersection of two aspects of Korea's modern history. One is the
inability to articulate the incommensurable experience of modernity,

and the other is the lament for the loss of the security of the past in the course of compressed modernization.

Under the authoritarian Confucian rule of precolonial Korea, where the ruler held all the power and consequently the ruled had none, people attempted to find temporary release of discontent or *han* not through verbal protest or political action but through shamanic rituals or transgressive, carnivalesque performing arts; from time to time, these activities precipitated peasant uprisings. After a brief experimentation with modern civil formulations in the late nineteenth century, Koreans were confronted with a hybrid form of colonial modernity, under the equally authoritarian Japanese rule. Under colonial rule, the popular Korean modes of aesthetic communication and the drama of communal resistance were contradictory to modern "scientific" administration, the rational narrative of print media, and the pursuit of individualism in the name of civility. This so-called modern administration was, in fact, an amalgam of modern European administration and Japanese appropriation of both Korean and Japanese conventions, designed to impose colonial law and order. Here two different systems of logic clashed. One was scientific rationality, which emphasizes true/false verification—the criterion of which was set by the colonial authority. The other was nonarticulative, aesthetic felicity, which adheres to cultural convention. As colonization emphasized modern rationality rather than cultural and aesthetic communication, Koreans were deprived of cultural language and accumulated a kind of historical *han*.

*P'ansori* is a performing art that emerged in eighteenth-century Korea and became fully commercialized by the late nineteenth century. *Sŏp'yŏnje* is one of the two major types of *p'ansori: tongp'yŏnje* is the eastern sound, and *sŏp'yŏnje* the western. While *tongp'yŏnje* is more masculine and grand, *sŏp'yŏnje* emphasizes *han* and sorrow. The art of *p'ansori* emerged along with the development of the nascent market economy. Though *p'ansori* singers were generally members of outcast shaman families of the Chŏlla region and built their repertoire on an oral tradition rich in popular expressions, from the outset *p'ansori* was a commercial art form rather than a spontaneous popular art. *P'ansori* was never directly subversive, but it challenged the literary tradition of

the ruling gentry. As the number of theaters in urban centers grew at the
turn of the century, *p'ansori* enjoyed increasing commercial success. As
Korea became colonized, however, Japanese *shinp'a* (*shimpa*) style theater[2] gradually replaced Korean theater, and Japanese police disbanded
*p'ansori* troupes in 1909.[3] Subsequently, throughout the colonial period *p'ansori* was in progressive decline; only a few singers survived as
itinerant entertainers in the countryside. The genre was almost erased
from the collective memory of Koreans until 1970, when the dissident
writer Kim Chi-ha adopted *p'ansori* rhythms in his monumental narrative poem *Five Bandits,* which satirically indicts the military regime of
Park Chung Hee. Because of its political component, *p'ansori* attracted
the attention of antigovernment activists, who saw it as a signifier of *minjung* culture and the spirit of resistance. At the same time, the South
Korean government skillfully preserved *p'ansori*— not, however, as a
vibrant, popular culture but as an "Intangible Cultural Asset," to be
strictly maintained under conditions of preservation set by the Culture
Preservation Law. This law was promulgated in January 1962, seven
months after Park Chung Hee usurped power through a military coup.
(Similarly, the adoption of a Japanese law of the same title was legislated
upon the recommendation of the Committee for the Protection of Cultural Properties at the turn of this century.) Following the proclamation
of the Culture Preservation Law, the military junta fully mobilized mass
media for the dissemination of cultural nationalism in order to create a
culturalist image that would serve as a means by which the junta could
unify the people.

   *P'ansori* thus became a site contested by the South Korean government's official cultural nationalism and the subversive cultural resistance movement. While the government disseminated *p'ansori* through
the various official media it monopolized, activists performed *p'ansori*
underground, with a revised narrative of protest. However, censorship
made this contest invisible, and the general populace consumed *p'ansori*
mainly as a nostalgia product. *Sopyonje* exploits this newly created aura of
*p'ansori,* together with the military regime's hyper-masculinist nationalist ideology. In fact, there is a striking analogy between the regime's
mode of operation and *Sopyonje*'s narrative structure. The capitalist development that deprived the nation of its voice and devastated its land

*narrative is allegory of the military gov'.*

in the name of nationalism is mirrored in Yu-bong's deprivation of his daughter's sight and the violation of her body for the perfection of this national art. This creates a double-edged, paradoxical allegory of a post-colonial nation: anticolonial nationalism fosters the self-construction of the feminine Other, which cancel each other out and thus accumulate cinematic *han*.

As postcolonial South Korea became more aggressively incorporated into the capitalist world order during the cold war period, the homogenizing force of modernity further silenced its citizens. The universalized scientism that drove South Korea headlong down the path of development invalidated conventional popular forms of communication as irrational, premodern, and therefore socially evil. Instead, the once organic popular culture was commodified as spectacle, under the label of "national culture"—to be displayed at museums and reproduced as a staged, performing art in an industrialized society. This commodified form of popular art was deprived of its significance as a communication through which *han* could be collectively released. The spectacularized "popular art" was an empty signifier, bereft of people's voices. In addition, the authoritarian military government, which pursued aggressive modernization, denied modern forms of articulation and imposed severe censorship of the most comprehensive kind under the National Security Law. In the absence of any means of transformative communication, national silence deepened in South Korea. Analogously, in *Sopyonje,* a Korean woman under a patriarchal system is doubly silenced—both by the patriarchy and by national complicity in the national silence. She becomes an emblem of *han.* The collective *communitas* of *Sopyonje*'s spectators can be located at the intersection of postcolonial silencing.

*old pop. culture ousted as dated in light of scientific modern ideology*

*Sopyonje* connects *han* to nostalgia. The film is set in Korea's postcolonial period, where American mass culture pushes its way deeply into the meager markets of the remote countryside. In the film the passage of time is suggested by the overlapping of the three traveling singers' hasty footsteps. These overlapping footsteps also represent the speed of Korea's rapid modernization. The film shows the compression of two centuries of Western industrialization into a few decades, pans this sequence in blurred details, and thus numbs any sense of history. Despite Yu-bong's prediction of the revival of *p'ansori,* the itinerant family barely subsists by entertaining drinking parties at restaurants in small towns and busking for a medical charlatan in a country market. The *p'ansori* family's peregrination likens the gradual displacement of popular art to the decline of spontaneous communal culture into a suburban entertainment form that helps promote medical advertising—a genre of capitalist mass culture. The family's life illustrates the transition from an organic popular culture to an inorganic commodity, from use value to exchange value, and it delineates the structural opposition through which the relation between tradition and modernity is constructed.

Marshall Berman notes that the word nostalgia was coined in the nineteenth century to describe a modern feeling that implies longing for the recent past destroyed by industrialization. Contradictory moments create a nostalgic impulse. *P'ansori* was born at such a contradictory moment, at the intersection of nostalgia and Korea's nascent capitalist development. A century later it was reborn as a "traditional," popular art form that was about to disappear because of Korea's intensive industrialization. Capturing this shifting time, *Sopyonje* presents a wide range of everyday activities in Korea's recent past: for example, at one point the itinerant opera troupe passes by on a rickshaw, a vestige of Japanese colonial rule. The itinerant troupe stages *The Tale of Ch'unhyang*, a well-known popular love story, on a makeshift stage in a rural marketplace. Spectators in the film are dressed in an awkward, hybrid combination of Western jackets worn over Korean clothes, and they wear Western style shoes on their feet. A traveling folk painter's pith helmet, a reminder of the European colonization of Africa and India, contrasts with the folksy blessings he bestows on his customers. Mixed in this kaleidoscope of things modern and premodern is the medicine hawker, who sells a panacea of equally hybrid, mysterious origin. A pushcart taffy seller clanking enormous metal scissors—a neighborhood fixture who used to exchange a few inches of taffy for a bundle of used personal items—is again a half-breed form of impersonal barter. This collection of scenes from Korea's very recent past allows moviegoers to luxuriate, reminiscing in the comfort of a movie theater about the hungry and destitute days of the Korean War years.

*Sopyonje* offers a visual tour of Korea's recent past, when all things indigenous were being replaced by commodities of Western origin;

everyday life was marked by a confusing array of hybridity. These items of everyday life have as much of an idealizing and unifying effect, as part of Korea's national history, as the nationalistic representation of *p'ansori* itself. The cinematic nostalgia here may not necessarily indicate a longing for the everyday life of the recent past. What is important is the social memory those materials embody or invoke. For the film's spectators, these nostalgic devices work not because the past is seen as utopian but because they confer validity on the sense of preindustrial community. The aura of emotional spontaneity and moral certainty the past is believed to have ensured allows aesthetic release and sublimation of *han*. In this sense, this newly memorialized past offers Korean spectators a sense of security and of home. Since the security of home exists only in the memory, Yu-bong's desire to relocate home by reclaiming the glory of *p'ansori* is practically impossible to satisfy. The tragedy is that Yu-bong struggles to make that impossibility possible by resorting to masculine violence against a woman.

Ironically, this tragedy is celebrated by the camera's nostalgic gaze, which captures the landscape of the memorialized past. John Frow argues that nostalgia seeks the absence that generates the mechanism of desire that lies in the ontological homelessness.[5] This sense of homelessness is represented by Yu-bong's arbitrarily assembled, itinerant family, trying to survive in a late capitalist society by selling its meager precapitalist artifact. As the camera follows them through the pristine landscape, urban spectators experience a sense of security while taking note of the inequalities between the city and the country, between center and periphery, and between the sense of now and the most recent past as "Othered" spectacle.

In fact, the film spectacularizes Korean rural life, centered on the marketplace, that was occluded by intensive capitalist development and eventually destroyed within the short span of three decades. Even mechanical transportation is absent from this recent past. Trains and buses enter the camera frame for the first time only toward the end of the film, as Tong-ho scours the countryside looking for Song-hwa. It is as if in the recent past Korea was a virgin land, so remote from modern technology that it was wholly unaware of technological innovations. The film ignores important historical facts: that Korea was the industrial

outpost of the Japanese Empire during the colonial period and that U.S.
bombing deforested and scarred this very land during the Korean War
with previously untested napalm. Instead, Im Kwon-Taek's typical long
shot of the homeless family wandering and singing through the beautifully tamed yet undeveloped natural setting offers a riveting visual feast.
The pristine landscape in which Yu-bong's homeless family wanders is
a wilderness that the camera idealizes with a tourist's gaze. Tourism
thrives on nostalgia that is drawn to places where there has been uneven
development. As I have discussed elsewhere, the film's aesthetic frame
exoticizes and eroticizes Korea by rediscovering it as "the sacred, uncontaminated, that is, undeveloped virgin land." It masks the intensely
developed industrial country that lies outside the camera frame.[6] In
other words, the film adopts the viewpoint of both the colonial male
gaze and the Othered feminine subject responding to that gaze. Under this self-primitivizing, internalized colonial male gaze, a daughter is
blinded for the perfection of a cultural nationalist artifact that fulfills the
masculinist desire of a father who has been shunted off to the margins
of that capitalist development.

  *Sopyonje* articulates Koreans' incommensurable experience of postcoloniality. The film attempts to sublimate the national *han* by recuperating a precolonial, aesthetic means of communication, *p'ansori*, as
it highlights the *han* of a victimized woman who bears the burden of
reclaiming national identity. In other words, the victimized woman is
given the role of the redeemer of the nation. This draws our attention to
the construction of gender, as well as of family and nation in postcolonial
Korea, represented in the film.

  In the colonial era, the contradiction between imposed modernity
and non-modern, indigenous culture disqualified traditional fathers and
their authority. They were judged unfit to be leaders of society because
they lacked modern knowledge and skills to transform the nation and
confront the powerful modern rule of the colonial master. The construction of the ill-equipped and inadequate father is quite evident in
modern novels written during the colonial period and in postindepen-
dence fiction. In these novels and short stories, fathers are generally
absent: for example, Kang Kyŏng-ae's "Underground Village" ("Chi-
hach'on," 1936); many of Pak Wan-sŏ's novels, from her very first, *The*

*Naked Tree* (*Namok*, 1971), to *The Unforgettable* (*Mimang*, 1990); and more recently Ch'oe Myŏng-hŭi's *The Soul Fire* (*Honbul,* 1996). Variations of the inadequate male authority include the intellectual husband dependent on his unskilled, prostitute wife in Yi Sang's *Wings* (*Nalgae,* 1936), and the sexually impotent male patriarch Ch'oe Ch'i-su, in Pak Kyŏng-ni's massive roman fleuve *The Land* (*T'oji,* 1973–98). At best the father figures of the colonial period are depicted as marginalized, emasculated, and wasted.

Since a great number of dispossessed heads of households emigrated, legally or illegally, during the colonial period in search of a way to survive, it is true that many Korean families suffered from the absence of a father. But it is also true that many women, especially young women, left home in order to reduce the number of mouths to feed; they had no illusions about the likelihood of being able to earn a living in the harsh colonial marketplace. In this sense, the absence of a fictional father is more than an accurate sociological representation of Korean households at that time. It serves as a symbolic representation of the absence of fatherly *authority* in the families of colonized Korea. These works of fiction narrativize the loss of masculinity in modern Korea under colonial rule.

In the absence of adequate fathers, the burden of the nation's future was placed on the shoulders of their sons, whose responsibilities continued well into the postliberation period—as is shown in the film *The Horse Carriage Driver* (*Mabu,* Kang Tae-jin, 1961).[7] It is noteworthy that a very similar pattern emerges as well in North Korean cinema classics, such as *Sea of Blood* (*P'ibada,* 1969) and *The Flower Girl* (*Kkot p'anŭn ch'ŏnyŏ,* 1972). The mother or—in the case of the latter—the young daughter sacrifices herself for the survival of the family against the enemy of the people, whether that is a greedy landlord or the Japanese Army. At the end of the struggle, the long-lost son/brother returns and identifies himself as a revolutionary. In the North Korean cinematic canon, all the credit for revolutionary heroism earned by the mother and the daughter is bestowed on the son/brother. Especially illustrative of this point are the novels of the "Immortal History" (*Pulmyŏl ŭi ryŏksa*) series, the hagiography of Kim Il Sung's guerrilla activities during the Manchurian war; these fill in the missing story of "the heroic son" hidden behind the story of the women's struggle at home. In other words, North Korean doctrinal literature, not unlike its southern counterpart, narrativizes the recuperation of Korean masculinity.

*Sopyonje* is a cinematic variation of this family saga of a colonized nation. Reading *Sopyonje* as an allegory of a multiply colonized, divided nation, we note that Yu-bong's family lacks cohesiveness and stability. As the head of an arbitrarily assembled family, Yu-bong also is a troubled patriarchal character. He challenged his mentor's authority by engaging in an affair with the man's mistress. As a result, he was excommunicated from the group of promising singers. Consigned to wander around the countryside, he attempts to reclaim the already waning glory of *p'ansori* in the marginalized and privatized circuit outside the limelight. Although Yu-bong adopts and raises Song-hwa and Tong-ho, his son often questions his patriarchal authority. Indeed, Tong-Ho poses a threat to his father's masculinity and fatherly authority as early as the episode in which Yu-bong makes love to Tong-ho's widowed mother Kumsandaek. In this scene Tong-ho gazes at the entangled couple through the darkness of the night, and the camera cuts to the boy's face, lingering on his intense gaze for a sustained period. Whereas Yu-bong once engaged his mentor in sexual rivalry and challenged his patriarchal authority, ironically it is now his adolescent son who challenges him.

Tong-ho's sexual rivalry with Yu-bong begins to surface more explicitly in the scene where Yu-bong slaps Song-hwa in the face for tolerating a drunken customer who forced her to pour alcohol for him and then stuck money in her bosom. Yu-bong's action breaks up the drinking party. As the still enraged Yu-bong flies out of the house, Tong-ho, who has been expressing his anger through fierce glares, steps forward and complains of his father's violent exploitation of Song-hwa. When Song-hwa tries to defend Yu-bong, Tong-ho announces that Yu-bong is not their real father.

This episode follows the scene where Tong-ho and Song-hwa sit on a branch of a magnificent old tree practicing the story of Ch'unhyang and her pregnancy from the *Tale of Ch'unhyang;* the two gingerly verbalize and explore their own sexuality. It is from under this tree that Song-hwa bids farewell to Tong-ho—and also from under this tree that Yu-bong, declaring that Tong-ho will never return, collects Song-hwa before he offers her the fateful poison. The all-encompassing branches of the ancient tree in which the two young people share their sexual interest invokes the image of a love nest; moreover, the enduring magnificence of the tree under which Song-hwa waits for Tong-ho symbolizes the extent of her devotion to him. But Yu-bong intervenes and prohibits this love between the adopted brother and sister. The famous long take scene—soon after the face-slapping one and prior to Tong-ho's departure—highlights the contest between the father and the son over the daughter/sister. In this scene the three sing and dance down a long, winding country road. The choreography signifies the relationship among the three. While the two men dance in crisscross fashion around Song-hwa, Yu-bong cuts into the space between Tong-ho and Song-hwa, thus foreshadowing his successful claim to Song-hwa. Before long, there is nothing Tong-ho can do but leave the family.

After Tong-bo's departure, Yu-bong resolutely regains patriarchal and masculine authority through violent means. For that reclamation he relies on "the Law of the Father." The enigmatic *kŏmungo* scene aids our efforts to understand this process. *Kŏmungo* is a traditional string instrument played only by literati and courtesans, as an accompaniment to their recitation of poetry. According to the mores of the Confucian caste system, the likes of Yu-bong—an itinerant *p'ansori* singer who performs before peasants—are not privileged to be in the company of the refined old man in the *kŏmungo* playing scene. The fact that we do not even know Yu-bong's surname attests to his lowly status. However, imagining Yu-bong (or Yu-bong's imagining of) sharing the high cultural space with the old man creates an imaginary homosocial space between Yu-bong and the old man—and, by extension, among the society of men the aristocratic old man represents. Occupying this space momentarily, Yu-bong gains the authority of the Confucian patriarchy and the high cultural male prerogatives this old man represents. This symbolic transformation of Yu-bong reconfigures the familial space of Yu-bong and Song-hwa along gender and class divides. The reconfigured and redefined relationship between Yu-bong and Song-hwa justifies Yu-bong's rape of Song-hwa as analogous to that of an elite male's ravishing of a homeless orphan girl.

This imaginary authority of the Father falls short of fulfilling the nationalistic agenda, perhaps because of the father's inauthentic authority and because of his betraying history. It is only after the death of Yu-bong, the inadequate father, and after a lengthy struggle of the victimized woman for survival and for perfection of her art, that the long-lost son returns. In fact, the film begins with the return of the son looking for his sister. It is of interest that Tong-ho's occupation is collecting medicinal herbs, an occupation related to healing.[8] Only with the return of the healer brother does Song-hwa's *p'ansori* reach its perfection. The intertextual amalgam of the fulfillment of national ideals, the sublimation of *han*, and human redemption by way of a woman's sacrifice is the climax of the film.

I must backtrack a bit in order to explain the complexities of the climactic scene. Once the incestuous relationship between Yu-bong and Song-hwa is established through the four scenes I discussed at the beginning of this essay, Song-hwa asks her father to teach her to sing the *Tale of Simch'ŏng*, the story of a filial girl who sacrifices herself so that her blind father will regain his sight. The heroine sells herself to sailors as a ritual sacrifice to the dragon king of the ocean. When Simch'ŏng is drowned, her father pays tribute to Buddha and regains his vision, and thus her filial piety is rewarded. At the climax of the *Tale of Simch'ŏng*, the immortalized daughter meets the father, who then opens his eyes. Up to this point, Song-hwa's repertoire consists of the *Tale of Ch'unhyang*, the narrative of a young courtesan who waits for her true love to return while resisting pressure from the local magistrate to serve him. With this request for a new role, Song-hwa appears to relinquish her love for Tong-ho and pledge her loyalty to Yu-bong.

However, toward the end of the film, when the brother and the sister (or, alternatively, the childhood lovers) meet again, Song-hwa sings a song from the *Tale of Simch'ŏng* as Tong-ho accompanies her on his drum. Performing the *Tale of Simch'ŏng* together, Song-hwa and Tong-ho aesthetically consummate their hitherto repressed and undeveloped love for each other, though there is no sexual consummation. Through this communion, Song-hwa's *han* is sublimated and humanity is redeemed. This is also the moment when Yu-bong's nationalistic goal of perfecting *p'ansori* is fulfilled. Ironically, the sublimation of *han* is achieved by way of the love that Yu-bong sabotaged by patriarchal and masculine authority. (It should be noted that in this scene Song-hwa wears the same clothes she had on when she first became Yu-bong's mistress.) The inauthentic sexual union between Yu-bong and Song-hwa is finally transcended; its place is taken by the authenticated love of the returned son. Like the revolutionary son in many North Korean narratives, who returns to complete the revolution and claim credit for winning the struggle, Tong-ho returns to authenticate Song-hwa's attempt to reestablish the preeminence of the national sound over the colonial music.

Sopyonje allows little room for Song-hwa's agency, however. Throughout the film she is portrayed as a victim: an orphan, the object of rape, and a filial daughter who fulfills her father's dream. Her character does not develop much and remains essentially flat. However, even the most masculinist narrative cannot totally victimize her. Song-hwa protects her love for Tong-ho by silently complying with Yu-bong. Absorbing Yu-bong's unforgivable violence is a form of silent resistance that enables her to keep the flame of her love alive. Song-hwa is the one who embodies the perfected art and who sublimates *han*—but at enormous expense. Is perfection of national art worth a woman's lifetime of misery?

## Aestheticism and Cultural Nationalism

In this section I turn to one of *Sopyonje*'s early precursors, *The Genealogy*. Reading the two films together helps illuminate the ways in which colonialism, aestheticism, cultural nationalism, nostalgia, and gender intersect in Im Kwon-Taek's work. *The Genealogy* is a watershed film in his career. Starting with this film, Im Kwon-Taek—who up to this point had mostly made B-grade action films—began to direct "serious films" that address various issues of Korean history, culture, and society. Curiously such a change in Im's career path was motivated, as Im revealed in an interview,[9] by the Quality Films Reward System (*usu yŏnghwaje*) implemented in 1973 as part of the Park Chung Hee regime's revision of the Motion Picture Law. This fourth revision legalized both severe film censorship and a quota system. Although this policy was designed to promote the dwindling domestic film industry, the incongruous ratio between the number of films produced and the number of exhibition days allowed further relegated domestic films to the margins of the market.[10] The quota system was imposed in tandem with the Quality Films Reward System, which gave film companies that produced "high quality" films special prerogatives to import and distribute foreign films. The Motion Picture Promotion Policy announced in 1973 defined "quality films" as follows: those that champion the Yusin Constitution, advance national identity and patriotism, promote the New Village Movement, and demonstrate a high level of literary artistry.[11] At the same time, Article 18 of the Presidential Decree amended to the Motion Picture Law spelled out eleven categories of censorship violations, chief of which was defamation of the state—which was equated with the regime—and its ruler. This severe censorship deprived Korean film directors of freedom of expression.

Under these circumstances, film companies relied heavily on box-office revenues from imported films for their financial survival, but in order to do this, they had to produce a certain number of domestic films. Consequently, film directors were under pressure to make "quality films" that were complicit in policies of the military regime, for the newly founded government agency known as the Motion Picture Promotion Corporation (MPPC) determined the financing of these films. Another option was to make low-budget commercial films. While Golden Age auteurs such as Shin Sang-ok chose the second route, Im Kwon-Taek chose the first. In 1973 MPPC financed Im's Korean War film *The Testimony* (*Chŭngŏn*, 1973), which received the Grand Bell Award. In the following year, again with support from MPPC, he made *The Wives on Parade* (*Anaedŭl ŭi haengjin*, 1974), which promotes the controversial New Village Movement—a government-initiated program to modernize the countryside. After a few years, however, Im Kwon-Taek turned away from propaganda films. His new focuses were "literary films" (*munye yŏnghwa*)—adaptations of well-received novels—and films that promote cultural nationalism. What saved Im Kwon-Taek from a career of propaganda filmmaking is his aestheticism, which is based on nationalism.

*The Genealogy* was adapted from a short story by the Japanese writer Kajiyama Toshiyuki. The film is anchored on the dilemma of the primogenitor of an old aristocratic clan, Sŏl Chin-yong, who oversees volumes of the clan's genealogy record (*chokpo*). However, the story is not about Sŏl but about Tani, a Japanese genre painter. *The Genealogy* is set in Korea during the Japanese colonial period. In 1939, at the height of imperial Japan's fascist rule, the colonial government imposed on Koreans the Name Change Order. (This was enforced under the slogan of *naisen ittai* [Japan and Korea as One Body], a motto intended to mobilize Koreans from all walks of life and make them Japanese imperial subjects.) In the film, Sŏl faces increasing pressure from Japanese colonial officials to adopt a Japanese surname and show his loyalty to Emperor Hirohito.[12] Sŏl has been donating large sums of money to the Japanese Army in hopes of protecting his clan from harassment. Nevertheless, the colonial officials are relentless. Finally Tani, a young colonial officer, is dispatched to Sŏl's house in an attempt to persuade him to alter his name. Tani is a young artist who paints pictures of Korean folk customs and of scenes from everyday life. He is serving in the colonial administration in Seoul as a way of avoiding being drafted into the military. Sŏl and his wife treat Tani with the utmost hospitality, even introducing him to their daughter Ok-sun. (Although the narrative explains that Sŏl needs his daughter there to serve as an interpreter, this is still a most unusual act for a traditional Korean patriarch.) It turns out that Ok-sun also has artistic talent and was trained by one of Tani's friends from art school.

The two young people are attracted to each other, but Ok-sun is already betrothed. As a means of increasing the pressure on Sŏl, colonial officials incarcerate Ok-sun's fiancé as a political prisoner. Brutal torture and the threat of conscription drive him insane, and the betrothal is annulled. As Sŏl maintains his resistance, the colonial authorities decide to draft Ok-sun as a military sexual slave—a "comfort woman." By chance, Tani discovers this scheme, and he thwarts it by finding Ok-sun a job at the Japanese Army procurement office. Sŏl's son Chang-won tries to persuade him to obey the Name Charge Order, because he fears for the security of his job. Moreover, Sŏl's grandchildren are barred from school because their surnames remain Korean. Sŏl finally changes his family's name—but then he kills himself immediately afterward. The patriarch whose authority has been claimed by colonial powers unleashes violence against himself—a contrast to Yu-bong in *Sopyonje*, who, under similar pressure, takes out his aggression on his daughter. After Sŏl's funeral, Tani confronts his superior and makes disparaging comments about Japan's bestiality and lack of civility. He is subsequently fired and then drafted into the military. *The Genealogy* demonstrates that Japanese as well as Korean civilians were victims of the fascist militarism of imperial Japan. It is not clear whether this film was meant to be seen as an indictment of the military dictatorship of the Park Chung Hee regime, though it certainly is—at least indirectly. At any rate, the regime, which bestowed the Grand Bell Award on this film, was apparently not capable of self-reflexivity.

Just as Tani and Ok-sun are spiritually connected through their shared appreciation of art, aestheticism connects empathic Japanese people with Koreans in this film. To clarify this relationship, *The Genealogy* actively mobilizes the thoughts of the Japanese critic Yanagi Muneyoshi (Yanagi Soetsu, 1868–1961)[13] as the spiritual arbiter between the colonizer and the colonized. Yanagi was a contemporary of both the doyen of Japanese folklore Yanagita Kunio (1875–1962) and the noted art critic Okakura Tenshin (Kakuzo, 1862–1913). Under the aegis of his teacher Ernest Fenellosa—who cast a special aura over the art of Japanese painting—during the early Meiji period Okakura initiated the movement to preserve traditional Japanese paintings and artifacts, which were being hastily destroyed to make room for new materials and art forms. Like Okakura, Yanagi chose art criticism for his career, and, like Yanagita, he became a leading figure in the Japanese craft movement. This preservation movement was modeled on the European craft movement, which developed in response to the destruction of craft work by nineteenth-century industrialism. The folklore movement rose in tandem with the craft movement and was an integral part of the nationalist ideology of countries such as Germany and Ireland that were at the margins of industrialism. Yanagi was absorbed in this modern aesthetic, and he is credited with developing the notion that Korean craft work represents an art form.

Unlike Okakura Kakuzo, the pan-Asianist who fought against Western imperialism even as he supported the Japanese colonial occupation of

Korea and Taiwan, Yanagi, who was active in the democratic movement of the Taisho period (1912–26), objected to Japan's colonization of Korea. He deeply appreciated Korean pottery and other traditional crafts. In an essay published in 1919, "Thinking about the Korean People," Yanagi identifies the most salient element in Korean art as the beauty of the curving line that symbolizes Koreans' sorrow, sadness, and hunger for love (from the people of other nations), and he offers sympathy and love to the Koreans. He also laments the disappearance of traditional Korean aesthetic values as a result of colonial control over public education.[14] In an essay written the following year, Yanagi mourns the colonial government's destruction of the Kwanghwamun Gate—the southern gate to the main palace of the Chosŏn court, which had a special place in the hearts of many Koreans.

Koreans have long admired Yanagi as an exceptional man, a Japanese intellectual sympathetic to their wishes for independence. However, not everyone has shared this sentiment. As early as 1922 the young Korean philosopher Pak Chong-hong vehemently charged that Yanai's concept of the Korean aesthetic is rooted in his view of Korea as a colony. Pak argued that Yanagi's thesis of the "beauty of sadness" shows his lack of understanding about the influence of Asian continental aesthetics on Korean art, the central features of which, he claimed, are physical dynamics and humor.[15] Pak's critique represented a singular assessment of Yanagi until 1974, when Ch'oe Ha-rim wrote a derogatory introduction to an anthology of Yanagi's work translated into Korean.[16] Nevertheless, the South Korean government, following the majority of Koreans' judgment of Yanagi's writings, posthumously awarded him the Jeweled Crown Culture Medal in 1984.

*The Genealogy* is a celebration of Yanagi Soetsu's aestheticism and humanism. In a sense, Tani embodies Yanagi, for he represents a humanism and an aesthetic steeped in imperial nostalgia. Tani wants to paint the disappearing beauty of Korean folk life. Emulating his appreciative gaze, the camera captures the beautiful rural landscape as Tani travels to and from Sŏl's rural home. Even the elaborate procession of Sŏl's funeral commands a long shot against the curving, feminized lines of the hills—the lines of sorrow. As Tani (in a Western suit) confides to Ok-sun (in Korean costume) his wish to capture the Korean sadness, the shot is from low on the ground in front of an ancient tree, and the camera looks up at Tani from beneath the tree trunk. Tani's lofty and larger-than-life stature is foregrounded by the gnarly roots and trunk of the imposing old tree, which takes up the right half of the screen. Clearly this shot maps out the relationship between modern, altruistic Yanagi/Tani and the aging, sorrowful, and feminine Korean objects of his benevolent gaze.

This self-orientalizing, nostalgic gaze and the grammar of the shot that portrays feminine sorrow and *han* through the tree represent an integral feature of Im Kwon-Taek's favorite cinematic diction, the one which he so effectively mobilizes in *Sopyonje*. Like Yanagi, Tani blames Japan for the destruction of traditional customs. Sŏl, who is familiar with Yanagi's work, shares Tani's deep appreciation of Korea, and this leads to a close friendship—between a colonial official and the colonized intellectual—and ultimately to Tani's being drafted. Even Sŏl reflects, on the night of his suicide, upon Yanagi's words about the Korean beauty of sorrow. (Actually this is the only time Yanagi's name is directly invoked in the film.) Like Yanagi, Tani offers his love to a Korean woman and rescues her from the grips of Japan's bestial sexual desire, fulfilling the formula that only the colonizing man can rescue the colonized woman. The aestheticism that rescues humanity from brutal colonial rule in the film thus raises a number of issues that appear regularly in Im Kwon-Taek's later films.

Yanagi's affection for Korean craftsmanship and his sympathy for suffering Koreans were truly exceptional and commendable, but he was not completely free from the influence of the intellectual discourse of his time and the implications of his position as a metropolitan citizen. In Europe, industrialization made handicrafts and their means of production obsolete. As handicrafts became objects of appreciation (and preservation), the lives of the disappearing craftsmen themselves began to receive attention, and nostalgia made its first appearance in Western Europe. Since industrialization did not begin in Japan until the 1880s, traditional modes of production still continued through most of Yanagi's lifetime. His nostalgia for the disappearing Korean craft and his notion of the aesthetic of sorrow need to be resituated. Yanagi's lament about disappearing Korean beauty may stem in part from the Japanese aesthetic sensitivity known as *monono aware*—the pathetic beauty implicit in heightened awareness of the transience of beauty. Moreover, his lamentation for this disappearance is set in a colonial context, inevitably raising the issue of ethnicity.

Noting the rise of the discourse of disappearance at the turn of the century in Japan, Murai Osamu argues that this discourse was an element of colonial discourse; it lamented the disappearance of ethnic minorities in Hokkaido and Okinawa yet also anticipated the total assimilation of those minorities—and the disappearance of their ethnic identity. In this sense, the craft movement in Japan gave support to a policy that fossilized the culture of people whose identity would eventually be eradicated.[17] Thus the discourse of the disappearing crafts of ethnic minorities within the Japanese Empire was not an innocent expression of sympathy and concern for the art of the disappearing ethnic minorities, but an incantation that anticipated the efficacy of such a discourse. This is precisely what lies behind what Renato Rosaldo termed "imperialist nostalgia": a yearning for the disappearing ways of life of colonized people that imperial advancement destroyed.[18] And in light of Murai's argument concerning the intellectual milieu of the craft movement in Yanagi's time, Im Kwon-Taek's representation of Yanagi's ideas and the Korean reception of Yanagi require a reassessment of the politics of aesthetics.

As Edward Said pointed out in *Orientalism,* when analogous nostalgic desire and attitude in metropolitan Europe was directed toward the colonies, they constructed the aesthetic of the colonized. The orientalist aesthetic constructs the cultures of the colonized as exotic, passive, and feminine. It does not neglect the cultures of the exotic Other, but it respects the representation it has constructed with confidence in the rational and masculine power of the self. Yanagi's characterization of Korean beauty as one which lies in the curving lines that signify the sorrow and sadness of unloved people (as if Koreans were children yearning for Japanese parental love) and his lament for disappearing Korean life and handicrafts resonate in the orientalist aesthetic. In *The Genealogy,* Yanagi's imperial nostalgia is powerfully invoked through Tani, but the gender code of orientalism is also activated. The lines of the feminized landscape are fully laid bare to the gaze of Tani, the quintessential colonial aesthete. Furthermore, it is the humanist Tani who loves the Korean

woman and rescues her from the system of military sexual slavery. This
film deviates slightly from an orientalist structure, however, to the extent
that Tani, the enlightened humanist, is depicted not as a masculine con-
queror but as a social misfit in militaristic, imperial Japan. Though he is
presented as a product of Japanese enlightenment, he loses confidence
in Japan's civility.

By contrast, Sŏl is not depicted as an inadequate patriarch but as a
rich and dignified one. He is also a champion of colonial hybridity. He
maintains a traditional Korean lifestyle, but he is intent on keeping up
with modern thought. Though he is not fluent in Japanese, he is knowl-
edgeable about the writings of Yanagi Soetsu. Sŏl's humanism is evident
in his touching request for farewell kisses from his grandchildren before
his suicide, and he is liberal enough about sex to allow Ok-sun's romance
with Tani—something the rigid and imperious Yu-bong would never
permit. He is even comfortable wearing a European soft hat with his
Korean dress. But this modern patriarch eventually must come to terms
with his powerlessness as a colonized Korean. He becomes increasingly
dependent on the colonizer Tani, who behaves more like Sŏl's adopted
son or son-in-law than a Japanese colonial officer. Indeed, Sŏl's family
welcomes Tani first as a lover of Korean culture and subsequently as a
lover of their daughter. Their relationship is foreshadowed in the ban-
quet scene on the night of Tani's first visit. The elaborate table setting
is intended to help introduce this young painter to Korean upper-class
culinary culture, but beyond that, the formalities are similar to those that
would be observed if the guest were a prospective son-in-law. Conversation during dinner is on a very personal level, leading Tani to confess
his bachelorhood and, implicitly, his eligibility for romance. Ultimately,
however, this "adopted son" cannot restore the father's authority. In the
end both the father and the son are destroyed by the bestiality of fascism.

Though it precedes *Sopyonje*, *The Genealogy* seems to go beyond the
binary aesthetic structure of Im's later film, which celebrates the local
and denigrates the foreign. *The Genealogy* interprets the national aesthetic in gendered terms. Its agenda is not to contest and overcome the
colonial through brute force but by using aesthetic rivalry to transform
the power relationship. Competing civilizations notwithstanding, Koreans themselves are complicit in this orientalist scenario. On the night

of his suicide, when Sǒl reflects on Yanagi's aesthetic thesis, his national consciousness is mediated by the words of a metropolitan intellectual. This allows us a glimpse of Im Kwon-Taek's aestheticism, which may be derivative of metropolitan aestheticism; this would explain his uncritical internalization of the orientalist aesthetic, signified in gendered terms, that appears in *Sopyonje*.

Alternatively, Im Kwon-Taek's indiscriminate adoption of Yanagi's discourse of disappearance can be situated within the cultural nationalist discourse of the 1970s, when *The Genealogy* was produced. This was the decade of South Korea's intensive industrialization, akin to that in Europe a century earlier. Urban industrialization required a massive labor force, and an urban working class emerged for the first time in Korean history. In order to meet the demand for labor and ease the pressures of this heavily compressed industrialization, the Park Chung Hee regime forced the modernization of the rural agricultural sector, under the banner of the New Village Movement. This led to the transformation of the rural scene. One of the most prominent changes was in the appearance of rural architecture. Thatched roofs gave way to corrugated tin ones, and clay walls to cinder blocks. The government ordered that the tin roofs be painted bright red, green, or blue. This forced modernization changed people's lifestyle overnight, at least in the visual realm.

In response to this rapid change, a sense of longing for home and security developed, as did nostalgia for the disappearing, preindustrial lifestyle—especially among rural workers who had migrated to the city. By the mid-1970s South Korean city dwellers began to witness the rise of the nostalgia industry in response to this longing. Taverns decorated with thatched roofs and gourd vines began to crop up in urban centers. These were called "folklife taverns" (*minsok chujǒm*), and they served regional cuisine and rice wine. This is only one example of the nostalgia industry in the quotidian space. The tourism industry, the recipient of enormous measures of government support, spectacularized the product of nostalgia as part of its commodification of sex.

The emergence of the nostalgia industry was not independent of the South Korean government's populist culture policy. As mentioned earlier, this was initiated by the promulgation of the 1962 Cultural Preservation Law and countered by the oppositional populist culture movement

that began in the late 1960s. Taking the Gramscian notion of hegemony
and the magical technique of commodity fetishism one step further,
Michael Taussig demonstrates some of the ways in which the modern
state deploys a magical technique of rule that conceals its iron fist in
a velvet glove.[19] The South Korean military junta, led by Park Chung
Hee—formerly an officer in Japan's Manchurian Army—carried out a
successful coup in 1961, but he lacked both political legitimacy and the
support of the masses. With the implementation of the new culture
policy, the junta, though it maintained a rigorously fascistic militarism,
managed to reinvent itself as a civilian government. It projected the self-
image of a sympathetic government committed to rejuvenating the popular culture that was destroyed by Japanese colonialism. This hegemonic
technique invoked popular support by appealing to the cultural nationalist sentiment. Just as nationalism in the colonized world derives from
the nationalism of empires—as Partha Chatterjee argues[20]— the notion
of popular culture was adopted in former colonies as a way to protest
against postcolonial military regimes and continue the struggle against
imperialism. South Korea's anti-imperial *minjung* culture movement in
the 1970s and '80s exemplified a counter-hegemonic construct.[21] Since
both hegemonic and counter-hegemonic constructs of the people and
popular culture are decontextualized inventions, the artifacts mobilized
as arbitrary signifiers are susceptible to commodification. This is the site
where the nostalgia industry thrives and becomes directly connected to
the tourist economy, which relies heavily on the production of simulacra.

Walter Benjamin's insight into the nuances of the reproduced artifact applies here. Reproduction technology casts an aura of authenticity
upon the original artifact. Yet at the same time, and precisely because
of mass dissemination and consumption of the reproduced art, it undermines the authority of that aura. Benjamin warns that this ambiguity is susceptible to dangerous and unethical appropriation in the
name of the aesthetic—as happened in the case of Leni Riefenstahl's
film venerating fascist rituals and celebrating the Third Reich. This is
where the subjective aesthetic judgment or Kantian sublime of dissoci-
ating ethical/political concerns must intervene. But Im's aestheticism
and cultural nationalism blur the boundary between the hegemonic and

counter-hegemonic inventions of national culture, and they indiscriminately appropriate popular cultural artifacts in the name of nationalism.

The Genealogy and Sopyonje narrativize the loss of masculinity under
colonial domination. They tell stories of men who, in their struggle to
restore national dignity and recuperate masculinity, resort to violence.
Sŏl preserves patriarchal honor by way of suicidal passive aggressiv-
ity, and Yu-bong sacrifices the opportunity of life and the dignity of
a woman. In this cinematic discourse of self-inflicted violence, the narrative constantly slips into self-orientalizing affirmation of imperialist
nostalgia and misogynist nationalism. These masculinist narratives leave
no option other than self-directed epistemological violence, which itself
holds out no hope of resistance or intervention. The blind obsession to
reclaim masculinity not only denies female agency but also forecloses
the possibility of creative interstices that might open up a new way of
imagining a nation, or even a post-nation. The road to the recovery of
colonized masculinity is not a path to healing but a highway to tragic
(self-)destruction.

## Notes

1. Victor Turner develops this term in his *Dramas, Fields, and Metaphors*
(Ithaca: Cornell University Press, 1974). Communitas refers to an anti-structural
sentiment, developed in the liminal stage of a ritual, in which role reversal
produces the effect of leveling and humiliation.

2. *Shimpa* theater (New Group Theater) was a newly emerging style of
Japanese theater at the turn of the century. It presented a mixture of Western and
Japanese modes, most notably Kabuki. Its most salient feature is an exaggerated
expression of emotion. For a discussion that relates *shimpa* to Japanese cinema,
see Komatsu Hiroshi, "Some Characteristics of Japanese Cinema before World
War I," in *Reframing Japanese Cinema*, ed. Arthur Nolletti, Jr., and David
Desser (Bloomington: Indiana University Press, 1992), 229–58.

3. Ch'oe Wŏn-sik, "*ŭnsegye yŏngu*" (A Study of *ŭnsegye*), *Ch'angjak kwa
pip'yŏng* 48 (summer, 1978).

4. Marshall Berman, *All That Is Solid Melts into Air: The Experience of
Modernity* (New York: Simon and Schuster, 1982).

5. John Frow, "Tourism and the Semiotics of Nostalgia," *October* 57 (Summer, 1991): 123–51.

6. See my "Nationalism and Construction of Gender in Korea," in *Dangerous Women: Gender and Korean Nationalism,* ed. Elaine H. Kim and Chungmoo Choi (New York: Routledge, 1998), 9–31.

7. For more detail, please see my "The Magic and Violence of Modernization in Post-Colonial Korea," in *Post-Colonial Classics of Korean Cinema,* ed. Chungmoo Choi (Irvine: Korean Film Festival Committee, University of California, 1998), 5–12.

8. For this insight I am indebted to Soyoung Kim.

9. Im Kwon-Taek, ed., *Sŏpyŏnje: yŏnghwa iyagi* (Sopyonje: movie book) (Seoul: Hanul, 1993).

10. Lee Young-il, *The History of Korean Cinema* (Seoul: Motion Picture Promotion Corporation, 1988), 184.

11. Kim Hong-dong, "Yŏnghwa pŏpkyu wa sich'aek ŭro pŏn chŏngch'aek ŭi hŭrŭm" (The History of the Motion Picture Law and motion picture policies), in *Hanguk yŏngwha chŏngch'aek ŭi hŭrŭm kwa saeroun chŏnmang* (The History of Korean motion picture policies and the perspectives of the future) (Seoul: Chimmundang, 1995), 154–155.

12. The Name Change Order was promulgated in late 1939 and imposed on February 11, 1940, one year before the war spread to the Pacific. Over eighty-four percent of Koreans complied. For more detail see Carter J. Eckert et al., *Korea Old and New: A History* (Seoul: Iljogak, 1990), 314–20. Sŏl Chin-yŏng was an actual person, known for his protest against the Name Change Order. Sŏl lived not in Suwon, as in the film, but in Koch'ang of North Chŏlla Province. When his grandchildren were threatened with expulsion from school, Sŏl committed suicide by jumping down a well. See Kim Tong-ho, "Iljeha ŭi ch'angssi kaemyŏng" (The Surname change under Japanese colonial rule), in *Ch'inilp'a* (The Collaborators), ed. Kim Sam-ung et al. (Seoul: Hangminsa, 1990), 301.

13. In Korea the name Yanagi Muneyoshi is more widely used, though in Japan he is known as Yanagi Soetsu. Although Yanagi Muneyoshi is an acceptable reading of the Chinese characters of his name, I follow the Japanese rendering in this essay.

14. Yanagi Muneyoshi, "Chosŏn saram ŭl saenggak handa" (Thinking about the Korean people)," in *Chosŏn ŭl saenggak handa* (Thinking about Korea), ed. and trans. Sim U-sŏng (Seoul: Hakkojae, 1996), 14–24.

15. Hŏ Yŏng-sŏp, *Chosŏn ch'ongdokpu* (Korean colonial government) (Seoul: Hanul, 1996), 296–97.

16. Ch'oe Ha-rim, "Haesŏl—Yanagi Muneyoshi ŭi hanguk misulgwan e taehayŏ" (Introduction: on Yanagi Soetsu's view of Korean art), in Yanagi

Soetsu, *Hanguk kwa kŭ yesul* (Korea and its art), trans. Yi Tae-wŏn (Seoul: 1974), 79–87.

17. Osamu Murai, "Nation and Narrative: The Narratives of the Empire and the Narratives of the 'Disappearing,'" (paper presented at the annual meeting of the Association for Asian Studies, Honolulu, Hawaii, April 1996).

18. Renato Rosaldo, "Imperialist Nostalgia," in *Culture and Truth* (Boston: Beacon Press, 1989), 68–87.

19. Michael Taussig, "Maleficium: State Fetishism," in *Fetishism as Cultural Discourse*, ed. Emily Apter and William Pietz (Ithaca: Cornell University Press, 1993), 217–74.

20. Partha Chatterjee, *Nationalist Thought and the Colonial World: A Derivative Discourse* (Minneapolis: University of Minnesota Press, 1986).

21. For more detail, please see my "The Minjung Culture Movement and the Construction of Popular Culture in Korea," in *South Korea's Minjung Movement: The Culture and Politics of Dissidence*, ed. Kenneth M. Wells (Honolulu: University of Hawai'i Press, 1995), 105–18.

Cho Hae Joang
Translated and edited by Yuh Ji-Yeon

CHAPTER 5

# *Sopyonje:* Its Cultural and Historical Meaning

## The Movie

No one involved in making *Sopyonje* (*Sŏp'yŏnje*) imagined that it would become the most popular domestic movie in South Korean history, quickly topping the box-office success of the same director's famed *The General's Son* (*Changun ŭi adŭl*). At the time of its release in April 1993, newspapers were reporting that the nation's filmmakers were principally aiming for prizes in foreign art film festivals rather than popularity at home, yet *Sopyonje* won rave reviews and the adulation of viewers all over the country. By October, the number of domestic viewers exceeded one million, and the film was being screened for foreign audiences at art theaters and on college campuses in many parts of the United States and Europe.

Briefly, *Sopyonje* focuses on a makeshift family over the course of three decades, from the 1930s through the 1960s: a father, his adopted daughter, and his stepson. The family ekes out a living performing *p'ansori* at parties and at the homes of rich aristocrats.[1] Performers have

134

traditionally been relegated to the lowest class in South Korea, and the family is scorned, ignored, and often humiliated. Once the country falls under the domination of American culture, the demand for *p'ansori* falls dramatically, and the family teeters on the verge of starvation. The father, however, clings to his art and insists on passing it on to his children. He trains them in *p'ansori,* the daughter as a vocalist and the son as a drummer. But the son, fed up with being poor and unable to fathom the father's motives, runs away from home. The movie follows his search, years later, for his sister, and it culminates in their reunion. Shot against a stunning rural backdrop, swelling with the heartbreaking strains of an original score that was deliberately reminiscent of—but not quite the same as—traditional South Korean music, and showcasing snatches of *p'ansori* and traditional folk songs, the movie was widely extolled as a major cultural achievement. The soundtrack album was also a great hit. Featuring the film's score, composed by Kim Su-ch'ŏl, as well as excerpts from the movie's soundtrack, the album gives listeners a sampling of traditional Korean music. Both the movie and the album were widely credited with reviving public interest in *p'ansori.*

The movie also generated scores of articles in South Korean news-papers and magazines. In addition to reviews, the South Korean press published updates on the movie's popularity and the public reaction, as well as interviews with the director, producer, principal actors, and the man who wrote the short story on which the movie is based. Four of the nation's major dailies weighed in with editorials, and most newspapers carried columns commenting on the social and cultural significance of the *Sopyonje* phenomenon.

Reprints of many of these articles, as well as a chronological list of them, can be found in *"Sopyonje" Movie Book,* a lavishly illustrated resource and fact book published in October 1993, just seven months after the movie's release.[2] Apparently aimed at fans hungry for detailed and up close information about the movie, it includes a long account of the film's production, beginning with Im Kwon-Taek's recollection that when he first read the story he knew it would be perfect for a movie. The *"Sopyonje" Movie Book,* based on journals kept by the production crew as well as individuals' reminiscences, records enough details about locations, conversations among the cast and crew, and other insider goings-on to satisfy even the most ardent fan. It also includes the full screenplay, interviews with members of the cast and crew, a guide to the locations where the film was shot, and reprints of editorials, columns, reviews, and articles. Moreover, it features blurbs from 100 fans about what *Sopyonje* meant to them, excerpts from college newspapers and Internet chat groups, and a detailed chronology of the director's life and career, including pictures of his family.

Edited by the director himself, the book is unique in South Korean publishing history: the first to focus so lovingly and in such detail on a single movie. (Books containing the scripts of fabulously popular television dramas, as well as some behind-the-scenes details, have also been published, however.) The range of references gathered in the *"Sopyonje" Movie Book* reflects the extensive public reaction to the film. On college campuses, for example, it provoked much discussion about South Korean culture and identity—one reason why a full section of the book is devoted to the reactions of the younger generation. It was seen as a positive sign that college students were so moved by the depiction of traditional South Korean culture. The female lead, O Chŏng-hae—an accomplished *p'ansori* singer making her acting debut—toured college campuses and sang the traditional South Korean lyrics while dressed either in blue jeans or a miniskirt. The idea, she often said, was to show young people that tradition need not be stuffy and boring. But what is the significance of this immensely popular movie? How should we interpret the remarkable reaction to it?

Most writers on the subject regard the movie and the ensuing public response as a trumpet call heralding the revival of South Korean culture. In articles such as *"Sopyonje* Is Ruining Korean Movies,"[3] they argued that the film's success in exploiting traditional culture gave the illusion that the South Korean movie industry was in revival, when in fact overall it was drawing its last breath in the midst of modern history's "cultural globalization," one with all the markings of a primarily Western-based culture. Thus the sensation raised by *Sopyonje* at this point in time is a deeply significant event in South Korea's cultural history. What does the emergence of such a movie in a society with little cultural capital signify? What meaning can be extracted from it? Does it contain the possibility of moving beyond cultural colonialism?

By focusing on the popularity of this domestic movie, I'd like to discuss postcolonialism in South Korean society generally, or, to put it differently, the self-generative potentiality of South Korean culture. Whether South Koreans are ready to throw off the colonialist mentality or *sadaejui*[4] and how such endeavors can be carried out are the issues I seek to explore here.

## Historical Background

The popularity of *Sopyonje* must be understood within the context of the decline of the South Korean movie industry in the 1970s and '80s. It appeared at a time when many South Koreans, young people in particular, had become thoroughly disappointed with domestic films. South Korean movies were regarded as boring, poorly made, and melodramatic to the point of becoming maudlin. Foreign films dominated the market.

South Korean movies have not always been out of favor with their home-grown audiences. During the 1960s, when directors such as Shin Sang-ok were active, viewers flocked to see domestic films. Throughout the 1960s, South Korean movies achieved great popularity by expressing the trials and tribulations of living life in the midst of rapid social change. But as television began to establish itself as a powerful amusement medium, South Korean movies started to decline. Television dramas reflecting South Korean society came straight into people's living rooms. So did comedies, sports, and other entertainment programs. In addition, many who had once produced movies moved over to television. The South Korean movie industry continued to atrophy even in the climate of rapid economic growth, and most moviegoers began to prefer foreign movies, even as they watched South Korean television dramas at home. (Actually, South Korean audiences are disappointed by more than just the domestic movie industry. Whether attending a play, a concert, or a dance performance, one frequently feels that one has somehow been mocked. South Koreans have been starved for too long of quality cultural works of their own, and many are now close to giving up.)

*Sopyonje* has great meaning precisely because it emerged in the midst of this culturally barren landscape. Made with tenacious craftsmanship and skill acquired over many years, this movie successfully bridges the gap the movie industry had created between itself and viewers. It shows us the possibility of the rebirth of the movie medium. *Sopyonje* may be the beginning of a revival of the culture industry. On the other hand, as it spurs emotional nationalism, it may simply be a reflection of an era that accelerates colonialist modernization. Final assessments of *Sopyonje* will not be determined by its producers but by audiences, movie reviewers, and cultural critics.

## "Searching For Our Culture"

It is widely accepted that *Sopyonje* became a hit because its principal theme is "searching for our culture."[5] Once an industrialized economy has advanced to a certain level, people begin to think about the "self" that they have lived without. This movie was released at precisely such a point in South Korea's history. From the exclamation that "Ah, our culture is good indeed!"[6] to the theoretical statement that "*Sopyonje* was woven by a self-inquiring consciousness that has begun gradually to surge forth,"[7] gratitude was fervently expressed that a "*minjok* movie"— one that "washes away our sweet sorrows with images filled with *toen-jang*-scented ocher earth"[8]—had been made.

Such comments reveal that "searching for our culture" is a great national desire. One passage in particular from the movie resonated in the hearts of many people: "Instead of being buried in the *han* clenched inside you, from now on sing the *sori* that transcends *han*." In these lines can be read the desire to find tradition and, within changed circumstances, revive it. In an attempt to examine further the discourse on collective sentiments, I asked college students who were enrolled in my course on cultural theory to write short essays on the film *Sopyonje* and the attendant phenomenon. The words of these students well illustrate the desire to "reinvent" tradition. They also provide other interesting viewpoints:

1) First, *Sopyonje* presented a fresh view of *p'ansori*, which was strange and unfamiliar to us even though it is part of our culture. I had

no idea that *p'ansori* was so emotional. If what we need to reestablish ourselves within the unilateral importation of Western culture and fashion is to make a new culture with tradition as its foundation, then this movie shows us the tradition that we need to find.

Another important point is that this movie transcended generations and touched everyone. Seeing middle-aged adults in their forties and fifties standing in line at theaters to watch this movie, one realizes that good movies are not the exclusive property of youth. That the movie transcended generations and touched everyone shows that *p'ansori* is the root that has been handed down through our everyday lives. Only through this movie did I realize this truth, and now the work of finding and revealing our roots in more areas must be started. (Class of 1988,[9] Kun-sik)

2) It was the first South Korean movie I had seen in quite a long time, and an excitement that I had not felt in quite a long time. During the singing scenes, I could sense my shoulders suddenly beginning to dance up and down. It felt like my body was being carried away on the rhythms of "*sori.*"

The extremely simple story line, the succession of plain scenes with no plot twists, the immature acting of new faces with no name value, what is it about the movie that despite all this gave me such excitement?

First, above all else, it was *sori. Sori* is not simply traditional South Korean music. There is definitely more to it than music. Our sensibility, the flow of emotions that linger in our collective heart, this dwells inside *sori.* It wasn't simply due to excitement that my shoulders danced as if of their own volition. It was because I felt that my mind was one with that of the characters on the screen, because the rhythms were the flow of my own mind, that it was possible. Of course there is a bit here of the "All of our culture is beautiful!" ideology as expressed by Yu-bong (the father character). The important thing is that the sentiment within *sori* is fully communicated to the audience and we can look at the self that we have lost.

Second, the background of the movie is another attraction. The shots in this movie are thoroughly Korean. They contain forms with simple, classic, and gentle lines. The rural landscape through which the *sori* family passes in its travels is the site of our lost lives and reveals the gentle emotions carried within that environment. When I see these scenes I feel great tranquility and ease. I feel the comfort of a baby who is finally resting on a bed after laboriously taking some faltering steps.

Ultimately this movie's excitement comes from its Koreanness. Its greatest attraction is that it calls up a nostalgia for "our culture" which cannot be found in a contemporary hectic lifestyle, a dull mass culture, or in a present thick with the marks of nation-less culture. If a new awareness of traditional culture and its successive revival is a repercussion of this movie, nothing could be more fortunate. But the more important thing is gaining the self-confidence to find the traces of my historical self right here where I stand. *Sopyonje* made me realize how greatly excited I could be by our own culture, and deeply impressed upon me that I cannot be anything other than a "Korean," and that the culture we must develop from now on cannot be cut off from tradition. (Class of 1990, Il-kwŏn.)

The meaning of "searching for our culture" is well expressed in these two essays. In a word, this is similar to a feeling of relief. First, the relief that comes from confirming that despite the invasion of foreign culture, one's own culture continues on; second, the relief that something ("Koreanness") can unite everyone across the chasms of generation, class, and other divisive factors. This seems connected to the relief that "we as an entity continue to exist." Put differently, "we exist" is a confirmation of self. There is great comfort in knowing that "roots" and a "we" that together can feel the same emotions still exist.

But this discovery of tradition centered on *Sopyonje*. Where is the commentary surrounding the "search for the self" headed now? There is, of course, the positive aspect of overcoming self-denigration. But where are South Koreans trying to go? An ethnocentric, sentimental nationalism that emphasizes a return to tradition can be dangerous. Essentialist traditionalism can easily veer off into fascism. For some responses to the questions raised here, let's turn to an essay by cultural critic Yi Se-ryong, titled "The Humanist Director Im Kwon-Taek, Who Found South Korean Identity in *Sopyonje*":

Im says that the much-discussed screening at the Cannes International Film Festival and the prize are secondary matters. Of first importance is that our South Korean audience feels the taste and style of *p'ansori*. Im describes this as his ambition, but he didn't have this ambition when he was making *Sopyonje*. "When I started I had the small ambition that it would be nice if a few people could be awakened to our culture. But when I finished, the reaction of the audience was so good that I developed this large ambition," said Im in his famously awkward speech. On the day of *Sopyonje*'s preview screening, the reaction of the audience was stunning. Reviewers famous for being stingy with their praise, reporters known for their pickiness, reticent junior directors, as one they were wiping away tears or their eyes were reddening in a rare spectacle. . . .

Just what is the "*sori*" that to the end wasn't lost throughout the wanderings of the *sori* family—Yu-bong, his adopted daughter Song-hwa, and his stepson Tong-ho—who made a living selling their musical talents? As Im explains it, *p'ansori* is the "rapturous sound that expresses our suffering and helps us to endure." So he focused *Sopyonje* on "how the *han* of those who wander in the midst of the beautiful landscape of southwestern South Korea seeps into *p'ansori* and is transformed into salvation and release." Even during liberation, when such songs as "Bessame Mucho" began to gain popularity and *sori* musicians barely eked out a living by playing in Western-style bands, the main character obstinately insists on *sori*. He clings to this *sori* that doesn't provide a living not only because it is our sound, but because when one sings good *sori* one forgets hunger, and isn't envious of riches and splendor. But time passes, and an old, weakened Yu-bong hopes that his daughter Song-hwa will reach the stage of "tǔgǔm."[10] The voice of Song-hwa, who is talented in *sori* and more than hardworking, is a fine voice but it doesn't meet Yu-bong's standard. Her *sori* isn't sufficient to make her a master singer. At the end of much consideration, Yu-bong blinds Song-hwa, planting *han* in his young daughter's heart. She finally obtains the *sori* voice her father could not achieve for her, but she wanders the country like a cloud in her sightless condition. There is another aspect worthy of attention in this movie that is regarded as a victory in aesthetics. This is the teacher/father's command to the daughter that "one must store up *han* and one must overcome *han*." This teaching is very important. This line represents Im's message that although *han* is a characteristic of our traditional culture, it must not be the ultimate goal of we who are living in the present. The reason is that *han*, arising from circumstances one cannot control, interferes with living like human beings. Therefore we must rate highly Im's borrowing of the movie character's mouth to say, "Instead of being buried in *han*, make *sori* that transcends *han*." That *Sopyonje* interprets the essence of *p'ansori*'s strength as the ability to burrow deep into *han* and then transcend it (into rapture) is masterful. To do this, Im expertly balances *han* and wit, giving us space to breathe. "The *sori* of *han*" provides sorrow and beauty, while wit provides laughter. Yes, it is precisely this *han* and this wit that are the special traits of South Korean culture and which stand as the two pillars that make this movie interesting and enjoyable.[11]

Yi Se-ryong regularly employs terms like "the breath of Koreanness," "the taste and style of *p'ansori*," "the harmony of rhythm and land," "the expression of our people's *han*," "salvation and release of *han*," "transcending *han* into rapture," and "the balance of *han* and wit" in this essay. His use of these terms is a sign he accepts "*han*" as the essence of Korean culture and develops his interpretation within that framework.

This kind of reading represents one of the most common perspectives in discussions about *Sopyonje*. The discourse in college circles about *han* and tradition that began in the early 1990s was broadened into public discourse by the screening of *Sopyonje*. It may well be that this movie played a big role in establishing "*han*" and "rapture" as uniquely "Korean." But this kind of definition is severely limiting. By restricting one's identity, one fails to see what one must really see. Those with strength do not restrictively define themselves. "The British," for example, may discuss in humor books how they are different from "the French," but they do not define their national personality in those terms alone.

The particular pitfall of this kind of awakening to nation in South Korea is that self-definition becomes that which the West does not have. Koreans have passed through several hundred years of modernization, and there is something terribly wrong in ignoring that historical accumulation and defining the self as what the West lacks. A self-definition that strips away the "First World" already dwelling within is most likely a self-deception and an illusion. Of course, the very fact that a group long subject to definition by others is now trying to define itself is an epochal event. That definition may quickly become yet another trap, however. Simplifying oneself to one word may provide a definite existence and identity, but finding security in setting up what is only an extremely small part of the self as the whole self—thus ceasing to inquire into the self—is very dangerous. At a time when self-inquiry should be more vigorous than at any other, nothing is as dangerous as such ready-made theories.

These theories surface in numerous places, as in the words of these students:

> 1) As the thought came to me that Westerners could not under-stand this movie, I felt pride. The shots were peaceful, there were no sex scenes, and the movie made me understand the preciousness of our culture. This is what a patriot is, I thought, a person who knows the worth of one's culture.
>
> 2) It was the first time I realized that South Korea had such beau-tiful music and such an emotion-laden landscape. I don't understand why South Koreans don't boast about such wonderful things. All this time we've had a treasure right in front of our eyes and haven't been able to see it.

These passages illustrate the typical thoughts of those who have fallen into self-denigration and are now trying to recover themselves. There is a relief that "our culture" exists, one which only "we" can understand, and yet the confirmation that "our culture" is good is made through Westerners. Nevertheless, the realization that "our culture" isn't too bad is a satisfactory first step, for essentialism can be used strategically in the process of overcoming self-denigration.

Fortunately, discussion about "searching for the self" continues. Some writers note that the quality and meaning of these emotions vary from one generation to another. For example, in "*Sopyonje,* Noise, and Kim So-wŏl,"[12] Yi Yŏng-mi points out that the movie is experienced in different ways by those in their fifties and sixties who directly underwent the degradation of poverty and colonialism, those in their thirties and forties who faced it only indirectly, and those in their teens and twenties who have no experience whatsoever with poverty or colonialism. For the older generation, Sopyonje evoked their forgotten past, but clouded in hazy nostalgia. To the middle generation, now of an age to understand their parents' suffering, it provided a sense of the continuity of life.

Moreover, Yi Yŏng-mi remarks that perspectives on tradition are also different from one generation to the next. She notes that the view that South Korean traditional cultural arts are no longer "the shameful and squalid smell of kimch'i[13] that must be discarded" but one of the "arts" that can rightfully be displayed anywhere in the world is beginning to take root among those who are under forty. She connects this to the traditional arts revival movement of the 1970s, the decade in which this age group began to enter college. As she points out, South Koreans are trying to free themselves from the colonial era in which all that was "ours" was seen to be "squalid." The voice of a generation trying to restore pride in "ours" is becoming louder.

But is the younger generation's image of "our culture" connected to han? This is not likely. Moreover, there are more than a few people within the younger generation who either have no image of "our culture" or who are trying not to have any image of "our culture" at all. As Yi Yŏng-mi notes, many in their teens and twenties buy the Sopyonje soundtrack after being impressed by the music in the movie—much as they come to appreciate Mozart after seeing Amadeus or opera after seeing Phantom of the Opera. To them, "our tradition" is simply another available artistic product, not something to hold more dear because it is "ours." Because aspects of the "feudal," the "modern," and the "postmodern"—usually conceptualized as being non-simultaneous—co-exist in South Korean society today, notions of "ours" and "nation" take on very different casts depending on the viewer. Reading a present in which the non-simultaneous simultaneously exist is the shortcut to finding the self. Revealing through difference—not erasing difference—is what's important. The alternative is to fall into yet another tyranny of conformity.

Much of the commotion surrounding *Sopyonje* was caused by generational difference. The father's generation may have finally realized that the West is not an adequate cultural goal, but many of the younger generation harbor great doubts about any return to the culture of their fathers. One student (Class of 1991, Yong-sŏk) goes further and asks whether we really have pride in our culture. For this student, the cry "No matter what kind of ruckus Japanese songs and Western songs raise, there will come a day when *p'ansori* reigns supreme"[14] reverberates with self-loathing.

In fact, *Sopyonje* does not really speak with a uniform voice. If one looks carefully at the characters depicted in this movie, it becomes clear that they are, in a way, very unfamiliar to us. Several students stated that even to their Korean selves, the movie's characters came across as strange and mysterious. The father character is bursting with pride in *p'ansori* for no apparent reason, steadfastly clinging to the conviction that "a time will come when *p'ansori* reigns supreme"—even though at that time it was a lowbrow art form that brought little more than scorn and a few pennies to its practitioners. *Han* is bequeathed to his daughter as if it were his dying wish. Whether or not that daughter understood him cannot be fathomed, and the final scene in which she sings *sori* with her younger brother all night long merely makes it more ambiguous. The daughter is depicted as if she were born only for *p'ansori,* never feeling hunger nor, despite her youth, sexual or romantic urges. The only understandable character in the movie is the younger brother, who runs away from home, complaining that *p'ansori* doesn't provide a decent living. Here is one student's reaction to this:

> When watching *Sopyonje* I felt hurt and sorrow and rather complicated emotions. It wasn't just because of the characters' struggle to maintain *p'ansori,* this piece of our past, or that the female character became blind, or that the circumstances of that time period were bad. Anyway, I can't reveal any more than that it hurt. Although if I've had this much education, I should be able to supply something for discussion, a mute person is just as comfortable as a blind person. (Class of 1989, Sŏng-gyu)

Probably not everyone who saw it was as touched by the film. One overseas Korean who had been away from the country for a long time said that watching this movie was like watching a "French" movie, and he asked, "When did Korea become so French?" What is the meaning of this question?

There are elements in *Sopyonje* that go against what is commonly considered to be the "national sentiment." One is the scene where the father blinds his daughter; this made many viewers uncomfortable. One student in my class, trying earnestly to understand, went so far as to say that the father could commit such an act because the woman was not his biological daughter. More than a few students saw it as a human rights issue. In a society that says "one's body is received from one's parents,"[15] one should be increasingly uncomfortable with this act the more one talks about "tradition." No matter that the prototype of Simch'ong[16] exists, artistic frenzy that can lead a person to blind a daughter is reminiscent not of something Korean but rather of a Van Gogh who cuts off his own ear. Despite their unease, however, few people complained about this scene. Does this mean that South Koreans are beginning to view Van Gogh-like artists, "modern" people with artistic temperaments, as acceptable and attractive?

Another scene that is difficult to comprehend from the perspective of the commonly understood "Korean sentiment" is the brother-sister reunion: after a night of singing *sori* together, they part without acknowledging their identities. However, viewers seem to have easily accepted this scene. Describing it as a refreshing betrayal, renowned novelist Pak Wan-sŏ offers unstinting praise. She writes that during the final scene, "I wanted to leave as I became edgy." She didn't want the emotions built up during the movie to be suddenly lost by an ending in which the characters hugged, cried, and recited lines such as "Sister! It's Tong-ho." The brother and sister's "meeting through music, hugging each other in their minds only, and stoutheartedly parting" is an "advance" and a "transcendence" that is superior to an "immature" meeting, she writes.[17]

Here is the convergence of Im's "humanism"—a very modern product—and viewers' fervent desire to throw off a feudal and/or refugee sensibility. Regarding the hints of an incestuous relationship between father and daughter, Im says, "It's not too important whether or not there was an incestuous relationship between Yu-bong and Song-hwa. After all, they are both people."[18] This is a "modern" view of humanity that departs from the feudal norm and sees people first and foremost as people. Regarding the brother-sister reunion, he says, "The reason that they meet but can't bring themselves to reveal their identities is that they know all too well that neither can be of any help to the other in the future."[19] This is definitely a view of humanity that is far from the "Korean" way of thinking. This "wordless parting" scene is an astonishingly new feature of South Korean movies, although it is found quite frequently in Italian and French art films. Considering that not too long ago South Koreans wept copiously while watching the televised reunions of families separated during the Korean War, this final scene is not "Korean" at all.

*[handwritten margin note: open-ended / new. / typical of / European / New-Wave / cinema]*

In reply to a student who, during an invited lecture at Yonsei University in fall 1993, asked Im why he didn't allow the brother and sister to unburden their hearts in reunion, he said that his personal familiarity with the drifter's life had taught him that there were times when it was better for separated relatives not to meet. The perspective on life he revealed here is connected to an Asian sense of human ties— that is, not to a Confucian ethic but to a Buddhist salvation that comes from renouncing this world and accepting fate. This is what Im has come to understand while living his life. And he shows that he clearly considers it to be the condition of all human beings, not the particular "something of Korean people who have been oppressed." His handling of the brother-sister reunion comes out of his modern and Buddhist perspective on life. Today's moviegoers, both young and old, prefer that kind of parting. Im told his own story honestly, and that it made a positive impression on viewers should not be overlooked.

The movie itself cannot really be said to display thorough mastery of cinematic language, however. First of all, it has an overabundance of sermonizing and discursive explanations. For example, consider lines such as "Don't stay in your *han*, but overcome it" and "There is the eastern style and the western style, but when you get to a certain level, the difference between them disappears."[20] Long passages contain such expressions as "I made your eyes go blind. Have you forgiven me?"

This kind of speech is onerous to modern viewers, who enjoy the subtle taste of ellipses. But apparently audiences still enjoy such sermons: I believe more viewers were drawn to the film because of them than were repulsed by them. In a sense, daring to preach sermons increased the movie's mass popularity. Where did Im find the confidence to do this? That kind of confidence is possible when one is faithful to one's own life.

In an article describing his travels with the production crew, Yi Ch'ŏng-jun (the author of the story on which the movie is based) describes the thoroughness of Im, who continued to interrogate the author even after he had come up with an answer or a solution. Not only the director but the entire film crew labored on the movie with complete craftsmanship.[21] The essayist Yi Yŏng-mi points to "professionalism" as precisely the quality that made the film attractive to youth. The artistry of the father character and the "skill" of the movie's production team—which possessed a level of craftsmanship not usually nurtured in South Korean society—played important roles in the movie's popularity.

Then doesn't *Sopyonje* reflect changed values and aesthetics even though it seems to mirror traditional values and aesthetics? And aren't those values and aesthetics, rather than being "characteristically Korean," actually closer to the scripts of the Western movies South Koreans have watched so often? Doesn't the line "When you reach the stage of *tŭgŭm,* you forget hunger and are not envious of riches and splendor" express the desire of a modern person who has come to demand more than material goods? By focusing on aesthetic obsession and the drifter lifestyle, doesn't the movie actually touch the sensibilities of modern urbanites who feel that "life is ultimately a sojourner's road and a lonesome journey"—especially those urbanites who are all the more lonely and fragmented due to a Third World development process yet still want to cling to their last remaining dreams? In this regard, aren't *p'ansori* and Korea's rural scenery the props that put "Korean" clothes on modern subjects? This movie's excellence lies in taking a very modern subject—"asking new questions about one's identity"—and developing it in a very modern way. Like Akira Kurosawa in *The Seven Samurai* and *Rashomon,* Im borrows a "traditional" setting but succeeds in making a modern movie with a modern subject. It may be that only now are South Koreans really entering the modern age.

Let's return now to our first questions: What is "tradition" and what is "Koreanness"? Was it to find "something Korean" that the pop group Sŏ T'ae-ji and Boys used the traditional Korean wind instrument, the *t'aep'yŏngso,* in the song "Hayŏga"? Is it an important attempt to find "ourselves" if South Korean children, stimulated by Sŏ T'ae-ji and Boys, develop an interest in playing the *t'aep'yŏngso*? Is the music of Kim Yŏng-dong "traditional Korean music" or "new traditional Korean music"? Is "new traditional Korean music" experimental music that is a form of the meditation music popular worldwide or is it experimental Korean music?[22] Are the "modern" and the "traditional" mutually exclusive or do they go together? It is said that "a succession of various experiments has brought a new feel and form to traditional Korean music—stereotyped as difficult and stiff and thus unpopular—and boldly put it in sync with today's modern public."[23] What kind of harmony is the harmony that *Sopyonje* has achieved between the "modern" and the "traditional"? What is the tradition that is on the verge of being remade through *Sopyonje*?

## Reading Movies in the Midst of Discourse Formation

*Sopyonje* does not provide final answers to these questions. However, it greatly touched the emotions of those South Koreans who are either feverishly looking for something or who have simply given up and fallen into slumber. That which has been hidden behind the rush of economic growth, that which has been rigidly suppressed by a generation struggling to survive or perhaps to fulfill ambitions, that something is beginning to wriggle. The movie has also jogged the self-consciousness of a younger generation that had resigned itself to wandering in an endless sea of floating "signs" unattached to either nation or community.

The movement to revive traditional culture is really an indication of modernity and an effort to rescue oneself. It's both an ideological ritual intended to help reclaim the lost past and an uprising against a materialist culture that turns humans into instruments. It's also a deliberate effort to differentiate oneself within a global homogenization. In other words, in the midst of profound restructuring of both the

national and world orders, it is the clear expression of a will to create
one's identity anew in a manner that better fits the times. "*Han*" and
"rapture" surface in the midst of such turmoil as if they were the
everlasting essence of ourselves. Some people become more enthusiastic
about efforts to essentialize tradition, while others begin to realize that
such essentializing is dangerous.

While the nascent movement to find oneself can be described as
"nationalism," it is a nationalism different from the "oppositional nationalism" in resistance to colossal foreign power that Koreans have
known in the past. As mentioned earlier, it is dangerous to force an identity to fit into something partial because the result may be even greater
isolation and alienation. The nationalism that remakes Koreans must
emphasize revitalization, cultural self-generation, and productivity. The
realization that "our culture is precious" must not be equated with the
struggles of a neocolonialist era in which the victim mentality becomes
the driving force; rather it must involve a postcolonial self-awakening
that tries to shed that mentality. As Im himself has remarked, had this
movie been released in the 1980s it would probably not have become
a popular success. South Korea's present situation demands a new leap
forward, and *Sopyonje* is culturally and historically important because it
provides the means to begin a serious discussion about the nature and
direction of this leap.

Witnessing the *Sopyonje* phenomenon, I became aware that many
people are ardently waiting for a storyteller who can tell "one's own
story." Whether they are tired of philosophical gags and fables or of
old-fashioned family tragedies, or whether they are fed up with rampant
materialism, many people are longing for something that comes out of
their own selves. Just as foreign plays in translation no longer attract
viewers, people want to hear words that speak to their own hearts. They
want to hear not translated speech but words that resonate deep within
their own lives. A movie without one's own voice chases away any and
all viewers.

Under current circumstances, when a South Korean movie wins
a prize in a Western film festival, this attests either to the country's
expanding national strength or to the enduring strength of orientalism.
South Koreans have lived for too long under the domination of Western

*Films marketed to foreign film critique, new westernized orientalism*

culture, and they have largely internalized the Western perspective on Asia known as orientalism. This perspective is now being imported to Asia itself, and it has become the lens through which Asians see themselves. The movies that have been made with the intent of winning prizes at Western film festivals have generally adopted an orientalist point of view. These movies emphasize things that fit Western tastes and exoticize Asian civilizations. Im Kwon-Taek's *Surrogate Mother* (*Ssibaji*, 1986) is one example. Pae Yong-Kyun's *Why Has Bodhidharma Left for the East* (*Dalmaga tongtchok kŭro kan kkadakŭn*, 1989) is another. But were there Koreans within those movies? The words that Koreans are so earnestly trying to say and hear cannot be found there.

Some commentators on *Sopyonje*'s success have seen it in terms of a kind of globalization slogan: "Finally something Korean has become universal." When modernization is a single route leading to a single peak, the slogan "What is the most Korean is the most universal"[24] may make some sense. But when people believe there is only one kind of modernization, there is also only one "subject" in the humanism that has been pursued. All humans on this earth struggle to be that "subject." Logically, just as what was "the most British" became "the most universal," what is "the most Korean" can also be "the most universal." But in reality, those in the margins always fall short of becoming that kind of subject. Competition with a "center" possessed of accumulated capabilities and overpowering capital can never be a fair game. No matter how South Koreans strive, it is still difficult within this global structure for them to produce work that is of the highest quality according to "universal" (Western) standards. And, upon reflection, there is no reason South Koreans should want to produce such a work. Would a South Korean movie attract a million viewers somewhere other than South Korea? An excellent movie emerges when its creator has an honest conversation with one viewer. Then the audience is not the anonymous masses or the "universal human" spread across the world but a group of individuals who share concrete historicity. In this sense, *Sopyonje* symbolizes the triumph of a local movie within a locality.

A turn toward postcolonialization is possible when one asks whether there is only one path toward modernization. Serious reflection regarding Western-oriented "development" had already begun even before the

First World War. The postindustrial West is now reflecting on a modernization that overemphasized one aspect of the "capitalist spirit"—i.e.,
"instrumentalist rationality"—and is trying to recover from the severely
colonized zeitgeist it constructed.[25] What is necessary now for South
Koreans, who have never created either a "capitalist spirit" or a "rationalism" but instead have been obsessed with instrumentalizing people in
order to increase productivity? There is an enormous difference between
a society where industrialization is indigenously driven and one where
industrialization has been forcibly transplanted. Doesn't that difference
become evident when the West begins a self-inquiry into its expansive
"modernity" while South Koreans cling to partial and abstract words like
"*han*" and "rapture"? They must think deeply about the impact of this
difference on the process of healing oneself. South Koreans must take a
good look at themselves and consider the possibility that they are simply
consoling themselves with idle talk. Instead of returning to "things Korean," they should now pursue, in a rapidly changing global structure,
an alternative modernity based on a new subjectivity. This is especially
important in an age where homogenization and heterogenization are
simultaneously happening at both local and global levels.

　　Although *Sopyonje* and Sŏ T'ae-ji and Boys are generally considered
to be diverse phenomena, I read in them identical meanings reflective
of the current era. I see Bob Dylan in Kim Min-gi's music, the Beatles'
harmonization in the songs of Tŭlgukhwa, Elton John's piano in the
instrumentals of Tongmulwon, and Deep Purple in the performance
of Shin Hae-ch'ŏl.[26] Of course my judgment may not be shared by
others. It is possible that Shin Hae-ch'ŏl hates Deep Purple—or has
never even heard of the band. But at the very least I hear a similarity
in their music; indeed, I think the world is becoming one in the sense
that the music of, say, Sŏ T'ae-ji and Boys is reminiscent of so many
different performers that it becomes impossible to identify any original
sources. To the point that debate over mimicry is now moot, South
Koreans have internalized things of the "First World" whether they like
it or not, and they live within those conditions. But South Koreans are
not yet Westerners, and Westerners are not Koreans. That distinction is
not easy to fathom, and neither is it an essentialist one. South Koreans
are being made different by outside forces, but they also are making

themselves different. If up to now a Western-oriented modernization has homogenized them, blurring the differences, then South Koreans must discard this full-blown "colonialist modernity" and search for the path toward an "alternative modernity," recognizing differences within and without.

The ultimate reason for writing this essay is because I want to see good movies of our own. I too want to have many Korean directors whom I love. South Koreans' collective misfortune has been to suffer the rapid pace of compressed development, leaving no time for self-reflection. In truth, South Koreans have lived bleakly for too long. Unable to endure such bleakness any longer, they then lived under a delusion: as if other people's culture were their own, as if others' dreams were their dreams, as if the events that occurred in other people's lands had also occurred in their own.

Both a new pair of spectacles through which South Koreans can see themselves and the "process" of creating new viewers with those glasses are needed now. It is the responsibility of filmmakers to make good movies, and it is the responsibility of moviegoers to attend good movies. The responsibility of a cultural critic is not to tell audiences how to view social phenomena, but to help people, standing within their own lives, to imagine freely.

# Notes

1. *P'ansori* is a traditional South Korean cultural form that can be compared to opera. Each opera consists of a lengthy series of songs that together tell a story. Unlike Western and Chinese operas, the story is usually told by one singer, who is accompanied by a drummer. There is no elaborate set, only the singer, who stands, and the drummer, who sits. Usually the only prop is a handheld, folding fan, which the singer uses for emphasis and drama. As the vocalist sings, he or she takes on the role of each character in turn. There are five extant operas, all of them based on famous Korean folktales. The best known (and the ones showcased in the movie) are the *Tale of Ch'unhyang* and the *Tale of Simch'ŏng. P'ansori* was a cultural form traditionally practiced by the lower classes; it was considered such "lowbrow" culture that no aristocrat would ever deign to learn it. Many practitioners of *p'ansori* are said to have been traveling performers who wandered from town to town. Although the

singers were scorned as inferior by the upper classes, they were often called to perform their art at parties and other aristocratic festivities. Today, *p'ansori* is recognized as a national cultural treasure, and several master *p'ansori* singers have been designated by the South Korean government as living human cultural treasures—a designation that brings some measure of public recognition and a nominal stipend. *Trans.*

2. *"Sopyonje" Movie Book,* ed. Im Kwon-Taek (Seoul: Hanul, 1993), referred to hereafter as the *Sopyonje* book. *Trans.*

3. Kang Chun-man, *"Sopyonje* Is Ruining Korean Movies," *Mal,* October 1993, 226. [This article was published too late to be included in the *Soponje* book. *Trans.*]

4. The term *sadaejuŭi* has historically been used to characterize the Chosŏn dynasty's relationship and attitude toward China, a relationship often likened to that between a little brother and his big brother. Today the term is commonly used to mean an overweening deference to and imitation of dominant nations, particularly the United States, that is comparable to a colonial mentality. *Trans.*

5. *Uri munhwa ch'atki* or "Searching for our culture" was a movement that arose in the 1970s on college campuses as students began to reconstruct and reinterpret traditional Korean cultural forms. The movement was a response to cultural colonialism and an effort to strengthen Korean identity. It focused not on the "highbrow" culture of court music and dance but on the "lowbrow" culture of agricultural peasants. Thus the cultural forms most widely taught were *t'alch'um* or mask dance—dramas with masked characters who often lampooned upper-class Korean society—and *p'ungmul*—a mix of drumming and dancing later popularized in modernized form by Kim Tŏk-su's *Samulnori,* a musical performance played with four traditional Korean percussion instruments. In recent years, the theme of "searching for our culture" has been widely popularized, as is evident in the enthusiastic public reception of Samulnori and other forms of Korean cultural expression as well as in numerous books that deal with various aspects of traditional cultural forms. *Trans.*

6. Kim Yu-jin, *Dongdae Sinmun,* May 5, 1993, qtd. in the *Sopyonje* book, 224.

7. Han Myŏng-hi, *Korea Daily,* July 25, 1993, "The Moon Waxes And Wanes, Wanes And Waxes," qtd. in the *Sopyonje* book, 161.

8. *Minjok* can be loosely translated as "nation" or "people" in the sense of a distinct group. It is often used by Koreans to refer to themselves as a people distinct from others. Toenjang is a fermented soy bean paste that is a staple condiment and seasoning in Korean cooking. It is also used figuratively, as in this passage, to evoke a rustic, traditional folk atmosphere and also to imply authenticity of Korean identity. The reference to ocher earth is used both literally and figuratively to evoke a traditional rural world seen as "home." *Trans.*

9. In South Korea, the class year denotes the year of entry into college, and it is a common identifier among students and alumni. *Trans.*

10. *Tǔgǔm,* literally "acquisition of sound," refers to acquiring the singing voice of a true *sori* artist, i.e., a sublime voice that represents the heart and soul of *p'ansori. Trans.*

11. Yi Se-ryong, "The Humanist Director Im Kwon-Taek, Who Found Korean Identity in *Sopyonje," Master Life,* April 1993, 32–37.

12. Yi Yǒng-mi, "*Sopyonje,* Noise and Kim So-wǒl," *Munhwa kwahak,* no. 4, 233–36.

13. *Kimch'i* is a staple dish in Korean cuisine and consists of vegetables—usually either cabbage or radishes—steeped in a hot, garlicky, red pepper sauce. The dish has a strong smell that many Koreans believe is offensive to Westerners. The admonition not to eat *kimch'i* or other garlicky foods before an appointment with foreigners remains a common one, and many Koreans still worry that foreigners, particularly Westerners, will find Korean food—and, by extension, the Korean people and all other things Korean—smelly and offensive. *Trans.*

14. This is a famous line uttered by the father in the movie; it was used widely in posters advertising the film. *Trans.*

15. This saying was often used to emphasize that one should take care of one's body out of respect for one's parents. *Trans.*

16. Simch'ǒng, a character in a traditional folktale, sacrifices her life so that her blind and widowed father may see. *Trans.*

17. Pak Wan-sǒ, *Kyung Hyang Sinmun,* May 29, 1993, qtd. in the *Sopyonje* book, 155.

18. *Sopyonje* book, 202.

19. Ibid., 204.

20. Eastern style (tongp'yǒnje) and western style (sǒp'yǒnje) are two styles of *p'ansori* developed in Chǒlla Province in southwestern Korea. *Sǒp'yǒnje,* whence comes the movie's title, is prevalent in the flat, agricultural, western region of the province. It has a style characterized as feminine, with many musical flourishes and ornamentation, whereas *tongp'yǒnje,* developed in the mountainous eastern region, has a simpler, more straightforward style characterized as masculine. *Trans.*

21. Yi Ch'ǒng-jun has said, "The short story was my responsibility, but the movie is theirs." See the *Sopyonje* book, 150–53.

22. Sǒ T'ae-ji is the leader of South Korea's first rap group. When the group debuted in the early 1990s, it provoked another round of discussion on whether Koreans were developing their own style of modern music or simply mimicking Westerners. The *t'aep'yǒngso* is a traditional Korean wind instrument with a wooden, flute-like body and a metal end that flares out like a trumpet. Kim Yǒng-dong composes music that mixes traditional Korean forms with modern forms.

His albums are generally classified as meditation music. The general public seems to view his music as "modernized traditional Korean music," as evidenced by the customary location of his albums in the traditional Korean music section at large bookstores and music stores. The background music for *Sopyonje* can also be labeled as such. *Trans.*

23. *Chosun Ilbo,* July 15, 1993.

24. This is a well-known saying associated with the push for "globalization," an effort spearheaded by the Kim Young Sam government. *Trans.*

25. See, for example, Michel Foucault, *Power/Knowledge: Selected Interviews and Other Writings, 1972–77,* ed. C. Gordon (New York: Pantheon, 1980), and Jürgen Habermas, *The Theory of Communicative Action I: Reason and the Rationalization of Society,* trans. T. McCarthy (London: Heinemann, 1984).

26. Kim Min-gi is a popular singer whose songs, especially "Morning Dew" (Ach'im isŭl), are associated with student movements and are known for poetic lyrics. Tŭlgukhwa is a group known for their harmonies and ballads, and Shin Hae-chŏl is a well-known rock singer. *Trans.*

*Julian Stringer*

CHAPTER 6

# *Sopyonje* and the Inner Domain
# of National Culture

Korean critics and foreign enthusiasts alike have been obliged to recognize that the international success many had predicted for the 1990s South Korean cinema did not materialize. While a number of individual titles were acclaimed at major film festivals, few were then picked up for wider distribution. Chris Berry, one of the most authoritative Western critics of Asian cinema, has suggested two reasons why the Korean film industry failed to achieve a breakthrough at this time.[1] On the one hand, he contends, an increased concentration of ownership in the U.S. and European art-house sectors resulted in a general unwillingness to take risks with internationally "unknown" product, meaning that Korean filmmakers met with unexpectedly severe resistance when negotiating overseas exhibition rights for their work. On the other hand, Korea had a hard time establishing a "new" identity for itself within highly competitive image markets because of its inability to differentiate its films from those produced by other East Asian countries.

Berry further suggests that the positive reception given at several recent film festivals to the stylistically excessive films of Kim Ki-young

(Kim Ki-yŏng)—such as *The Insect Woman* (*Ch'ungnyŏ,* 1972) and *Killer Butterfly* (*Sarin nabi rŭl tchotnŭn yŏja,* 1978)—signals a reversal of this situation. Kim's movies have been greeted enthusiastically on the globalized art-house cinema circuit, whereas works by other Korean directors have been denied similar exposure. Consider the case of Im Kwon-Taek's *Sopyonje* (*Sŏp'yŏnje,* 1993). A historic movie by any standards, this representative text of the New Korean Cinema, habitually proposed by critics as "the next big thing" in world cinema history, was a great box-office hit domestically. It was also the recipient of a number of international film festival prizes and the first Korean film ever to be included in the permanent collection of the Museum of Modern Art in New York. Subsequently, though, it failed to make the rounds of the European and U.S. art theaters.

In Berry's judgment, *Sopyonje* stalled on the cusp of international greatness because it was perceived as being too much of a known quantity for foreign audiences. While Kim's flashy, highly individualistic works beckoned and winked from the global stage, Im's utilization of a more familiar realist aesthetic (however beautiful) was not "new" enough to suit the culinary tastes of the international marketplace. According to Berry, *Sopyonje* suffered from the fact that its use of cinematography was too reminiscent of the "ethnographic" strain of contemporary Chinese cinema—that branch of mainland filmmaking epitomized most spectacularly by Zhang Yimou's *Red Sorghum* (*Hong gaoliang,* 1987), *Ju Dou* (1989), and *Raise the Red Lantern* (*Da hong denglong gaogao gua,* 1991), and by Chen Kaige's *Yellow Earth* (*Huang tudi,* 1984). This is a cinema of what Berry variously terms "ethnic," "exotic," and "orientalist" attractions. Offering "primitive" representations of the national past (ancient rituals, feudal customs, peasant lifestyles), titles like these might easily be mistaken as providing models for *Sopyonje*'s narrative and pictorial strategies. According to this logic, Im's film did not secure the requisite breakthrough for Korean cinema because it looked too much like other Asian movies.

While not necessarily disagreeing fundamentally with Berry's assessment of the recent fate of Korean cinema abroad, I suspect he has slightly overstated his case. Even if *Sopyonje*—or more recent examples of what has come to be known as the New Korean Cinema such as

Park Kwang-su's *To the Starry Island* (*Kŭ sŏm e gago sipta*, 1993), Hong Sang-su's *The Day a Pig Fell Into the Well* (*Twaeji ga umul e ppajin nal*, 1996), or Yi Ch'ang-dong's *Green Fish* (*Ch'orok mulgogi*, 1997)—has not quite achieved all that was expected of it, the film can still enhance Western interest in the Korean national cinema. As I want to argue, *Sopyonje* has something to tell us about the dynamics of cross-cultural looking relations, so it should not be written off too quickly, left to rot in festival limbo, or banished to the margins of film historiography. When considering the reception of Asian cinema today it is important to keep in mind alternatives to the official story, to "remember" paths not taken or opportunities regrettably lost. If we do not, then Western understanding of Korean cinema becomes a parroted discourse, a form of knowledge determined primarily by the uneven power relations showcased whenever and wherever moving images are trafficked internationally.

In addition, prioritizing the stylistic excess of Kim Ki-young over the studied realism of Im Kwon-Taek sidesteps an important issue. Simply put, the distinct national images marketable transnationally these days do not as a matter of course have to promote "new-ness" or a sense of contemporary life. In contrast to the work of the 1960s and '70s film movements Berry references—such as the French New Wave, New German Cinema, and the New Latin American Cinema—filmmaking in East Asia in the 1980s and '90s does not have to be identified ostensibly on the basis of its up-to-date pyrotechnics, because many directors there are utilizing heritage and historical elements in highly suggestive ways. Indeed, this may well be the paradigm shift in the perception of "new cinemas" signaled by the astonishing success of the Chinese Fifth Generation. Because the homogenizing forces of globalization have inculcated in all of us an intense desire to get back to the past, representations of local life situated in historical time are now just as likely to be attractive to foreign audiences as more modern tales. Certainly, Im Kwon-Taek's realist period melodramas fit the bill. It is no accident that after the ethnic, exotic, and orientalist attractions of *Sopyonje*, his next film, *Festival* (*Ch'ukche*, 1996), concerned similarly "traditional" subject matter: burial rites in regional Korea.

This situation creates both opportunities and limitations. Positively,

titles like *Sopyonje* are important for educating overseas audiences in
the ways of unfamiliar lands and peoples. Alternatively, they can easily
lead to reductive, stereotypical, and perhaps even racist perceptions of
a nation's culture. As the critical dialogue about these issues advanced
in terms of the transnational circulation of Chinese cinemas over the
past fifteen years has shown, the dangers of cultural objectification are
ever-present. There is always the chance that artists and audiences will
subscribe to orientalist standards of value, thus perpetuating the vicious
cycle Yingjin Zhang has observed in the case of ethnographic Chinese
film-making: "favorable reviews at international film festivals lead to the
production of more ethnographic films, and the wide distribution of
such films facilitates their availability for classroom use and therefore
influences the agenda of film studies, which in turn reinforces the status
of ethnographic films as a dominant genre."[2]

The implications of this argument have been thought through most
fully by Rey Chow in *Primitive Passions,* her book on contemporary Chinese cinema.[3] Chow discusses how various filmmakers employ strategies
of self-exoticism so as to gain access to international image markets. As
her work demonstrates, the representation of native cultures on the
global stage is an extremely complex phenomenon, fraught with ambivalence and refusal. If we want to do justice to the significance of such
intelligent, popular, and powerful films as Im Kwon-Taek's historical
melodramas, we would do well to be aware of the existence of a number
of distinct instabilities. These can be put in the form of a series of questions. What special artistic strategies do particular films utilize to resist
objectification? By what means can such films shield the national past
from an encroaching global culture? Are unique audiovisual aesthetics
read in divergent ways by differently situated audiences?

One way of exploring such questions is to acknowledge that when
ethnic, exotic, and orientalist movies are projected in international are-
nas they advance a key contradiction of the nationalist project. As Ernest
Gellner writes, "nationalist ideology suffers from pervasive false consciousness. . . . [I]t claims to defend folk culture while in fact it forges
a high culture; it claims to protect an old folk society while in fact helping to build up an anonymous mass society."[4] Similarly, heritage movies
commodify the histories they attempt to preserve; by contrast, historical

narratives manipulate cross-cultural looking relations, even as they salvage the site-specific—the local and distinct—for the global marketplace.
There exists throughout this process a tension between insider and outsider forms of knowledge, between what one culture knows about itself
and other cultures would like to find out. Critical analysis can help explore such interactions by exposing their embedded power relations. As
I have suggested, "traditional" films—"nationalistic" titles of the kind
made at regular intervals by Im Kwon-Taek, for instance—may teach
us about these things in ways that more flamboyant, idiosyncratic titles
may not.

In discussing these issues in relation to the specific case of *Sopyonje,*
I want to start by entering as evidence my own personal encounter with
the film. When we showed *Sopyonje* at Indiana University in the spring
of 1996, the post-screening discussion raised an interesting problem of
cross-cultural analysis. The film had been introduced by a Korean studies
faculty member in terms of its representation of *p'ansori* music.[5] Yet
while expressing much interest in the characteristics of this unfamiliar
folk art, a number of audience members later admitted to feeling a little
confused and disappointed by how the film actually uses *p'ansori*. To be
more precise, we—most of whom were non-Koreans—felt "cheated"
by the film's climactic moment: the reunion scene between the blind
woman Song-hwa (O Chŏng-hae), and her surrogate brother Tong-ho
(Kim Kyu-ch'ŏl).

Let me set up the terms for this debate by briefly describing how
the narrative of *Sopyonje* leads up to the pivotal reunion scene. The
film concerns the life of three wandering *p'ansori* performers: Tong-ho,
Song-hwa, and their nonbiological father Yu-bong (Kim Myŏng-gon).
Forced to lead a life of poverty and hardship in postwar Korea, the
trio travels across the country practicing and refining their art. One
day, after Yu-bong has been particularly hard on Song-hwa, Tong-
ho runs away. Though he eventually finds work collecting herbs for
a pharmaceutical company in Seoul, Tong-ho actually spends much of
his adult life looking for his sister. In the meantime, Yu-bong, fearful
that his daughter will abandon him, blinds her by feeding her a lethal
dose of the herb *buja*. Now completely dependent on her father, Song-
hwa devotes herself to her music. After Yu-bong dies, Song-hwa drifts

FIGURE 6.1.
*Sopyonje:* Tong-ho and Song-hwa practice their *p'ansori*

in and out of a few brief affairs, but fundamentally she remains alone. Tong-ho eventually locates her, and the two perform *p'ansori* together during the course of a very emotional evening. However, though they are reunited through their music, neither openly acknowledges having recognized the other. Tong-ho returns to Seoul the next day, and Song-hwa heads once more for the open road, accompanied this time by her young illegitimate daughter.

The reunion scene constitutes the emotional center of the entire film and works on several different levels. To begin with, it provides a powerful example of the melodramatic imagination, illustrating a key generic tendency. With regard to its storytelling capabilities, melodrama often plays with temporality and the viewer's privileged knowledge of various characters' comings and goings to create poignancy, tragedy, and, ultimately, tears: events seldom happen "on time," personal awareness comes "too late," everything could have been so different "if only. . . ."[6] Such feelings are underlined in *Sopyonje* by the relation of the scene

FIGURE 6.2.
*Sopyonje:* Performing *p'ansori* in the marketplace

in question to the film's narrative structure as a whole. Song-hwa and Tong-ho's face-off after so many years apart is organized so as to parallel earlier scenes. Most obviously, the moment of their reunion "answers," both thematically and stylistically, the very start of the plot, wherein Tong-ho listens with great sadness to an older woman's *p'ansori* during one of his earlier sorties. Consequently, Tong-ho's later "return" to a comparable situation—this time with his sister in place of the elderly woman—has already been foreshadowed, filled with poignant memories of what might have been. Further, this sense of emotional buildup and release is matched by our understanding that the melodramatic bringing together of the two young family members provides Song-hwa with the outlet for her perfected singing style. By this stage of her tragic life, Song-hwa has suffered enough to be able to perform her *p'ansori* with utter conviction. The words she sings in this penultimate scene are delivered with an astonishing intensity that draws waves of tears from many viewers, a feeling only enhanced by the fact that the tale Song-hwa is telling (of a woman who sacrifices herself for her blind father) closely parallels the turns her own life has taken.

The scene can also be taken as superbly indicative of Im Kwon-Taek's authorial presence. Set in a small dark room, it appears on first acquaintance to be shot in a conventional "international" manner: a one-hundred-and-eighty degree line establishes the space where the two characters perform, shot-reverse shot configurations map out the nuances of their interaction, camera distances move from long shot to close up as emotions are expressed more deeply. However, while these formal characteristics contrast subtly with the shooting style of the earlier scene mentioned above (Tong-ho's meeting with the elderly woman is filmed with a zoom lens and a minimum of editing), they also need to be considered in relation to the film's soundtrack as well. Halfway through the *p'ansori* recital in the reunion scene, there is a startling effect that indicates a curious stylistic decision. Im chooses to shut off all diegetic sound, compelling his characters to be mute. We see Song-hwa sing her song and we see Tong-ho bang his drum, but we no longer hear them. A non-diegetic, "traditional" Korean piece—performed on flute and synthesizer—is brought to the front of the mix, and the most climactic moment of this musical reunion is denied to the listening subject. In other words, at the very moment the central characters are most connected to each other, at the very moment they express their familial bonds most passionately through song, and at the very moment all of this has been carefully built up and structured by the narrative as a whole, *Sopyonje* gives its audience mood music. No wonder some of us felt cheated. With all the fuss made up until now about the authenticity and beauty of *p'ansori*, why don't we get its full expression at this crucial juncture?

In short, what some of us felt at that screening in Bloomington in 1996 was that here is an example of a film not quite delivering all we had been led to expect from it. Sure, we could rationalize our response, appreciate that there are perfectly good aesthetic reasons for blocking the soundtrack in this way. Because we see the rapture of a blind woman experiencing an easing of her pain, doesn't the emphasis on sound manipulation approximate Song-hwa's own heightened sense of perception? Yet we also couldn't help feeling that perhaps we just didn't "get it." Given the narrative's overall reliance on the importance of Korean national culture, there seemed to be a level to *Sopyonje* that, as foreigners, we did not have access to.

This thought also came to me when I subsequently read some of the English-language critical reviews. For example, according to the Korean music critic Yi In-won, the word *imyŏn*—equivalent to "the inside" or the "inner meaning"—is frequently employed by *p'ansori* artists. For practitioners of the form, *imyŏn* refers to how "the sound, rhythm, tone and technique of their singing must all convey the inner meaning of the narrative."[7] *Sopyonje* beautifully suggests an "inner" dimension to *p'ansori* through its matching of life and art: its protagonists express through song what they experience and feel in their everyday lives. But some critics have responded to this appeal to the interiority of a national cultural form in a curious way. Chung Choong-hun, writing in praise of how *Sopyonje* resurrects a lost folk art, decrees that the film is a "modern masterpiece" because of how Im "has managed to 'visualize' *p'ansori*. Here is where Im's genius lies and it may also explain in part why the film has sparked such a reaction from audiences."[8] Pyeon Jang-wan takes a remarkably similar line, claiming that "the sounds in the film have the effect of sounds shown. In other words, the range of observation is magnified by the coalescing of the scene and its sound: sound expands its aural territory into that of the image, so much so that it can be said that the sound is seen and the visual is heard."[9] The sound is seen and the visual is heard. What does that mean exactly? How can sound be visualized? (Are we talking here about synaesthesia?). And how is it possible to give aural expression to an "inner" narrative meaning?

In her book *Strains of Utopia*, Caryl Flinn suggests that film music is often taken to express the "inner" life of culture through its ability to re-claim a lost past. Flinn describes how music, especially non-diegetic music, appears to stray farthest from the "ideology of the visible" because its "source within the film's fictional world cannot be accounted for." Music is often linked to utopian notions through its non-referentiality and through affective economies which open up a more perfect imaginary sphere for the viewing and listening subject. Because utopia is itself "etymologically linked to the non-representable since it a 'no place,' a society that cannot be put into representation (much less practice), but only described and alluded to," a variety of critical discourses have worked to uphold "music's ability to conjure forth remote, impossibly lost utopias."[10]

The way in which the "inner meaning" of *p'ansori* is obliquely suggested through its sonic denial in the climactic reunion scene of *Sopyonje* may provide one such instance of the construction of a lost utopia. The film's unexpectedly good showing at the domestic box office, as well as the release of a very successful soundtrack CD, has created an aura of spiritual value around its heritage and historical elements. What was once a regional folk music, then subsequently an endangered cultural form, has now been culturally reconstructed as a living, breathing national treasure. Such a shift in how *p'ansori* music has recently come to be framed so as to symbolize the very endurance and vitality of Korea itself bears all the hallmarks of a nationalist project. Moreover, in keeping with all nationalist projects, its effectiveness is reliant upon boundary classifications, upon barriers of inclusion and exclusion. When the film is unspooled outside Korea, foreigners like myself may be moved by the beauty of the reunion scene; but if we are confused by the shift from diegetic to non-diegetic sound, that only goes to show how little we appreciate the terms of this cultural recoding.

Yi In-won's words on the "inner meaning" of *p'ansori* are echoed in the language subaltern studies scholar Partha Chatterjee uses in his writings on nationalism. In *The Nation and Its Fragments: Colonial and Postcolonial Histories,* Chatterjee reacts against one of the central formulations of Benedict Anderson's classic study of the subject, *Imagined Communities.* Chatterjee has one central objection to Anderson's argument:

> If nationalisms in the rest of the world have to choose their imagined community from certain "modular" forms already made available to them by Europe and the Americas, what do they have left to imagine? . . . I object to this argument . . . because I cannot reconcile it with the evidence on anticolonial nationalism. The most powerful as well as the most creative results of the nationalist imagination in Asia and Africa are posited not on an identity but rather on a difference

with the "modular" forms of the national society propagated by the modern West.

Chatterjee goes on to theorize further the distinction between "inner" and "outer" domains of anticolonial nationalism, with the latter being located so as to offer a sphere of resistance to subjects structured within the orbit of postcolonialism:

> The material is the domain of the "outside," of the economy and of statecraft, of science and technology, a domain where the West had proved its superiority and the East had succumbed. . . . The spiritual, on the other hand, is an "inner" domain bearing the "essential" marks of cultural identity. The greater one's success in imitating Western skills in the material domain, therefore, the greater the need to preserve the distinctiveness of one's spiritual culture. . . . [N]ationalism declares the domain of the spiritual its sovereign territory and refuses to allow the colonial power to intervene in that domain. . . . [T]he colonial state, in other words, is kept out of the "inner" domain of national culture; but it is not as though this so-called spiritual domain is left unchanged. In fact, here nationalism launches its most powerful, creative, and historically significant project: to fashion a "modern" national culture that is nevertheless not Western.[11]

These words may very well describe the ideological project of *Sopyonje*: to utilize modern technology so as to preserve the perceived distinctiveness of a spiritual culture. Certainly, Chatterjee's assertions lie at the heart of the issues we were fumbling toward during that post-screening discussion in 1996. By seizing the affective and spiritual possibilities of film (representable) and musical (non-representable) language, Im's movie tries simultaneously to both project and protect a unique Korean folk culture.

That *p'ansori* is being advanced by Im Kwon-Taek as representative of the authenticity and emotionalism of the national culture is evidenced by the visual and aural symbolisms of other scenes as well. At one point, a military-style parade advertising a new form of music passes down the

middle of a street where the three itinerant *p'ansori* performers are working. The band, comprising such non-Korean instruments as trumpets
and trombones, is representative of the military, economic, and musical
colonization that has stopped Korean songs from remaining popular in
the postwar period. Earlier, Yu-bong had railed against American and
Japanese music, and now along comes confirmation that such forms are
indeed threatening his family's very existence. Aside from indicating the
decline in support for "traditional" Korean culture, the parade band
march also resonates with another open-air market scene. Here, the
*p'ansori* performers accompany a man selling Western-style medicine in
order to make a little extra money, yet the herbs being peddled are not
the real thing. The medicine is as false and inauthentic as the foreign
music. By contrast, Yu-bong will later give a different local herb, *puja*, to
Song-hwa. This herb *is* effective: it successfully blinds Song-hwa, thus
forcing her to devote her life to the perfection of authentic *p'ansori*. The
message is clear. When placed against the culture of the foreigners and
those who will listen to them, Yu-bong's music and medicine (though
horrendously destructive) are real, not fake.

When the reunion scene between Song-hwa and Tong-ho chooses
to deny the listening subject the thrill of "really" hearing the *p'ansori*,
Im seems to be constructing an "inner domain" of "essential" Korean
culture. Significantly, as *p'ansori* is an oral, acoustic form of cultural
expression, there is the implication that it cannot properly be caught
by technological means of reproduction. The singer must not be heard
singing her innermost life, and the drummer must be silent. The climactic emotions of the reunion scene are left unheard, unconsummated—
except perhaps to those national subjects who have already experienced
their cultural power and who will therefore already recognize the stories
that lie behind them. Outsiders can feel the pull of the emotions, but
they are excluded from taking part in the "inner" expression. With this
brilliant manipulation of sound mixing at a crucial stage of the narrative, Im Kwon-Taek appears to open up a space where the affective
capabilities of melodrama can be experienced and felt by the national
subject.

In *Sopyonje* the movement of the narrative as a whole in relation to its musical arrangement also supports this project. There is a gradual shift of emphasis away from individual desires and on to the importance of social bonds and obligations. The suggestion is that the community (the family/nation) provides the locus where true inner feelings reside. The previously mentioned first scene, for example, depicts Tong-ho listening to an old woman perform a *p'ansori* about the singer's desire to follow her lover wherever he may go. In a later flashback, Song-hwa and Tong-ho sing another song of love, shouting out lyrics describing how they have been abandoned. These two themes are picked up again in the major love song, "Ch'unhyang," that structures most of Song-hwa's subsequent performances. This *p'ansori* tells the story of a poor woman who falls in love with a noble man; instead of marrying her, however, he leaves her behind and moves to Seoul in order to further his career.[12] But by the time of the final reunion song between Song-hwa and Tong-ho, the emphasis has switched from personal desire to family loyalty. As recognition stirs in the blind Song-hwa, she is singing the words to "Simch'ŏng," a *p'ansori* version of a folktale which narrates the story of a daughter who sacrifices herself for her father—much as Song-hwa has been forced to do in her own life. Again, the reunion scene is so effective partly because it represents the culmination of a narrative process that has built up themes of loyalty and desire and then resolved them in a satisfyingly melodramatic fashion.

In line with the overall narrative utilization of a complex double temporal framework, the reunion scene itself exhibits a highly sophisticated structural use of music. It combines two components of the film's sound design, collapsing into one both the opening section of the fully stated *p'ansori* and the flute/synthesizer tune that has been heard intermittently throughout. This tune, which has already been used in a variety of different mixes, connotes sadness and grief. (Just before the reunion, for example, it underscores a parallel scene where Yu-bong admits to his daughter that he blinded her—a confrontation that sets up Song-hwa's more demonstrative one with Tong-ho.) The song, "Ch'ŏnnyŏnhak," composed by Kim Su-ch'ŏl, tells the story of a bird that accumulates wisdom and grief by living for one thousand years. The switch from the diegetic *p'ansori* to the non-diegetic use of this song in the reunion scene, then, presents a second level to the "inner" domain of meaning. A *p'ansori* that is so emotional as to go unexpressed is superseded by a tune about the accumulation of grief and understanding over an untold number of years.

To say this is to recognize that *Sopyonje* appeals to the affective economies familiar to Koreans through the concept of *han*.[13] It is here that Im Kwon-Taek's admirable attempt to "visualize" the "inner" domain of national culture through his manipulation of the sound mix in this scene from *Sopyonje* is joined by wider discourses of gender and class. Clearly, the film supports the notion that the burden of national grief in Korea is borne most of all by women, because women are the ones who have suffered most historically. This belief is verbalized explicitly enough by Yun-bong to Song-hwa just before he dies. Grief is accumulated through life, he tells her, and you cannot separate the two—you can only express grief through the life of your singing. It is no surprise, therefore, that *Sopyonje* ends on a fatalistic note. In the very last shot of the film, as Song-hwa walks down another snow-laden road, she is accompanied by her young daughter, thus suggesting that *han* lives on through the female line. By implication, it is women who can most vividly symbolize the inner spiritual domain of a national culture struggling against the evils of colonialism.

Chatterjee's broad claim is that within the dynamics of postcoloniality, women's emancipation is appropriated in terms of resistant nationalisms rather than through a "modular" form of colonialist nationalism. In the process, though, he has to struggle with the celebration of the inner domain of colonized society as a site of essential identity and resistance even when its constituent features are themselves patriarchal. As if illustrating this point, *Sopyonje* may be said to construct an inner domain of spiritual culture that has not yet been conceptualized outside of gender ideologies that are politically reactionary and historically incongruous. Chungmoo Choi (whose use of Chatterjee resembles my own) reports that in the film "a young woman is blinded and raped by her adopted father in the name of artistic perfection." She then goes on to note the "striking similarities" between Yu-bong's aspirations for Song-hwa's artistic maturation and South Korea's drive for economic enhancement:

The capitalistic development that deprived a nation of its voice and devastated its land in the name of nationalism is mirrored in the father's deprivation of his daughter's sight and in his violation of her body for the perfection of national art. In other words, the capitalistic development destroys a national body in the name of nationalism, while the spiritual essence of a nation is believed to be maintained only through the destroyed body. This creates a double-edged, paradoxical allegory of a postcolonial nation: anti-colonial nationalism can be achieved only through the self-construction of the feminine Other.[14]

& destruction

While I would not be as quick as Choi to equate the character of Yu-bong with a straightforwardly capitalist mind-set, her thought-provoking words on *Sopyonje* identify some key social instabilities. Specifically, it is interesting to ask how differently situated audiences may identify with the feminine Other's virtuous suffering. What emotional ambivalences constitute the mix of attraction and repulsion many Korean and international viewers will feel toward Song-hwa? Most intriguingly, what of the double-edged, paradoxical nature of both male and female subjectivity? Women are not the only ones who may cry while watching emotional melodramas like *Sopyonje*. How does the need to self-construct a "destroyed body" impact on the perceived masculinities and femininities of distinct audience members?

Because such questions lie outside the immediate concerns of this essay, all I want to do here is state that raising them will of necessity complicate any monolithic reading of the film's possible meanings, as well as Im Kwon-Taek's avowed desire to make nonideological, humanist films. Titles like *Sopyonje* are everywhere penetrated by the conflicts and contradictions of political struggle. Let me quote at some length Im's own response to a question about what *han* signifies or represents for the Korean people:

> *Han* is not a concept that Koreans can agree on. I can't even count the number of books that have been written about *han*. In fact, I don't think there can be a definitive answer to your question: however, *han* is a specific emotion that has profound links to the history of the Korean people, and as such, might be a difficult concept for non-Koreans to

grasp fully. You say that *han* permeates throughout *Sopyonje*. Well, it's not a perfect piece of work and every time I look at it, I see ways in which it could have been made better, but I feel that it is an important film because it has succeeded in giving voice to *han* and making it felt, albeit in a limited fashion, among people who have not shared the common history. To me, that is deeply meaningful.[15]

These comments provoke two trains of thought. First, as *han* is not "a concept that Koreans can agree on" but which most Koreans are nevertheless likely to experience, the withholding of Song-hwa's voice through the non-representability of mood music opens up a space for social fantasy: the "hidden" *p'ansori* in the reunion scene calls forth a myriad different emotional investments around a common perception of feeling. Second, since Im himself suggests that there is no common consensus on the meaning of *han*, it might be the case that the term can only properly be understood in terms of the fragmentary or ambivalent nature of Korean national identity (who are these "people" who have not shared the common history?). That is to say, there is no such thing as a unified entity called "the Korean people" who all experience the same sense of *han* when watching *Sopyonje*.

A severe contradiction comes into play here. As Isolde Standish has pointed out, women's embodiment of the Korean nation's accumulated *han* resonates in the context of the aims of the *minjung* cultural movement.[16] If that movement itself was on the wane by the early 1990s (the wind taken out of its sails by successful labor and democratization campaigns), it had managed to sensitize the nation to the perceived uniquely spiritual value of such folk arts as *p'ansori*. Michael Robinson, in words that recall Chatterjee, puts it like this: "Placing the concept of the *minjung* at the center of a countervision of national identity is an attempt to free Korean nationalism from its ties to a universalist path of Westernization and capitalist development as well. This vision posits that material progress linked to capitalist development is antithetical to the "true" nature of Korean identity more appropriately centered on the culture and identity of peasant-producers, the *minjung*."[17] *Sopyonje* can only present this notion of "true" national identity by objectifying it, by mediating one of its oral, acoustic forms of cultural expression through means of technological reproduction, and then by gendering it female.

Before exploring this contradiction in a little more detail, though, it is well to acknowledge that the appeals of *Sopyonje* for diverse Korean and international audiences are also shaped by class issues. The film's selection of *p'ansori* as a national symbol derives in part from its radical difference from anything produced in the West. Although the basic plots of some of the stories can certainly be found in other countries, the text and style of singing in *p'ansori* appear to be unique to Korea. In addition, the music reflects the tastes of both elites and common people. (Along with allusions and quotations from classical Chinese literature, it carries explicit references to sexual and other popular matters.) Up until the late 1980s, large segments of the middle class were sympathetic to the working class, and they advanced the interests of the *minjung* (that is, the masses, past and present) against the government elites. Soon after liberalization, however, a range of factors, such as an increasing number of work stoppages and a general slowdown in the economy, made some of the middle class lose much of its sympathy for the working class, even as many members of the working class were themselves being absorbed into the middle class. *P'ansori,* as a symbol that could incorporate the shared experiences of both elites and commoners, rather than their opposition to each other, thus came to have great appeal.

However, while the use of music in *Sopyonje* has stimulated many Koreans to feel and preserve the inner domain of a shared national culture, the film reproduces some of the same contradictions that plagued the *minjung* movement itself. In the 1970s and 1980s, student activists wanted to make ordinary Korean peasants the subjects of history, but they attempted to do this by recontextualizing, reframing, and so objectifying peasant culture. The students both learned from the peasants but also aspired to steer them in the "proper" political direction. Middle-class students tried in vain to be something they weren't—peasants and workers—while arguing that they could never be Korean until they had been educated about the *minjung*.[18]

A similar dilemma confronts *Sopyonje*. The film's massive domestic and stalled international success only works to recontextualize and commodify the folk culture it claims to preserve. While celebrating the oral

and acoustic authenticities of *p'ansori*, the film drags it into the modern
world of Dolby sound and compact disc. (Indeed, this objectification of
"early music" through the cinema's technologically advanced "ideology
of the visible" is itself a result of the conditions of cultural modernism.)
It has been reported by a personal source—although I have been unable
to verify the truth or otherwise of this statement—that the singing style
in the movie is actually not *Sŏp'yŏnje* (the western school that prevailed in
the Chŏlla or Honam region) but rather *Tongp'yŏnje* (the eastern school
that prevailed in the Kyŏngsang region); if true, this would provide a
 perfect example of contemporary filmmakers inventing tradition for the
modern era. Whatever the facts regarding this particular claim, though,
there can be little doubt that *Sopyonje* manipulates cultural symbols so
as to construct national identities in the present.

Consider the grain of the *p'ansori* voice itself. The sound design
of *Sopyonje* mixes together three different female voices so as to give
the impression of one coherent, if gradually more intense, aural texture.
The first voice belongs to O Chŏng-hae, the lead actress, who herself
is an accomplished singer of *p'ansori*, trained under one of the true
masters of the form, Kim So-hŭi. By contrast, much of the singing in
the second half of the film is provided by a government-designated
apprentice, and the singing during the climactic reunion scene was
provided by An Suk-sŏn, a "Korean National Living Treasure" (*Ingan
Munhwaje*—literally "Human Cultural Property"), one of a group of
people designated by the South Korean government as outstanding
performers of "traditional" arts.

Armed with such background knowledge, how should the film's acts
of objectification be handled? It may be necessary to remain skeptical
of the ways in which *Sopyonje*'s commodification of folk music links up
with the state's own attempts to preserve national culture as a means of
legitimizing itself. While the film has done well on its touristic rounds of
the international film festival circuit (Tokyo, Berlin, Nantes, Shanghai,
Hong Kong, Hawaii), *p'ansori* has also been useful to the Ministry of
Culture. Since 1963 this organization has attempted to link "traditional"
culture to the policies of the state rather than to the aims of the *minjung*,
through the terms of the National Cultural Properties Preservation Act.
The result of this move is that the museum-ification of working-class

culture allows the state to proclaim itself as the sponsor of modern forms of folk expression. Folk culture is thus removed from the people and attached to the modern nation's narratives of capitalist becoming.

This may very well be how the release of the *Sopyonje* CD functions within Korea, and how the film itself functions within transnational image markets. On a textual level, too, we should be aware of how the film's sound design masks the process of cultural objectification by hiding its means of technological reproduction. For example, consider the celebrated scene where the three central characters perform the song "Chindo Arirang" as they walk down a long country road. This five-minute sequence shot is executed in a single static take. The singers slowly dance toward the camera, but the camera itself doesn't move. Yet the sound mix doesn't vary either. No matter where the three characters are on the road, we can hear their voices loud and clear; there is no "logical" correlation between camera distance and volume. Or again, a close listen to the soundtrack CD will reveal the presence of the

FIGURE 6.3.
*Sopyonje:* The family travels through the countryside . . .

FIGURE 6.4.
*Sopyonje:* . . . and sings spontaneously (the "Arirang" sequence)

acoustic properties of electronic reproduction. As *p'ansori* is sung into
the microphone, the performer's voice can be heard echoing around
the sound booth.

Im Kwon-Taek's use of editing accentuates this process of cultural
objectification. There are, for example, three scenes composed in a
similar manner to the reunion scene that has been the subject of this
essay: the opening scene, where Tong-ho and an elderly woman face
each other in a dark room; the scene where Yu-bong learns a *p'ansori*
from a junkie friend in order to teach it to his daughter; and the scene
where Yu-bong tutors Song-hwa on how to perform with maximum
emotion. A comparison of these four scenes in chronological order is
most revealing. In "visualizing" *p'ansori,* there is a marked shift away
from the use of the long-take and toward the intervention of editing.

In the first scene, for example, Im makes only one edit—a functional
reverse cut—otherwise using a slow circular pan and zoom-in as a
substitute for more conventional shot-reverse shot patternings. The

use of the long-take emphasizes that the song is being preserved as it happens, in real time. By the final reunion scene, however, there is a sustained use of editing. Even though this moment is supposed to provide us with our clearest and most direct access to Song-hwa's emotions, it is completely broken up. The result is that the cutting into performances which have elsewhere been represented through the long-take only serves the film's objectifying tendencies. At the very moment it reveals its "inner meaning," *p'ansori* is manipulated through ideologies of editing and sound mixing.

It should be clear by now that through the process of engaging with *Sopyonje* cross-culturally after a screening at a specific reception site, I have reevaluated how its climactic reunion scene works. I no longer feel disappointed or cheated; rather I am impressed with how Im Kwon-Taek and his composer, Kim Su-ch'ŏl, have manipulated the soundtrack so as to suggest the presence of national thematics. If I wanted to be supportive, I would say that in drawing attention to the distinction between diegetic and non-diegetic music at this moment, *Sopyonje* is aware enough of the dangers of cultural objectification to be able to deny audiences the thrill of "really" hearing, and so experiencing, this unique cultural form. The point is not simply that *p'ansori* cannot be expressed directly through Dolby sound—so much that Im doesn't want it to be reduced to the status of a simple commodity. He wants to preserve its "inner meaning," its spiritual core and life. I now consider that this scene seeks to avoid the cultural objectification of *p'ansori* music by opening up an inner domain of national culture for viewers and listeners. To what extent the scene actually manages to avoid the contradictions of objectification once it enters international image markets, however, I'm still not sure.

We return, then, to the question of the desirability, or otherwise, of a title like *Sopyonje* providing Korean cinema with a level of global exposure. Does Im's film reinforce the status of ethnographic filmmaking in Korea? Does it lead outsiders to reductive, stereotypical, and perhaps even racist perceptions of the national culture? While I have been trying to think through some of the questions raised initially during a screening of *Sopyonje* at a university campus in the U.S., I am more than willing to recognize that a number of objections could doubtless be leveled at my argument. For example, it is probably the case that many viewers will simply not have noticed the shift from diegetic to non-diegetic sound during the final reunion scene—or it will not have struck them as particularly inappropriate—and so my reading becomes another exercise in overinterpretation based upon dubious notions of "national allegory." As a Western film student, my sensitivity to formal questions (as well as my own "orientalist" fascinations?) may produce rupture where no rupture actually exists.

In addition, there is the larger question of cultural specificity. To me, the fragmentary nature of this final song—its replacement by a nonverbal piece of mood music—exposes the fragmentary nature of the nationalist project. Yet *p'ansori* is itself often experienced in Korea in fragments. Since musical texts are full of allusions to classical literature that is now obscure, as well as to old folk songs and tales, Koreans themselves may experience some difficulty in following and making them out. I have been informed, for example, that an FM radio station in Korea used to talk about and play *p'ansori* for thirty minutes every afternoon at 5:00 PM, but that it did so in excerpts because an entire performance might take several hours, with singer and audience resting and eating at intervals throughout, only a few modern South Koreans are enthusiastic enough to sit through one in its entirety. Consequently, it is probably not in the least bit strange that the crucial sample of *p'ansori* singing in Im's film ends after a mere minute or so and that the non-diegetic flute playing rounds off the scene. Excerpts from *p'ansori*, rather than whole performances, have been adopted as symbols of national culture.

Such possible objections do not invalidate the interpretation of *Sopyonje* offered in this chapter. Equally, my interpretation does not invalidate the importance and interest of other kinds of readings. I have considered in some detail issues of objectification so as to show how the representation of native cultures on the global stage is an extremely complex phenomenon fraught with ambivalence and refusal—a truism Im Kwon-Taek himself appreciates only too well. Im's words quoted below reiterate one of Rey Chow's main points about the recent international reception of New Chinese Cinema; for directors like Chen Kaige and Zhang Yimou, the question of visuality, of looking and being looked at, structures self-perceptions of the national culture. Im has witnessed the

extraordinary global success of Chinese cinema at first hand, and he has
learned his lesson.

> My personal desire has been to capture elements of our traditional cul-
> ture in my work, and I have been doing so bit by bit. In a world becom-
> ing increasingly homogenized—they call it a global village nowadays,
> don't they?—and amid the current of internationalism, what happens
> to the culture of a people who have kept themselves, for the most part,
> historically self-contained? The fear is, of course, that most aspects of
> Korean culture that are not favored by the terms of this new inter-
> national, and more aggressive, culture may be absorbed, and in the
> end disappear. Korean culture is geographically and anthropologically
> specific, but I believe that it must be revived and brought into the
> international context; it must makes its colors *visible* and find in what
> is most unique, what is also the most universal. As Koreans what we
> can depict the best in the medium of film are the very elements and
> experiences of our lives, which will necessarily find their roots in our
> culture and traditions. *If we do not make these visible, who will look?*
> Indeed, who can? Through film, we can and we must reveal the col-
> ors that are our own, and this is particularly important in a global
> context.[19]

Increasingly these days heritage and historical aspects of distinct national
cultures are being utilized to achieve such goals. Just as recent mainland
Chinese movies like *Swan Song* (*Juexiang,* 1985), *Woman Demon Human* (*Ren gui qing,* 1987), and *Farewell My Concubine* (*Bawang bieji,*
1993) draw on local musical and gender traditions to engage complex
issues of national and cultural identity, it may be worth considering how
sound/image, class, and gender relations are treated in other Im Kwon-
Taek films such as Ticket (*Tik'et,* 1986), *Surrogate Mother* (*Ssibaji,* 1986),
and *Adada* (*Adada,* 1988). Such explorations would help initiate among
scholars of Korean film some of the same debates that have energized
discussion of transnational Chinese cinemas over the past fifteen years.
At the very least, sustained consideration of particular cross-cultural encounters should highlight the political efficacy of Im Kwon-Taek's work,
regardless of how we decide to evaluate it artistically or sociologically.

# Notes

I should like to thank Cheon Hosang, Roger L. Janelli, Kim Jeongmee, Michael Robinson, and Shin Jeeyoung for their help, support, and advice.

1. Chris Berry, "Introducing 'Mr Monster': Kim Ki-young and the Critical Economy of the Globalized Art-House Cinema," in *Post-Colonial Classics of Korean Cinema*, ed. Chungmoo Choi (Irvine: Korean Film Festival Committee, University of California, 1998), 46.

2. Yingjin Zhang, "Chinese Cinema and Transnational Cultural Politics: Reflections on Film Festivals, Film Productions, and Film Studies," *Journal of Modern Literature in Chinese* 2, no. 1 (July 1998): 121.

3. Rey Chow, *Primitive Passions: Visuality, Sexuality, Ethnography, and Contemporary Chinese Cinema* (New York: Columbia University Press, 1995). See also some of the essays in Sheldon Hsiao-peng Lu, ed., *Transnational Chinese Cinemas: Identity, Nationhood, Gender* (Honolulu: University of Hawai'i Press, 1997).

4. Ernest Gellner, *Nations and Nationalism* (New York: Cornell University Press, 1983), 124.

5. For background information on *p'ansori*, see Marshall R. Pihl, *The Korean Singer of Tales* (Cambridge, Mass.: Council on East Asian Studies, 1994).

6. See Steve Neale's article on this topic, "Melodrama and Tears," *Screen* 27, no. 6 (November-December, 1986): 6–23.

7. Yi In-won, "P'ansori: An Unexpected Revival," *Koreana* 7, no. 2 (summer 1993): 77.

8. Chung Choong-hun, "Im Kwon-Taek's *Sop'yonche:* Traditional Art Strikes Chord in Modern Audiences," *Koreana* 7, no. 2 (summer 1993): 75.

9. Pyeon Jang-wan, "*Seo Pyun-Jae,*" *Cinemaya* 20 (summer 1993): 27.

10. Caryl Flinn, *Strains of Utopia: Gender, Nostalgia, and Hollywood Film Music* (Princeton: Princeton University Press, 1992), 6, 10.

11. Partha Chatterjee, *The Nation and Its Fragments: Colonial and Postcolonial Histories* (Princeton: Princeton University Press, 1993), 5–6. Cf. Benedict Anderson, *Imagined Communities: Reflections on the Origins and Spread of Nationalism* (London: Verso, 1983).

12. Tong-ho himself follows this path as an adult, signaling the ambiguous nature of his character. This brother resists the oppressive law of the father, yet he also abandons his sister to a grisly fate.

13. Isolde Standish cites a working definition of *han* from M. Shapiro's *The Shadow in the Sun: A Korean Year of Love and Sorrow* (New York: Atlantic Monthly Press, 1990), 11: "the result of injustices perpetrated by, among others, parents, friends, siblings, a colonial ruler, an occupying army, past governments, the present government, and those who in crucial moments failed to display

sincerity." See Isolde Standish, "Korean Cinema and the New Realism: Text and Context," in *Colonialism and Nationalism in Asian Cinema*, ed. Wimal Dissanayake (Bloomington: Indiana University Press, 1994), 87.

14. Chungmoo Choi, "Nationalism and Construction of Gender in Korea," in *Dangerous Women: Gender and Korean Nationalism*, ed. Elaine H. Kim and Chungmoo Choi (New York: Routledge, 1998), 22–23. Choi repeats her claim that Yu-bong rapes Song-hwa in her chapter on *Sopyonje* and *The Genealogy* in the present volume. Does he rape her? It seems to me that *Sopyonje* is characterized by the use of structural ambiguities, or antinomies, that may resonate differently for different (cross-cultural?) audiences depending upon their cultural expectations and competencies. In his article on censorship and the "antinomian text," Richard Maltby reports a student's claim that the previous time she saw *Casablanca* (1942) she didn't feel the Humphrey Bogart and Ingrid Bergman characters had slept together, but on viewing it again she felt they had. Similarly, while acknowledging the force of Choi's argument, I am on occasion inclined to believe that Yu-bong does not in fact rape his adopted daughter: mistreat, abuse, and blind, yes, but not rape. The point is that the "antinomian text" allows for both readings. See Richard Maltby, "'A Brief Romantic Interlude': Dick and Jane Go to Three and a Half Seconds of the Classical Hollywood Cinema," in *Post Theory: Reconstructing Film Studies*, ed. David Bordwell and Noël Carroll (Madison: University of Wisconsin Press, 1996), 434–59.

15. Qtd. in "Between Blockbusters and Art Films," Harvard Asia Pacific Review [on-line journal], available from http://www.cinekorea.com/ImKwon Taek/harvinter.html.

16. Standish's definition of *minjung* is taken from an unnamed Korean theologian: "the *minjung* are those who are oppressed politically, exploited economically, alienated sociologically, and kept under-educated in culture and intellectual matters." Standish, "Korean Cinema and the New Realism," 86.

17. Michael Robinson, "Enduring Anxieties: Cultural Nationalism and Modern East Asia," in *Cultural Nationalism in East Asia: Representation and Identity*, ed. Harumi Befu (Berkeley: Institute of East Asian Studies, University of California Press, 1993), 182–83.

18. As Mao once put it, "the task of learning from workers, peasants, and soldiers comes before the task of educating them. . . . [T]he only way to educate the masses is by being their student." See Bonnie McDougall, *Mao Zedong's Talks at the Yan'an Conference on Literature and Art: A Translation of the 1943 Text with Commentary* (Ann Arbor: Center for Chinese Studies, University of Michigan, 1980), 68, 73.

19. Qtd. in "Between Blockbusters and Art Films." Emphasis added.

*Yi Hyoin*
*Translated by Kyung Hyun Kim and Mison Hahn*

CHAPTER 7

# *Fly High, Run Far* and Tonghak Ideology

## *Fly High, Run Far* and Im Kwon-Taek's Other Films

In my judgment, Im is like a weather vane.[1] On another occasion—recalling the modernist poet Kim Su-yŏng's satirical reference to people who neither actively resisted nor entirely surrendered to the effects of Korea's harsh political climate—I compared Im to grass, for he often "lies down before the wind, and gets up before the wind." His films have impressed me, literally opening up a new world, but at the same time they made me feel that I had been betrayed. This is especially true of the ones based on Korean history and ideology that Im produced under the regimes of the two military dictator/presidents, Park Chung Hee and Chun Doo Hwan, for they fail to take any conclusive position. After gesturing toward critique, they always end with an equivocal statement, such as "No one was right" or "It depends on the individual." That is why I now compare him to a flexible weather vane, turning with the political wind whichever way it is blowing.

In 1991, around the same time that the Soviet Union and the Eastern Bloc were falling apart, the South Korean military regime was also coming to an end.[2] This was a time of ideological confusion, and no one knew where to turn. Those who were looking for some new ideological stability regarded Im's *Fly High, Run Far* (*Kaebyŏk*, 1991) as an important film. Whether or not he realized its full significance, it also meant a great deal to Im himself. *Fly High, Run Far* is the film in which he reveals his own political viewpoint more fully than in any of his other works from the 1980s and the 1990s that treat ideology and history. However, *Fly High, Run Far* has not commanded much attention either from serious Korean film culture or from general audiences, and it remains a relatively obscure film. It is not my objective in this essay to propose it as an unrecognized masterpiece. Rather, my intention is to use *Fly High, Run Far* as a representative text to investigate the underlying ideological analysis of Korean history that informs Im's work during the last two, transformative decades of the twentieth century.

The most conspicuous feature of Im's films since about 1980 is the prevalence of history and ideology as foregrounded themes. Most of them deal with the lives of Korean people as they suffered through foreign invasions, the ravages of colonialism, and the imposition of alien ideologies. Following *Pursuit of Death* (*Tchakk'o*, 1980) and *Gilsottum* (1985), *The Taebaek Mountains* (*T'aebaek sanmaek*, 1994) is Im's final and in some ways summary version of these explorations of past history. We can also recognize cognate concerns in films that are not ostensibly historical, such as *Come, Come, Come Upward* (1989)—which circuitously approaches the conflict between religion's practical, social goals and its purely spiritual values—or *Sopyonje* (1993)—which also scrutinizes the social meaning of Korean culture under siege by colonial intrusions. Informed by the context of such works as these and resonating with them, *Fly High, Run Far* articulates the underlying philosophical principles that appear in more or less latent forms in these other films. Here Im comprehensively assembles questions of ideology, religion, and culture that he explores only tangentially elsewhere, covering them from a wider angle and from a more clearly enunciated secular viewpoint. Im speaks more openly in this film about the essential characteristics of

Korean culture, about how we Koreans should view our lives and find the right way to deal with our social reality.

## "Human being equals heaven." "Death is life."

*Fly High, Run Far* takes place in the second half of the nineteenth century, during the last stages of the feudal Chosŏn period, a time when the lower classes were severely exploited, the economy was faltering, and the political system was thoroughly corrupt. During this period the imperialist countries—Japan, China, and Russia—were competing with each other for the spoils of Korea, which had just been forcibly opened to the West. The film is centrally concerned with the social meaning of the Tonghak or "Eastern Learning" belief system as it was developed by Ch'oe Che-u.[3] A member of an upper-class [*yangbang*] family fallen into decline, Ch'oe left home at the age of twenty and wandered the country for ten years before establishing Tonghak in 1860. His ideas represent a combination of various religions of the time—especially those practiced by the most oppressed classes (the *minjung*), who hoped for a better society—including Catholicism and its belief in salvation, and *Silhak*,[4] another new ideology of the period. Though Ch'oe claimed a divine basis for Tonghak and asserted that heaven had chosen him for this project, he also appreciated the significance of including elements of contemporary folk beliefs in this new religion. Moreover, he believed that by imitating the methods of Catholic missionaries—who provided education and medical treatment to the underprivileged along with doctrinal instruction—he could transform the hierarchical, exploitative society characteristic of contemporary Confucianism.

Ch'oe's summary declaration, "The way is the heaven's way, but the learning is Tonghak," meant that though Tonghak, like Catholicism, served heaven, its key principles had to be derived from the actual world in which it came into being. The most significant differences between the Tonghak idea of salvation and the Christian one were the timing of salvation and the relationship between the believers and their god. Though the Christian concept of salvation referred to life "after death," Tonghak called for *huch'ŏn kaebyŏk:* the opening up of a new world

on this earth. The *huch'ŏn kaebyŏk* ideal and its anticipation of a new
world also included a critique of the deficiencies of Western civilization.
Ch'oe Si-hyŏng, the historical successor to Ch'oe Che-u who became
the main character in *Fly High, Run Far,* proclaimed the new religion's
credo: "The idea of *huch'ŏn kaebyŏk* is to create a world where everyone
can live in harmony. The limitations of *sŏnch'ŏn kaebyŏk* [opening up of
a new world after death] is that though everyone possesses the faculty of
reason, they must compete against each other in this life in their search
for self-realization."

The way that believers relate to god in Tonghak was heavily influenced by traditional Korean humanism, which differs substantially
from Western humanism. European humanism developed when people
were liberated from the idea of the ontological priority of a supreme de-
ity, but the essence of Tonghak humanism is the principle that human
beings are just as important as heavenly realities. Tonghak maintains
that a new world will open up when heaven, nature, and human beings serve each other faithfully. This beautiful, broad-minded, idealistic
attitude is also compatible with lived reality. Considering the fact that
we only recently began to realize that nature has been destroyed by the
instrumental, egotistic rationality of Western Enlightenment, Tonghak
humanism clearly outstripped the cognitive potential of Western humanism in the mid-nineteenth century—when Western imperialism was also
at its zenith. Tonghak's answer to the exploitation intrinsic in Western
Enlightenment is vividly illustrated in the scene in *Fly High, Run Far*
where Ch'oe Si-hyŏng recalls his youth in Chŏkjoam. When he says to
his wife, "I don't know why I feel so sorry for the broken branch or for
the injured worm in the field," he metaphorically invokes the followers
of Tonghak who were suffering under miserable living conditions and
governmental suppression; he also implies that Tonghak humanism was
an indispensable philosophical foundation of the struggle for a new,
properly humane society.

Despite this fundamental axiom, the social turbulence of the period
in which Tonghak was born and attempted to establish itself inevitably
generated conflicts for those who tried to put it into practice. For
example, the political militancy of its most oppressed followers was not
always compatible with the humanistic principles of Ch'oe Si-hyŏng

himself, who believed that *huch'ŏn kaebyŏk* was only fully possible after social reform had elevated the minds of the people; that is to say, Tonghak humanism was not always understood in exactly the same way by the leadership and by the followers.

To fully comprehend it, Tonghak humanism must be studied from both a sociopolitical and an ideological perspective. From an ideological point of view, the essence of Tonghak comprises two ideas: "I myself am heaven" and "The movement naturally follows the rule of nature and the logic of the agricultural society."[5] Taoist observations regarding the rule of nature, belief in a new world, the notion of reaching utopia through spiritual discipline, and belief in faith itself are all combined here. On the other hand, from a sociopolitical vantage, the Tonghak idea is an ethical movement of social and political forces, an anticolonial and nationalist project that pragmatically tolerated ad hoc combinations of popular Confucianism, shamanism, and folkloric hocus-pocus.

*Fly High, Run Far* focuses primarily on the ideological aspect of Tonghak, the equivalence of the human and the divine. As a result, the film does not deal adequately with the peasant wars—known as the Tonghak War—it occasioned, nor does it investigate why Tonghak's followers so readily embraced militant strategies.[6] In other words, *Fly High, Run Fair* supports the precept of Ch'oe Si-hyŏng's *kaebyŏk:* the belief that the new world will come only when people reform their thoughts and lives. And it negates the radical tendency of those commoners who placed a higher priority on fighting against wretched social conditions and political oppression. The film's idealist, nonmilitant reading of Korean history is consistent with the politics of Im Kwon-Taek's other films, such as *Pursuit of Death* and *The Taebaek Mountains.* For Im, the most important elements in Tonghak are its specific humanism and the native thought—a heritage of several thousand years of Korean culture—preserved in it. This aspect of Tangun thought emphasizes the harmony of humans and the universe. As *Tangun Ch'ŏnbukyŏng* (*The Celestial Text of Tangun*) declares: "It was born from nothing, split into three at once, and has become the source of infinity." The heaven is yang, the earth is yin, and humanity is both yin and yang—meaning that from one source comes eternity. This ideology of harmony lies at the heart of the didactic component in Im's aesthetic.

## Contempt for Collective Political Struggle:
## Im's Understanding and Misunderstanding of
## Tonghak Thought

*Fly High, Run Far* traces the life of the second Tonghak leader, Ch'oe Si-hyŏng, from 1864—when the first leader, Ch'oe Che-u was executed—until his own execution in 1898. A fugitive who is constantly being pursued, the cinematic Cho'e Si-hyŏng finds the truth for himself and tries to convey it to his fellow Koreans, but he is finally killed by the government. Im follows the chronological order of historical events and frequently uses subtitles to supply important background information. As a result, the film often has the feel of a documentary. Even though Ch'oe Si-hyŏng's life is dramatic, narrative interest is sustained by the historical situation rather than by the portrayal of the main characters. Moreover, the film's exposition is different from that of classic Hollywood cinema. This does not mean that the film is Brechtian or in any other way radically avant-garde, only that the loose organization of cause and effect relations results in a similarly loose narrative clustering of episodes. The director's intention is clear. By following chronological order in the narrative of Ch'oe Si-hyŏng's life and minimizing the techniques of classical narrative, Im is able to emphasize a moralistic didacticism. He once commented on this in an interview.

> I have always thought that no matter what it is, ideology should not claim the lives of people. Tonghak was a religion that people could use to solve their problems by respecting each other. . . . *Kaebyŏk* was intended as a message that earthly matters should be resolved on the condition that people be respected. . . . The criticisms of the film came from people who thought that the film should have focused on the Tonghak Peasant War [1894–95]. . . . From a religious point of view, however, the war was a minor incident considering that this newborn religion had only recently begun to flourish. That is why it was controversial. . . . *Fly High, Run Far* shows what Ch'oe Si-hyŏng's ideal was. I think we need to pay more attention to Ch'oe Si-hyŏng's religious world.[7]

But the question remains whether the Tonghak religion and the Tong-hak War can be separated. To find an answer to this question, we need to discuss two main issues: the domestic reception of *Fly High, Run Far* and debates about Tonghak in the film itself. (Though we cannot deny Im the right to choose his subject matter, the audience is also free to criticize his ideological orientation. Audiences can also revise or contest that critique according to their own wishes.)

Im was able to see the Tonghak movement and the Tonghak War as separate issues because he believes that the essential principles of Tong-hak were not the main motivation or cause of that war. This is consistent with the position he has usually taken against large-scale political strug-gles that entail the loss of human lives. Im's dismissive attitude toward mass political struggle and his repudiation of movements that lead to bloodshed is in accord with Tonghakan religious principles, but it can also be understood as a reflection of Im's own life. His family suffered grievously around the time of the Korean War because one of his uncles was a leftist, and anticommunist sentiment forced Im to keep this a secret until very recently. Moreover, Im's point of view was also undoubtedly influenced by the political upheavals of the period when the film was made: the disintegration of the Soviet Union and the eastern European countries, and increasing demands for democracy in Korea.

Im had impressed many critics, including myself, with an earlier film, *Pursuit of Death,* which persuasively portrays the havoc that can be wreaked by people who are obsessed with ideology. However, *The Taebaek Mountains* and *Fly High, Run Far* do not demonstrate equiv-alent thematic clarity and force. *The Taebaek Mountains* suffers from condensation of the epic scale of its source novel, and *Fly High, Run Far* appears to be a simple juxtaposition of historical incidents. In particular, *Fly High, Run Far* was unfavorably received by peopled allied with the pro-democracy movement, of which I myself was a member, because we regarded Tonghak as a radical political movement rather than an episode in the development of Korean religious thought. When these movies were released, we considered the negative depictions of the leftists in *The Taebaek Mountains,* and of progressive militant characters such as Kim Kae-nam and Chŏn Pong-jun, under the command of Ch'oe Si-hyŏn, in *Fly High, Run Far* very unfair. Because the political tenets of the pro-democracy movement—which were based both on Marxist theory and on the *minjung* theory of other Korean leftists—were still in the formative stage, we did not have solid support for our opinions. Of course, few of us in the pro-democracy movement paid much attention to *Fly High, Run Far,* nor were we culturally mature. Korean film critics showed little interest in *Fly High, Run Far*'s interpretation of history, but eventually some younger critics (most of whom were then in their thirties and just getting their careers underway, though who are now the leaders of Korean film criticism) chose to obsessively criticize the film. Belonging both to the *minjung* movement group and to the film critics' circle, I found myself ill at ease with that critique. I was similarly torn when I was the only one who openly defended Chang Sŏn-u's *A Petal* (*Kkotnip*, 1995), a film that uses as subject matter the May 1980 Kwangju massacre, when the military government killed as many as 3,000 people. I also felt uneasy when those who had nothing to do with the pro-democracy movement assailed the political positions of films like *Fly High, Run Far* and *A Petal.* During the period when the *minjung* belief in the dialectical historical process that would spontaneously transform Korea into a classless society was lost, most of those critics had themselves done nothing to preserve it, and it was self-serving for them now to use the terms of this process to attack films like these. Recognizing the unsureness of my own political convictions, I found it difficult either to defend or criticize them. And so my reading of *Fly High, Run Far* here cannot remain simply on the level of textual analysis. I must consider the sociopolitical context surrounding it and other Korean films with similar topics.

Even fiction films must be subject to reproach if they fail to provide appropriate historical grounding, even when audiences are conversant with the facts of the historical moment in which they are set. And the controversies surrounding *Fly High, Run Far* and *The Taebaek Mountains* are complicated by the absence of consensus among Korean historians regarding the facts these films deal with. Indeed, no film dealing with Tonghak, or for that matter any modern ideological movement in Korea, is above criticism. For example, *The Southern Army* (*Nambugun,* Chŏng Chi-yŏng, 1990)—which portrays communist partisans resisting to the bitter end during the Korean War—was criticized by leftists in

Korea as "a de facto anticommunist film" and by right-wingers as "a communist film." *The Taebaek Mountains* was sharply attacked by the right wing while it was being shot, though it was not criticized from the right after it was released.

If *Fly High, Run Far* did not draw as much attention as *The Taebaek Mountains* or *The Southern Army,* most likely this was because it dealt with a period more historically distant. At the time of its release in 1991, Im was chiefly known as the director of the very popular genre action film *The General's Son* (*Changgun ŭi adŭl*). Moreover, *Fly High, Run Far* was eclipsed by other popular films of the time, such as *Silver Stallion* (*Ŭnma nŭn oji anŭnda*, Chang Kil-su, 1991)— which portrays the suffering of a Korean woman during the Korean War—*Road to the Racetrack* (*Kyŏngmajang kanŭn kil*, Chang Sŏn-u, 1991)—which sarcastically rebukes Korean intellectuals—*Marriage Story* (*Kyŏlhon iyagi*, Kim ŭi-sŏk, 1992)—a romantic comedy of a "new generation" couple—and *Berlin Report* (*Berŭllin rip'ot'ŭ*, Park Kwang-su, 1991)—which critiques ideological conflict in the Korean peninsula allegorically, through the story of two Korean children, a boy and a girl, who are adopted by a French family, and so eventually brought face-to-face with European political tensions. Nevertheless, *Fly High, Run Far* does reaffirm Im's disdain for mass political struggle.

It is difficult to deny that the Tonghak War would not have taken place without the previous establishment of Tonghak as a religion. The religious principles of Tonghak—"Human beings equal heaven" and "a new world on earth"—were popularly translated as "economic and social equality" and "a new world with equal rights where no one starves." In light of these precepts, the historical Ch'oe Che-u and Ch'oe Si-hyŏng repeatedly warned their followers against precipitous use of Tonghak as a tool of real praxis to overcome hardship. In the film, this is shown through the conflict between Ch'oe Si-hyŏng and other group leaders, Yi P'il-je and Chŏn Pong-jun. Im's portrayal of this conflict asserts, in effect, that Yi P'il-je and Chŏn Pong-jun's revolutionary actions actually destroyed Tonghak and misdirected its principles. Im's decision to focus solely on the leadership to understand the formation of Tonghak thought prevented him from seeing that Tonghak was molded from many diverse voices. In fact, Tonghak was not given enough opportunity to establish its own body as a religion. Compared to Christianity, Buddhism and Confucianism—all of which were influential in Korean society in that period—Tonghak had much less time to establish its internal intellectual system or bridge the enormous gap between its ideal and the reality in which it found itself. It is probable that anonymous community leaders involved in local struggles played a crucial role in the rejection of Tonghak's idealism and its lack of immediate political impact.

However, Im's occasional misreading of history and his single-minded focus on the Tonghak leader do not nullify the overall significance of *Fly High, Run Far*. Tonghak was, after all, a religious mode of thought, and Im emphasized this central component. Yet if we treat Tonghak as a major stream within the context of modern secular thought or subsume it under nationalism, we can easily fall into the complementary error of overlooking its religious makeup. It is similarly inaccurate to think that Tonghak precepts were the sole ideological basis of the Tonghak War. Nonetheless, the question remains: What led Im to prefer Ch'oe Si-hyŏng's Tonghak rather than that of Chŏn Pong-jun (which was much more popular with the masses)? Im's claim that his choice was right cannot be justified any more than the obverse claim that only Chŏn Pong-jun's Tonghak was authentic. So why did Im choose Ch'oe Si-hyŏng's? He claims that he does not believe in any ideology and expresses contempt for all of them, yet he fails to recognize that he himself effectively chose an ideology when he promoted one aspect of Tonghak over another. In themselves, his hatred of ideology and his focus on the negative repercussions of its praxis in real life manifest an ideological bias.

## *Fly High, Run Far*'s Narrative and the Discourse of Paradox

The narrative structure of *Fly High, Run Far* comprises two main elements: the life of Ch'oe Si-hyŏng and the contemporary historical situation, though any account of Ch'oe Si-hyŏng's life cannot be separated from its historical context. Im portrays Ch'oe Si-hyŏng as an ordinary person, one who does not disdain menial chores and hard work. Ch'oe's wife also is no different from ordinary women who wish for a happy family and a normal life, but because she is married to a Tonghak leader, her family is fragmented. Not only is she separated from her children, she also has to learn to live with Ch'oe's concubine. While the drama of Ch'oe's life makes up the principal narrative, a subplot involves two police officers—a father and his son—who pursue Ch'oe across two generations. The father goes after him for the reward his capture will bring (he hopes this will compensate him for the financial loss he suffered through his attempt to bribe his way to promotion), but, ironically, he is mistaken for a Tonghak follower and killed. His son then pursues Ch'oe to avenge the father's death, though he finally surrenders to him. (These characters are reminiscent of the former policeman in *Pursuit of Death* who chases a partisan leader for years. Through the agency of such obsessive characters, Im has often been able to further highlight the principal characters who are opposed to them.)

Meanwhile, Ch'oe Si-hyŏng attempts to defend and extend Tonghak and lead it to a meaningful intervention in Korean history. In response to a question raised by an emeritus monk in Chŏkjoam Temple, he says, "The heaven is the spirit. The spirit includes yin and yang, which comprise the human. This human being is the subject of the world." He believes that humans will only become the true subjects of the world when society values them equally. His belief that heaven is everywhere informs the tolerance that encourages Ch'oe to forgive the officer who tried to kill him; from his perspective, even the assassin is part of heaven. The opportunities provided by Confucianism and Buddhism to guide humanity have proven so inadequate that now people no longer care for each other; another "opening up of a new world"—another *kaebyŏk*—is desperately needed. The axiom of Tonghak humanism that "human equals the heaven" offers another opening, articulating a new prospect for people and the world.

These are the ideals of Tonghak thought that Im so desperately wanted to announce to the world in *Fly High, Run Far*. Yet the project is paradoxical because the film portrays Ch'oe—both as a human being and as the leader of Tonghak—as a loser. Though Im presents him as a humble and respectable man who considers human beings as heaven, he fails to do full justice to the contradictions of the historical Ch'oe's life. For example, in the film, his jealous concubine prevents him from visiting his wife when she is seriously ill, and he is obliged to abandon his own children. In his public life, he approves an uprising even though he disagrees with it in principle, and at his death he has failed to gain much respect as a religious leader. In the film's final scene, his execution is witnessed by only a few followers, along with his wife and his concubine. Yet in actuality, Chŏn Pong-jun was popularly celebrated as a national hero and a champion of the peasants' cause. As a consequence of these historical and cinematic incongruities, *Fly High, Run Far*'s discourse becomes paradoxical. Im criticizes violence and the kind of blind faith in ideology that Ch'oe's life manifests, but his proposal that Tonghak humanism supplies an alternative or corrective appears to have no narrative justification.

Im's own favorite principle is that one should respect human values. Nevertheless, he shows his lack of confidence in mass political struggle by presenting Tonghak as a metaphor for the needs of contemporary Korea. After listening to Ch'oe speak on the principles of Tonghak, the old monk facing his death in Chŏkjoam states, "Tonghak is young and Buddhism in this land is old"—as if to imply that Tonghak is the only solution that can save people on earth. The historical Ch'oe had practical reasons for strongly opposing Chŏn Pong-jun's request to approve an uprising in 1894: He disapproved of the failed uprisings two years earlier, and he realized that the renewal of revolutionary violence would give Japan an excuse to invade. But, most importantly, he thought it was against the principles of Tonghak. However, in the film Ch'oe states that "A new world will not open up without changing the way we think and live." It is clear that Im is articulating his own thoughts here, using Ch'oe as his mouthpiece. But it is not clear what Im thinks of the historical Ch'oe's subsequent approval of the uprising despite the fact that he knew it would ultimately fail and claim many lives. Granted, it is not easy to discern Ch'oe's motives. Perhaps he heeded his followers' determination to rebel by interpreting it as "the mandate of the heaven." The principle of Taoism that "one should act in accordance with the movement of nature" must also be considered. Paradox is common in the discourse of Taoism, but it is believed to reflect the truth. In this case, the logical progress seems to be, "It is wrong, but we have to do it knowing that it is wrong; therefore, it is right." This is logic of a dimension beyond both Confucian ideology and Western rationalism. Other interpretations—perhaps more reasonable than this one—are also possible. For example, a central principle of Tonghak is to "serve people as heaven," and so when most of the people favor rebellion, it cannot be rejected. Additionally, if a leader does not grant the people's request, he would probably lose his position regardless of the results. But whatever the interpretation of the historical Ch'oe Si-hyŏng's attitude may be, Im maintains in the film that blind faith in any ideology is insupportable. It is not his objective to uncover historical truth or investigate the transformation Tonghak achieved in the turmoil of the years between 1864 and 1898. He seems to have begun the project with a categorical repudiation of any ideology and any praxis that claimed people's lives. Im's humanism is thus not much different from the Tonghak humanism of Ch'oe Che-u and Ch'oe Si-hyŏng: "Human being equals the heaven."

## Conclusion

Im has never been a right-winger or an anticommunist, and he has never advocated a social structure that values capital more than people—indeed, he has criticized societies, indirectly and metaphorically, that did so. (The films *Ticket* and *Sopyonje* best illustrate this point.) Im's intention in *Fly High, Run Far* was to send a sympathetic warning to the leftist movement, which was very active in Korea in the 1980s. He did not present an overtly negative view of the intellectuals and the young students who were struggling for democracy during this period. Instead he wanted to point out that no ideal thought can neglect the logic and praxis that people are the ultimate value. But at the time of the film's release, many Koreans regarded the attitude he expressed in *Fly High, Run Far* as reformist or defeatist. It probably is not surprising that he was misunderstood. His humanism might have been more positively received if he had also highlighted the hardships of the poor and those who work for social change, rather than placing all his emphasis on humanism. For despite his humanism, he was less than generous when it came to depicting the difficult challenges and pains endured by people who have idealistic agendas and practices.

## Notes

1. In preparing this essay, I relied on several books and articles for background information: Cho Tong-il, *Hanguk munhak sasangsa siron* (Essays on the history of Korean thoughts on literature) (Seoul: Chisiksanŏpsa, 1978); Pak Yŏng-suk, *Hanguk kodae misul munhwasa ron* (Essays on the history of ancient Korean art) (Seoul: Iljisa, 1976); Yi Hyoin, *Hanguk ŭi yŏnghwa kamdok 13–in* (13 Korean film directors) (Seoul: Yŏllin Ch'aektŭl, 1994); *1894–nyŏn nongmin chŏnjaeng yŏngu 3* (*A Study of the 1984 Peasant War, no. 3*), ed. Hanguk yŏksa yŏnguhoe (Association of Korean History Studies) (Seoul: Yŏksa pip'yŏngsa, 1993); and Yi Yi-hwa, "1894–nyŏn nongmin chonjaeng chidobu yŏngu" (A Study of leader groups in the 1894 Tonghak War), in *1894–nyŏn nongmin chŏnjaeng yŏngu 5* (A study of the 1984 Peasant War, no. 5), ed. Hanguk yŏksa yŏnguhoe (Seoul: Yŏksa pip'yŏngsa, 1996).

2. Roh Tae-woo (1988–93) was the last president who rose through the military ranks. Kim Young-sam (1993–97) was the first civilian president since 1961.

3. Originally developed as a philosophy that would protect Korea against Western learning (*sŏhak*), Ch'oe Che-u's movement became a popular instrument for promoting xenophobia and reform among the peasantry. See Bruce Cumings, *Korea's Place in the Sun: A Modern History* (New York: Norton, 1997), 115–20. *Trans.*

4. It would be difficult to claim that *silhak* was a new ideology in the nineteenth century, for as early as the seventeenth and eighteenth centuries it was already a powerful philosophical and political discourse advocating political and social change—albeit not always successfully. For a descriptive analysis of *silhak*, see Carter J. Eckert et al., *Korea Old and New: a History* (Seoul: Ilchokak, 1990), 164–71. A few *silhak* scholars continued to demand radical reforms and open-door policies throughout the nineteenth century, urging King Kojong to increase Korea's contact with the outside world. *Trans.*

5. U Yun, "Tonghak sasang ŭi chŏngch'i, sasang jŏk sŏnggyŏk" (The Political and ideological characteristics of Tonghak ideology), in *1894–nyŏn nongmin chŏnjaeng yŏngu 3*, 236.

6. The Tonghak Peasant War (1894–95) is of paramount importance in Korea's modern history. Led by Chŏn Pong-jun, who appears as a minor

character in *Kaebyŏk*, thousands of disgruntled peasants rebelled in Chŏlla Province, and before long the revolt spread to other regions. The rebels fought for modernization, and their demands included elimination of slave registers, fair taxation, and land redistribution. Unable to quell the uprising himself, King Kojong panicked and invited Japanese and Chinese troops into Korea. The rebellion was put down, but the foreign soldiers stayed, provoking the Sino-Japanese War in 1895 and the subsequent colonization of Korea from 1910–45. *Trans.*

7. Cited in Yi Hyoin, *Hanguk ŭi yŏnghwa kamdok 13-in,* 18–19.

*Kyung Hyun Kim*

CHAPTER 8

# Is This How the War Is Remembered?: Deceptive Sex and the Re-masculinized Nation in *The Taebaek Mountains*

In *Land of Exile* (*Yuhyŏng ŭi ttang*), a short story by Cho Chŏng-nae published in 1981, Mansŏk, the protagonist, has a secret he has been keeping for thirty years. This fragment of his past contains images that juxtapose passionate sex and bloody violence. Just the thought of these images, so haunting and still vivid, freezes him. He has drifted from one construction site to another for decades, and his memories are no longer reliable, but he still recalls the smell of prohibited sex that intoxicated and infuriated him when he stood as a voyeur at a scene of sexual intercourse between his wife and an initially unidentified man.

> Mansŏk almost cried out. He couldn't identify the man, whose buried face was turned away. But the one on her back, moaning, eyes tightly closed, mouth half open, was his very own Chŏmnye. . . . Arms crossed over her breasts, blanching with fear, she waddled to a corner of the room. Mansŏk, eyes blazing and teeth clenched, stepped closer to her. Cornered, unable to retreat further, the woman trembled, her nude body shriveling before his eyes.[1]

Mansŏk's fear quickly translates into uncontrollable rage when he rec-
ognizes the man as his commander in the northern People's Army into
which he had been recruited. He empties the chamber of a machine gun
into the couple. When he is through, the room has become "a sea of
blood where two sprawled corpses spewed forth their intestines." But
in killing the pair he has lost both the woman he loves and a man he
admires. Fearing a court martial, he immediately leaves his hometown
in Chŏlla Province.[2] Even after the war is over and the People's Army
has long since retreated, Mansŏk does not dare to return home. As a
former soldier of the Communist Party, he was responsible for order-
ing the executions of landlords. With the sons of the landlords now
back in power, he would surely face decapitation. Deprived of home
and ideology, both lost forever at the moment of irretrievable violence,
Mansŏk now spends his life on the road, where there is only hardship.
Because of that incident, Mansŏk also lost his masculinity: he became a
victim, never able to reclaim either his home or a salient fatherhood.[3]
For Mansŏk, this is how the war is remembered. The Korean War is
here reduced to a series of voyeuristic images, irrevocably articulated in
sexual terms.

This intricate webbing of sex and violence is a prominent phenomenon in contemporary films about the Korean War. For instance, in
both *Silver Stallion* (Ŭnma nŭn oji annŭnda, Chang Kil-su, 1991) and
*Spring in My Hometown* (Arŭmdaun sijŏl, Yi Kwang-mo, 1998), the prostitution of a mother to an American soldier instigates the violent revenge
of a son through whom the story is told. In this essay, I devote my attention to Im Kwon-Taek's *The Taebaek Mountains* (*T'aebaek sanmaek*,
1994), a film about the Korean War that also frames sex as a destructive
and deceptive element that induces broken homes, intensifies rivalries
between brothers, and reframes masculinity. Every sexual impulse in
the film ignites guilt and shame. The guilt is borne by women, however,
not men, and subsequently the matching of deceptive sex and senseless
violence affirms the phallocentric discourse. By amplifying the horror
of sex and denying pervasive desires, the film protests the contaminat-
ing process of women and the dislocation of families. In other words,
by focusing on abhorrent, illicit, and transgressive sexual encounters,
the film's crisis becomes the men's crisis, justifying the restoration of

"tradition" and order under a recharged masculinist identity. In *Dangerous Women* (1998), Chungmoo Choi writes that by disdaining local women who have become sexualized, the "Korean male is complicit with the colonizer."[4] The stark naked body of Chŏmnye, along with numerous representations of "shameful" women copulating with men other than their husbands, strikes an ignominious image that is so shameful only the women's deaths can mend the damage and restore the honor of men and of the nation.[5]

That *The Taebaek Mountains* is "new" in the historical context of Korean cinema may be beyond dispute, for it was one of the films that reengaged the Korean War, which had been nearly forgotten in Korean cinema. During the 1980s, cinematic depictions of the Korean War were scarce. Among the films that received critical and/or popular attention during that decade, only two feature scenes from the war: *That Winter So Warm* (*Kŭ hae kyŏul ŭn ttattŭthaetne,* Pae Ch'angho, 1984) and *Gilsottum* (Im Kwon-Taek, 1986). And even these films package the war as only memories, in flashbacks that pivotally dramatize melodramatic tensions in the featured families; there is no attempt to engage it ideologically. Of course, the vigilant censorship board then known as the Public Performance Ethics Committee discouraged any depiction of the war that failed to carry messages of anticommunism. *Seven Female Prisoners* (*7 in ŭi yŏp'oro,* Yi Man-hŭi, 1965), a Korean War film that for the first time attempted to depict soldiers of the People's Army humanely, was found to be in violation of the then-terrifying anticommunist law.[6] The arrest of its director, Yi Man-hŭi—one of the most popular filmmakers at that time—and the severe excising of the film ordered by the censorship committee made any future engagement with the Korean War outside the formulaic ideological circuit of anticommunism impossible, despite Yi's eventual release.[7]

In the 1990s, as the political mood began to shift toward liberalization, the Korean War became once again one of the most popular historical events on screen. *The Southern Army* (*Nambugun,* Chŏng Chi-yŏng, 1990) opened the floodgate of films that critically retraced Korea's modern history. If there was one element that distinguished the new Korean War films from the ones that dominated theaters in the 1960s, it was the erasure of North Koreans as enemies. Dichotomous depictions of the war that simplistically characterized all North Korean communists as villains and all South Korean nationalists as virtuous victors had long since become unfashionable. The New Korean Cinema reengaged the Korean War by focusing on the previously taboo subject of underground partisan guerrillas in the south. Chŏlla Province, a mountainous region known for intense local guerrilla activities during the Korean War, had been neglected in the popular culture for most of the postwar decades, but it became the primary setting for *The Southern Army, To the Starry Island* (*Kŭ sŏm e kagosipta*, Park Kwang-su, 1993), and *The Taebaek Mountains*.[8] This directed attention away from spectacular war images and toward internal conflicts within a community or a family, allowing the gender question to resurface in cinema. The films produced during the Golden Age of Korean cinema in the 1960s desperately sought to reconstruct Korea's masculinity that was devitalized when Korea's military sovereignty (along with its cultural subjectivity) was relinquished to the U.S. upon the outbreak of the Korean War in 1950.[9] In the 1990s, realistic representations of men who lost their virility and authority during the war proliferated.

The films of the 1990s distinguished themselves by demythologizing the heroes. Nothing could better embody the image of an emasculated man than some of the main characters in the Korean War films from this period. For instance, the final image of *The Southern Army* is of Yi T'ae (played by An Sŏng-gi), a socialist guerilla ostracized by his platoon. Standing outdoors in the bitter cold, he holds a rifle to his chin, contemplating suicide. The humble image of Old Hwang in *Silver Stallion*, a feudal aristocrat who is embarrassed not only by American soldiers but also by local prostitutes who dare to use vulgar profanities against him, is also a memorable imprint of the war. As male authority dissipates, women too are consistently victimized, brutalized, and betrayed.

I argue in this essay that even as these new Korean War films display gender identities that are more complicated and less auspicious than the ones from films of the 1960s, they still project a nationalist agenda that imagines a salient form of masculinist identity. *The Taebaek Mountains* is no exception. Here Im holds firm to the hope that the nation will overcome the chaos of the war, which has contaminated the Korean landscape with artillery pockmarks and Korean women with scars of sexual rape in the process of achieving a patched up patriarchal system. By featuring lurid images of naked women as well as the patricidal and sadistic actions of violent men, Im Kwon-Taek—along with other directors of Korean War films—proposes that the father's absence and/or futility has allowed the women's transgressions. Like his other films that so brilliantly dramatize the perverted narrative of the nation by depicting a repressed and dysfunctional family (one need look no further than *Sopyonje*), *The Taebaek Mountains* effectively re-inscribes and legitimizes the need to restore patriarchal authority.

Not only do the Korean War films of the 1990s—*The Southern Army, Silver Stallion, To the Starry Island, The Taebaek Mountains,* and *Spring in My Hometown*—represent the nation's crisis through the characterization of traumatized males, they also revise the dominant historiography of the Korean War by focusing on internal conflicts. The overriding official view in South Korea placed strong emphasis on June 25th, 1950, as the onset of the war—the day North Korea staged a surprise attack along the thirty-eighth parallel, thus violating the international treaty then acceded to. By contrast, these films emphasize the tensions among the local populace in South Korea. As Kim Pŏm-u, the protagonist of *The Taebaek Mountains,* asserts, the concentration of land ownership in the hands of a few landlords who had collaborated with the Japanese was one of the principle causes of the war. Representations of the North Korean People's Army are generally absent from these films. Instead the focus shifts to the southern region, where dramatic tension is promulgated between a feudal patriarch and a subaltern woman (*Silver Stallion*), between a nationalist army camouflaged as communists and innocent villagers who are branded as "commie-sympathizers" (*To the Starry Island*), or between two brothers with competing ideological persuasions (*The Taebaek Mountains*). Also absent are heroic images of the war: the arms of a marine reaching desperately out from a trench to rescue his wounded comrade, handsome faces of South Korean pilots in red scarves who risk their lives to carry out dangerous missions, and vicious and raw expressions on the faces of North Korean soldiers who are motivated by nothing more than killer instincts. Indeed, in *To the Starry Island,* when soldiers who represent themselves as communists are unmasked, they prove to be South Korean soldiers who deceived the naive southern villagers in order to induce them to identify themselves as communists before they were massacred. Such films inscribe a new meaning of the war, blurring distinctions between the "enemy"—merciless communist soldiers—and "us"—South Korean men of distinguished valor. Korean cinema had finally accepted that the list of blame for the war was indeed—as Bruce Cumings puts it—"multiple" and "long," and that it included Japanese, Americans, Soviets, and Koreans themselves.[10]

Im Kwon-Taek's *The Taebaek Mountains* attempts to locate the origins of the war in the 1948 Yŏsu-Sunch'ŏn Rebellion, staged two years before the war's overt outbreak.[11] Himself born and raised in a leftist family in Chŏlla Province, Im finally had a chance in the mid-1990s to create a more detailed picture of the liberation period (1945–50), a time marked by intense ideological struggles. Im wanted to make this film immediately after the novel on which it is based became a bestseller in the late 1980s, but he had to wait until the inauguration of a post-military government before beginning work on this project.[12] Probably no film director was in a better position than Im to adapt Cho Chŏng-nae's epic novel. Aside from having grown up in Chŏlla, Im was capable of raising the enormous production budget required for an epic, and he shared the nationalist and humanist vision Cho proffers in the novel. Moreover, by the 1990s, he was the only active director who had lived through the war years. Although some of Im's earlier efforts—*The Hidden Hero* (*Kippal ŏmnŭn kisu*, 1979) and *Pursuit of Death* (*Tchakk'o*, 1980), for example—focus on the lasting impact of ideological conflict, *The Taebaek Mountains* is the film that allowed him to rethink the origins of a conflict that haunted him for decades. After the enormous box-office success of *Sopyonje* the year before, he had a greater measure of financial freedom than he had ever had before. His budget to recreate this historical epic represented, at the time, the most money ever spent on a Korean film.[13] Although times had changed, Im's central themes had not. Once again he placed much emphasis on the difficulties of maintaining liberal humanism and searching for a corresponding national identity.

FIGURE 8.1.
*The Taebaek Mountains:* Kim Pŏm-u, center, represents the nation's hopes.
On the left, Yŏm Sang-jin, the socialist guerilla and on the right, his brother,
a violent rightist

Certainly *The Taebaek Mountains* represents Korean cinema's re-
newed interest in questioning the past, but perhaps its most salient
feature is its stylish reprisal of a hackneyed convention of melodrama
to motivate the story.[14] The film's principal characters find themselves
caught up in personal, internal, and ideological conflicts in the period
from 1948 to 1950—the three critical years that preceded full-blown war.
While Yŏm Sang-jin is a highly educated guerilla commander in the
communist "partisan" army encamped in the mountains, his younger

brother Sang-gu is a vulgar right-wing leader of the local Anticommunist Youth League in their home village of Pŏlgyo, collaborating with the police to quell the local socialist insurgency. Not uncommonly for the time, the seeds of family conflict have already been sowed.[15] Sang-gu is repressively brutal, and by unleashing violence against communist families he intends to emerge from the shadow cast by his older and more intelligent brother. This surely exploits the familiar convention in which the younger brother, the bad son, becomes irrationally violent in his attempts to dispel the pressures imposed by the specter of an older brother who excels in every aspect of life. Usually in this melodramatic narrative structure, the immoral or useless son is ultimately redeemed or eliminated. Yet unlike, for example, the Robert Stack character in *Written on the Wind* (Douglas Sirk, 1956), who is accidentally killed by the character played by Rock Hudson—a friend who is like a brother to him—Sang-gu remains alive, though Sang-jin confronts him with a pistol at the end of the film and would be justified in killing him, for he is a brutal rapist and a murderer. Instead the two brothers fight, allegorizing the present-day divided Korea, where antagonists quarrel with each other without actually pulling the trigger.[16]

Despite their ideological differences, the brothers share a measure of common ground through their nationalist friend Kim Pŏm-u. Kim is the son of a landlord, but he is also an intellectual, and he maintains his moderate ideological position in the face of terrorist and coercive tactics designed to induce him to join either the rightists or the leftists. At the end of the film, the two brothers are forced to leave Pŏlgyo, but Kim remains firmly tied to his homeland. The stories of these three characters are deftly woven into Korea's turbulent history. Ideological impulses, in the form of communism, nationalism, and reactionary terror, break down the harmony of this small town. Distrust and inhumanity are all that survive in this lifeless place, where the only public gatherings are guilt-ridden, anticommunist marches. Traditional divisions between the peasantry and landowners, between male and female, and between domestic space and the public domain are continually in flux, instilling fear and anxiety in the town.

Im accentuated the perception of fear by shooting many scenes at night. Night and day are visually juxtaposed as radically different from each other, yet they are also inseparable. The significance of nighttime dramatically changes the temporal order of the farming community, which normally functions only in daylight. Night has become so transgressive and disorderly that a curfew is declared, prohibiting people from going outside after sunset. Yet both socialist guerillas and right-wing terrorists defy this ban. Although ideologically disparate, their daily schedules are similar, for their clandestine activities are most effective at night. Civilians are rounded up by the rightist youth guards at night, tortured in darkness, and killed. When the terrorists are not "at work," they either drink or play cards in their dark quarters. Taking advantage of the rightists' enjoyment of their nocturnal leisure, the partisan guerrillas make surprise attacks, rob villages, and establish espionage contacts once night has fallen. In one sequence, the radical shift between day and night is profoundly articulated. Sang-jin's army takes over a village near Pŏlgyo each night, but when the nationalist army retakes control of the village after sunrise, the people who collaborated the previous evening are rounded up and punished. And the villagers who terrorized people by randomly sending some of them off to their deaths during the day are killed as soon as the day has ended and the socialists return. The village, eventually inhabited only by women, children, and the elderly, is burned to the ground, forcing the villagers to leave. The constant exchange of power—Pŏlgyo itself is taken over by socialists twice in the film—disrupts order and ethics, endangers people's lives, and fragments homes. Nighttime activity not only produces indiscriminate killings, it also, as I will argue, promulgates multiple instances of disorderly sex that crucially underscore the central themes of the film.

In *The Taebaek Mountains,* the alternating takeovers of public space by socialists and nationalists inevitably affects domestic space, for it is no longer immune from brutality and violation. Homi K. Bhabha's concept of "unhomely" can perhaps provide a useful theoretical intervention here. As explained by Bhabha, this awkward word connotes a postcolonial, transnational identity; it captures the "estranging sense of the relocation of the home and the world in an unhallowed place."[17] "Unhomely" does not signify homelessness but rather an uncanny feeling, vacillating between familiarity and unfamiliarity—even when one is "at home"—because the world has been so rapidly transformed. Here I use

FIGURE 8.2.
*The Taebaek Mountains:* At night time, socialist guerillas rule. . . .

the term slightly differently from the way it was originally intended—
deducting the "transnational" component Bhabha emphasized—and
employ it to depict the unstable subjectivity produced in *The Taebaek
Mountains* that both belongs in a home and is dislocated from it. The
"home" is now permanently associated with a sense of eeriness and
blessedness. The discursive maneuvers of power dislocate and differently
configure many preexisting hegemonic paradigms. Transgressive sex,
which proliferates when many homes suffer from patriarchal absence,
unravels the threads that bind people together. In the film, "unhomely"
becomes a contagious "disease," which contaminates the entire village
through psychological ruptures and which is transmitted through sexual
acts that are hardly the norm.

As I mentioned briefly above, by foregrounding two brothers in
direct conflict with each other, *The Taebaek Mountains* institutional-
izes its thematic foundation on classic sibling animosity. The acrimony
between the two is precipitated by the older brother's success and by

FIGURE 8.3
*The Taebaek Mountains* . . . But during the day, their sympathizers are shot

the younger brother's jealousy and patricidal urges. Sang-gu feels that his older brother consumed all of their mother's love and then ignored him. (Even Sang-jin acknowledges, when his brother is appointed to an important right-wing post, that he had seriously underestimated Sang-gu's abilities.) Sang-gu, on the day he receives word of his appointment as the new captain of the local youth league, comes home drunk. He proudly brags to his mother that he is no longer inferior to his high-ranking brother on the other side of the conflict. Seeing Sang-gu in a good mood, the mother requests his permission to send some rice to Sang-jin's starving family. The mood changes abruptly. Sang-gu flatly refuses his mother's plea, and, in a rage, he reveals the real reason for his hatred of socialism: Sang-gu, who constantly refers to his brother only as "*ppalgaengi*" (commie) or "*kaejasik*" (son of a bitch), announces to his mother that had his brother been a rightist, he himself would have become a *ppalgaengi*. This clearly demonstrates that his engagement with anticommunism is motivated not by a firm belief in right-wing

causes but by deep-rooted hatred for his brother. Sang-gu laments the
fact that the family was able to sponsor only one son's formal education
throughout college, forcing him to drop out of elementary school. In
effect, both his right-wing cause and his brother's leftist sympathies
spring from the same source: their family's poverty.

Several critical sequences clarify the strategy by which Im Kwon-
Taek articulates the dangers of contracting the "unhomely"—which
ultimately destroys home, community, and nation. After the Yŏsu-
Sunch'ŏn Rebellion is quelled, a new "sheriff" arrives in Pŏlgyo to put
down the communist insurgency. Lim—the captain of the military forces
newly dispatched to the region to minimize the impact of the communist
guerrillas and reinstitute social order after the rebellion—is dissatisfied
with the efforts of the local police. The red-baiting search begins once
again; the community is terrorized, and communist sympathizers are
executed without benefit of trial. Lim declares that "all the villagers who
stayed in town [during the brief socialist takeover] are communists." He
goes on to demand that reluctant local officials "gather all the residents
at the schoolyard" after sunset.

Lim's intrusiveness is heavily accentuated. He clearly speaks in an
"extra-territorial" accent, a northern Korean dialect that is particularly
distinctive in this southern village. As we later find out, he had also
been personally victimized: his house in North Korea was destroyed,
and his landlord parents were executed after the communists found
them guilty of treason. His *official* disdain for the left-wing, which
is firmly rooted in a *personal* vendetta against communism, further
implodes the boundary between public and private in the village—a
boundary that was already imperiled even before Lim's arrival there.
This outside threat to Pŏlgyo not only radically widens the rift between
leftists and rightists, it also creates tension within the nationalist camp—
among politicians, landlords, military officers, and police. Lim's seizure
of power and his assumption of local authority allow his "unhomely" to
proliferate throughout the town. The intrusion of Lim as a ruthless
force, disrupting and reorganizing the local power structure, is also
framed in a melodramatic convention: Lim bickers constantly with
the local police chief, whose obesity and comic gestures excessively
underscore the ineffectiveness of the local tyrant.

The anger and anxiety induced by Lim's loss of his parents affect the lives of people in Pŏlgyo. Though its origin is hundreds of miles away, Lim's "unhomeliness" works its way into Pŏlgyo throughout the next three sequences, wielding an incredible impact on the local populace. After Lim's official orders are disseminated, many villagers are rounded up in the schoolyard. In the darkness, a flashlight indiscriminately surveys the crowd, rehearsing the "finger-pointing" schema to find out who is to live and who is to die. The selection of the communist sympathizers here clearly has no legal or rational basis. The desperate outburst of a woman whose voice rings out in the dark—"It's her. She is the one who informed on my husband. . . . My husband was killed because of you"—becomes sufficient reason to create yet another victim. By contrast, Sang-gu allows a woman named Oesŏdaek to live simply because he finds her attractive—despite the fact that since her husband Kang Tong-gi is a socialist leader it would have been justifiable to have her shot.

The shift between public and private continues in each subsequent scene, where the sadistic pleasures of sex and violence underpin the tensions of the film. In the next episode, which takes place in an interrogation room at police headquarters, Chuksandaek, the wife of the socialist Sang-jin, answers Lim's questions. Lim does not seem to be concerned with the whereabouts of Sang-jin; instead he accuses Chuksandaek of being a "commie sympathizer." When Lim suggests that she should have discouraged her husband from engaging in socialist activities and encouraged him to focus on feeding his family, she boldly corrects the fearsome captain. "Let's get this straight," she asserts. "It is because of hunger that people become communists; it is not because they are communists that people go hungry." Lim physically attacks Chuksandaek, and she retaliates by biting his ear.[18] Here the film concedes that Korea's national historiography of underdevelopment and poverty during the colonial and postcolonial phase has inevitably found an ally in socialist politics. But one should also note that Chuksandaek's resistance is motivated not by a desire to defend her communist agenda but by her courageous protection of her husband's public ideology and her private body against Lim's threat. Her stance ensures that her sexuality is unexposed, allowing her to achieve honorable purity and thereby immunity from criticism. By comparison, as we will see, Oesŏdaek's "failure" to ward off Sang-gu can be rectified only by her suicide.

*The Taebaek Mountains* depicts a period—the late 1940s—when sex was rigidly circumscribed, yet in the film, ideology intervenes and makes sex pervasive and excessive. There are three crucial scenes of sexual intercourse, and all of them—even when they are physical expressions of love and desire—lead to violence and death. One rape scene quickly follows the interrogation episode. Oesŏdaek, asleep at home, is rudely awakened by Sang-gu, who insists that she repay him now for her freedom. At nighttime, violent rape takes place, and the "unhomely," which entered the village with the arrival of Lim, now continues its circuitous "intercourse," invading the female body. In the scar tissue of Sang-gu's poverty and inferiority complex, the "unhomely" virus finds a vulnerable and penetrable host, transforming him into a carrier who disseminates the virus and contaminates the village. Sang-gu's patricidal feelings toward his older brother are transferred into misogynistic

FIGURE 8.4.
*The Taebaek Mountains:* Chuksandaek bravely resists Captain Lim's terror

violence directed against women whose husbands are absent. He rapes and tortures women of leftist affiliation to fulfill his job description as a right-wing youth guard.

Ideological instability, oedipal anxiety, and sadistic violence all undergird the troubles of a nation where homes are psychologically and ideologically fractured. Sang-jin's family and Sang-gu's family are already split into two houses—unusual given that nuclear families were not yet standard—and only their mother can cross the ideological boundaries between the two houses. (Since the father is dead, it is the mother, the affectionate and benevolent one, who delivers food from one house to another and hides Sang-gu when Sang-jin returns from the mountains after the socialist takeover.) Confucian unity or harmony is now gravely threatened. Because "home" can no longer be conceived of as a coherent whole, Sang-gu seeks other means of self-fulfillment. He literally invades another broken home, which is already suffering from the absence of the father. By raping Oesŏdaek—whose husband Kang Tong-gi has joined Sang-jin in the mountains—and forcibly taking her on as his mistress, Sang-gu accomplishes two things. First, when he assumes the role of surrogate husband in a socialist home, he gets revenge on his brother and tries to sexually compensate for the phallic absence created by both Kang and Sang-jin. Second, he transfers the profane "virus" of the "unhomely" to another household already tormented by a family's disruption.[19] We remember that this all began with Lim's intrusion and his order to gather up all the villagers. The psychological anxiety that frustrates Kang's masculinity (a condition that also afflicts Sang-gu) compounds with the external ideological factor, exacerbating the village's instability.

Oesŏdaek's "contaminated" body is now incompatible with her "pure" spirit, and in the end her only alternative is death. Later, when rumors of Oesŏdaek "sleeping with the enemy" has spread to the mountains, Kang forsakes his duty and travels to his home in Pŏlgyo. There he finds the naked Sang-gu, who has usurped his position next to his wife, and Kang fires at him—a clear violation of the code of undercover guerrillas, who must remain anonymous and silent. Once again, transgressive sex and deceptive gaze—not unlike the predicament of Mansŏk discussed at the beginning of this essay—lead to violence and death, though Sang-gu is not killed. But once the vision of her illicit sex is exposed to her husband, Oesŏdaek can no longer live. Later, after the People's Army's occupation of the village, and when the return of her socialist husband from the mountains is immanent, she commits suicide. Sex cannot be confined to the private realm. It has translated into discourses of power, primarily enacted and inscribed in a woman's body—once again the ventriloquist site of fiercely contested ideological warfare.

Im's treatment of sex in *The Taebaek Mountains* is extraordinary. Sex is central to the narrative, for it moves the plot, complicates relationship between characters, and heightens ideological tension. Another sexually explicit scene involves Ha Tae-ch'i, a loyal leftist soldier and a former resident of Pŏlgyo. His house, ironically situated next to Kang's, has already been ravaged by Youth League terrorists. In a scene where Sang-gu rapes Oesŏdaek once again, we hear a woman screaming from outside, and there are loud noises of household items being broken. Next door, Sang-gu's subordinates are destroying Ha's house, wife, and children. Both Oesŏdaek and Ha's wife pay heavy prices for their husbands' ideology; their bodies are punished and their homes "unhomed."

Now it is Ha's turn to spread the "unhomely." Camouflaged as a merchant selling wood, he travels to a commercial town, where he initiates contact with a widowed tavern-keeper, Market Lady, who welcomes him. Ha is following an official order from his guerrilla army to use the woman as a spy to get medicine needed by his comrades, and the Market Lady seeks the phallic replacement of her absent husband. Their different agendas complicate their sexual relations. In a sexually explicit sequence, Ha's loyalty to the party is perversely projected as his entire body repeatedly moves up and down, in perfect rhythm with the woman's pleasurable moans from below. Afterward, exhausted from his "labor," Ha finds blood dripping from his nose. The Market Lady tells him: "You are now responsible for lighting me up. Never will I let you go."

Several significant issues are raised here. First, the newly established romantic relationship between Ha and the Market Lady replaces Ha's real family in Pŏlgyo, which has already been ravaged and exiled. Second, women, not men, shoulder the guilt for sexual transgression. A comparison of this relationship with the one forcibly forged between Sang-gu and Oesŏdaek illuminates this point. Although Oesŏdaek has no choice but to sleep with the brutal right-wing leader, she feels such guilt and pain that she must kill herself. By contrast, even though his wife's misfortunes are directly related to his socialism, Ha displays no guilt when he begins his new romantic relationship with the Market Lady. Ironically, the Market Lady shows more sympathy toward Ha's family than he does; at one point she tells him that she has tried to find Oesŏdaek and give her some money. Third, transgressive sex and desire always produce a female victim. Even the Market Lady pays a price for seeking sexual pleasure and replacing her absent husband. The police arrest her, and she is freed only when she agrees to become a double agent, collaborating with the police and betraying Ha and the socialists. There are neither "white men" nor "brown men"—Gayatri Chakravorty Spivak's sarcastic description of people who compete to save "brown women"—to rescue the Market Lady.[20] She is a femme fatale—promiscuous and dangerous—who cannot be left alive in this phallocentric universe. After the town is liberated by the socialists, she is seized as a spy—and shot to death by none other than Ha Tae-ch'i himself. Ha offers her a brief apology but he doesn't hesitate to pull the trigger, punishing her for a crime that originated with her first embrace of him and his "unhomely." *The Taebaek Mountains* demonstrates that ideology intrudes into people's homes, showing the erosion of boundaries between public and private spaces, and the division of the village into at least two distinct ideological terrains inseparable from each other.

A different kind of relationship than those discussed above is the one that exists between Ha-sŏp, an intellectual and an undercover agent for the guerrillas, and So-hwa, a shaman's daughter who is sympathetic to socialism. Unlike the other sexual relationships, the one between Ha-sŏp and So-hwa is genuinely romantic. Yet it is also clandestine. The pair cannot take a public stroll together, and Ha-sŏp can only visit So-hwa surreptitiously, in the course of "official" business trips in which he engages her to deliver messages to his wealthy parents. So-hwa, born after her father died and thus a marginal figure in the village, has long been a secret admirer of Ha-sŏp. He surely exploits her love and trust to advance his own ends, but he is also a socialist, free of class biases, and he sincerely loves her. They have widely divergent views of shamanism, however, and this leads to protracted debates between them. Despite So-hwa's insistence that her belief is real, Ha-sŏp claims that it is bogus; indeed, he tells her that as the future wife of a socialist cadre member she should abandon "poisonous" religious myth. As if to confirm her belief that there is a world beyond rigid Marxist historical determinism, she becomes unexpectedly pregnant with Ha-sŏp's child.

Yet two people forestall the relationship between the two from becoming a "productive" one: Sang-gu and Ha-sŏp's mother. Right-wing violence—exercised by Sang-gu—literally aborts the child carried by So-hwa, and the feudal order of rigid class distinction—insisted upon by Ha-sŏp's mother—blocks any possibility of their marriage. Suspicious of So-hwa's frequent visits to Ha-sŏp's parents, Sang-gu tortures her, extracting evidence of espionage and collaboration—that is, serving as an agent for the transferral of funds from Ha-sŏp's parents to the socialist cause. When Sang-gu kicks So-hwa's gut as he tortures her, Sohwa miscarries her child. While she is hospitalized following the miscarriage, So-hwa receives a visit from Ha-sŏp's mother. Though initially sympathetic, the mother finally tells So-hwa, "I heard that you were pregnant with Ha-sŏp's child. Not many people know what has happened. . . . Ha-sŏp must also never know. . . . As you know very well, you could never marry him. That could never happen. So, you must forget about him. I am sorry about what has happened, but do not blame me for it." As Ha-sŏp's mother makes these unabashed statements, the camera lingers on So-hwa's face in a medium close-up. She never opens her mouth, but through her silence we understand her pain as a subaltern woman who is not sure whether her miscarriage is a relief (at the loss of a child who was destined to be a bastard and thus marginalized, not unlike herself) or a source of grief. This particular loss serves fair warning that right-wing terrorists will root out any "impregnation" by socialism. And the mother's demand that she stay silent about the child of course signifies that feudal power will ensure that such a "mistake" between a *yangban* (aristocrat) son and a *ch'ŏnmin* (low-class) shaman will not even be whispered about in public. All the sexual transactions explicitly visualized in the film—the one between Oesŏdaek and Sang-gu, the one between Ha and the Market Lady, and the one between

So-hwa and Ha-sŏp—produce death, demonstrating the impossibility of climbing out from under the weight of ideological loyalty, rigid class structure, and political terror.

How does a feudal leader respond to sex that is becoming more dangerous and rampant? One community leader in *The Taebaek Mountains,* Kim Pŏm-u's landlord father, like Old Hwang in *Silver Stallion,* no longer possesses the authority he once had, for tenant farmers are increasingly challenging traditional ethics and systems. However, in a departure from the structure of *Silver Stallion, The Taebaek Mountains* develops and strengthens the role of the landlord's son. Kim Pŏm-u emerges as a young man who insists on wielding power himself. As both a liberal, intellectual nationalist and a landowner, Kim Pŏu refuses to be drawn into the crisis that threatens the nation's phallic presence. No melodramatic tension erupts in Kim Pŏm-u's house; he is a filial son, willing to negotiate between the rioting tenants and his sick father. He quickly fills the power vacuum created by his father's illness. Through this episode, Im Kwon-Taek cautions that oedipal anxieties and precipitous challenges to the feudal patriarchal order produce only senseless violence. And he demonstrates that national order must be restored by people like Kim Pŏm-u, the young liberal son of a nationalist landlord, and a man who is neither rebellious nor anxious.

Im dramatizes two versions of family in *The Taebaek Mountains:* one that suffers from the absence of the father and another that benefits from stable patrilineal heritage. A reverse image of the house of Sang-gu and Sang-jin, which lacks a father and is dependent on the mother, Kim Pŏm-u's house is without a matriarch. While Sang-gu's patricidal feelings toward Sang-jin, his surrogate father figure—at one point in the film, Sang-gu declares that he will be much better off when his brother is dead—unleash right-wing terrorism and sadistic rape in a fractured home, Kim Pŏm-u's house produces hope for the nation's future. In the opening scenes of the film, when the guerillas taking part in the Yŏsu-Sunch'ŏn Rebellion briefly control Pŏlgyo, Kim Pŏm-u's father is tried in the people's court on charges of being a landlord. Although it appears he will be executed Sang-jin spares his life by recalling that he was a patriotic landlord who was fair to his tenants. The elder Kim's life may be saved, but as Kim Pŏm-u later acknowledges, the humiliating

proceedings kill his spirit. From this point on, the elder Kim is bed-
ridden, and he becomes increasingly decrepit and voiceless. His son
develops as a leader, negotiating with the tenants, attending business
meetings with other community overseers, and making crucial decisions
about land distribution. Even though he comes from the landowner
class, Kim Pŏm-u refuses to support right-wing causes, nor does his
friendship with Sang-jin lead him to become a left-wing subscriber. The
film depicts a period in which people were forced to choose between
two radical politics, yet Kim Pŏm-u offers an alternative. The two
households frame two dramatically different pictures, not so much along
the axis of ideology but rather along the lines of family stability. Kim
Pŏm-u's choice of liberal nationalism makes him a tempting target for
political repression by both rightists and leftists, yet he remains above
the psychological traumas that torment and fragment Sang-jin's house.
Maintaining a filial relationship with his ailing father also reaffirms Kim
Pŏm-u's position as the de facto leader of the village, even though he
possesses neither Sang-jin's military authority nor Sang-gu's terrorist
power. He knows that eventually history will be on his side, as long
as he can hold firm to the tenets of humanism and nationalism. Im's
portrait of Kim confirms once again the agenda of a nation that must
re-masculinize under the ideologies of liberal democracy, while avoiding
self-destruction.

The Taebaek Mountains anchors one of the important national
transformations Im sought during the 1990s. In the 1980s, his sensitive treatment of women's issues helped earn him the reputation of
international auteur, yet in the ensuing decade his films concentrated
on masculine crises and tensions. Starting with the popular three-part
series The General's Son (Changgun ŭi adŭl, 1990–92) series, he continued to frame history through male protagonists in Fly High, Run Far
(Kaebyok, 1991) and Sopyonje (1993). The Taebaek Mountains remains
within this trajectory. One of the most significant cruxes in the film is
not that women are simply contingent to the plotline that foregrounds
three male characters—Kim Pŏm-u, Sang-gu, and Sang-jin—but that
they are consistently sexually victimized without being given a chance
to speak or act for themselves.

Among Im's films, Gilsottum (1985) perhaps best demonstrates Im's sensitivity toward gender issues. Framing the war from a contemporary perspective, *Gilsottum* foregrounds Hwa-yŏng, a woman in her fifties who is comfortably settled in her upper-middle-class life, with a loving husband and two teenage kids. Almost by accident, she runs into her former husband, Tong-jin, whom she thought had died during the war. Over thirty years have passed since their last meeting, and Hwa-yŏng's present life contrasts sharply with Tong-jin's. He has had a difficult life as a worker. His present wife is blind, his three grown sons are blue-collar workers (he has two younger sons who are still in middle and high school), and he has incurred a fatal disease as the result of a lingering war wound. All of this separates him from Hwa-yŏng, who is elegantly dressed and drives a sedan—at a time when automobiles were still a luxury.

Despite their differences, however, they try to mend their fractured pasts because they have a common goal: to find the son they lost thirty years earlier. Aided by the Korean Broadcasting System's campaign to

FIGURE 8.5
*Gilsottum:* Hwa-yŏng refuses to recognize her son

reunite families separated during the war, they succeed in relocating their son. However, he is a miserable and vulgar man, a drunken butcher and a wife-beater. Indeed, his status is even lower than Tong-jin's. Deeply disappointed at the outcome of their search, Hwayŏng refuses to accept this man as her son, despite convincing scientific evidence that he is. She decides to return to her home in Pusan and forget that she ever lived in this place, which has been devastated by the war. In the film's final scene, Hwa-yŏng stops her car in the middle of a country road, unable either to proceed forward or turn around. Torn between past and present, Hwa-yŏng finds no room for negotiation, and she decides not to look back. This ambiguous ending is perhaps the finest, antisentimental treatment of emotional material Im has achieved. The film presents a realistic portrait of a woman; she is neither a caricature nor an appendage to the male characters.

Unlike *Gilsottum*, which employs a woman's dilemma as the central narrative element that affects the entire story and influences other character's actions—even at the expense of rejecting the recuperation of family—*The Taebaek Mountains* imagines a nation guided by phallocentric liberalism, where the harmonious, traditional universe of the prewar period can be restored. The film ends with Kim Pŏm-u and So-hwa talking to each other for the first time since her miscarriage, in the midst of mayhem as the communists retreat from Pŏlgyo once more—this time from the Americans, who have entered the war. The destruction cannot be contained, even by Sang-jin, whose specific orders not to harm civilians are ignored. As buildings burn, people are massacred, and women ravaged, Kim Pŏm-u and So-hwa fall outside the film's critique. The only "non-ideological" characters, they are also the only ones who are still able to talk, for everyone else's voices have lost legitimacy. Their humanitarian and "pure" intentions draft a sacred property of *minjok* (nation), proposing the present-day hopes for a new Korea in search of an uncontaminated past. What is interesting here is that *minjok* is synonymous with the kind of liberalism that must set itself free from socialist agency. So-hwa performs a *gut* (shamanistic ritual) at the end, comforting the souls of the newly deceased Oesŏdaek and her husband Kang, who had requested this service. So-hwa's ritual also reminds us of her grief over her aborted child. By mourning death, life will be remembered and celebrated. Yet unfortunately life privileges the "pre-ideological" past where, the film has conveniently forgotten, landlords ruled and tenants suffered, men talked and women were silenced, fathers disciplined and children were punished.

Together So-hwa and Kim Pŏm-u provide final images unlike the prototypical endings of other Korean War films such as *Silver Stallion* and *Spring in My Hometown,* which depict the forced migration of their principal characters. Kim Pŏm-u and So-hwa have no reason to migrate or de-territorialize. As everyone else rushes madly through the fiery streets of the village, he watches serenely as she attempts to heal wounded souls. Kim Pŏm-u admits to So-hwa, who has just finished an all-night performance of *gut,* that he was impressed by her performance of the ritual. But he asks how she can "spend so much energy on dead people when so many people alive are suffering?" So-hwa replies that *gut* is for the living and for their *han.* Here, with his ultimate focus on the two characters of nationalist and native heritages instead of on Sang-jin and Sang-gu, Im implies optimism. The "unhomely" conjured up throughout history may not be completely resolved even through ritualistic practice, but there remains hope for life as long as humans are not completely annihilated. What is important here is that life is valued and celebrated through the remembrance of the dead. Recall that one of the deaths So-hwa mourns is that of Oesŏdaek, a victim left unprotected by her socialist husband and then ravaged by a disturbed right-winger. Having slept with both a leftist and a rightist, she suffers a fate not unlike her nation's, which has similarly fallen prey to two competing ideologies. Ironically, only self-destruction can salvage the significance of her life. Her fate parallels that of her country, which, having "slept" with both America and Russia, underwent a devastating civil war that produced mass self-destruction.

In Rey Chow's analysis of the Chinese Fifth Generation film *To Live* (Zhang Yimou, 1994), she states that "the imperative 'to live' through endurance becomes what *essentially* defines and perpetuates 'China' " (her emphasis).[21] What is remarkable is that both endurance and survival are identified as the foundational discourses of China. As does *The Taebaek Mountains, To Live* reframes its public history from the viewpoint of a private family and depicts exigent individual sufferings through the contours of radical national history. Despite the loss of his wealth, his daughter, his son, and his treasured timber puppets to the turmoils of the Chinese Civil War, the "Great Leap Forward," and the Cultural Revolution, Fu Gui—*To Live*'s principal character—remains optimistic to the end. Despite humiliation and tragic losses, it only matters that Fu Gui still lives. The box in which he used to store his puppets now contains little chicks he has purchased for his grandson. As noted by Chow, the empty box symbolizes "tradition," which "continues to live nonetheless by supporting new life—both the grandson and his chicks."[22] In *The Taebaek Mountains*, the "tradition" rendered through *gut* is an emblem that contains life through the remembrance of death. The tension between the left-wing and the right-wing remains unresolved in the Korean film, much like the present national status of Korea—which is still constrained by such archaic notions as "the communist north" and "the anticommunist south." Yet Im's humanism confidently reverberates with the faith that the nation will endure and live, despite instability, violence, and even genocide. In a contemporary era dominated by contempt, greed, and suspicion promulgated both by distrust between the two Koreas and intensive industrialization, Im's continuing faith in people may itself be impractical and unreasonable. But this is precisely why Im and his films have persevered while others have not.

## Notes

1. Cho Chŏng-nae, "Land of Exile," in *Land of Exile: Contemporary Korean Fiction*, trans. and ed. Marshall R. Pihl, Bruce and Ju-Chan Fulton (New York: Sharpe, 1993), 212–13.

2. This province, located in southwestern Korea, is a traditional farming area; it was the site of a fierce ideological contest during the Korean War. It is also the homeland of both Cho Chŏng-nae and Im Kwon-Taek. See chapter 1 in this volume for further description of Chŏlla Province.

3. After turning over his malnourished, six-year old son to an orphanage, Mansŏk, decrepit and wretched, returns to his hometown, where he suffers an anonymous death.

4. Chungmoo Choi, "Nationalism and Construction of Gender in Korea,"

in *Dangerous Women: Gender & Korean Nationalism,* ed. Elaine H. Kim and Chungmoo Choi (New York: Routledge, 1998), 17.

5. The only Korean War film that falls outside this conventional characterization comprising reputable men and shameful women is *Spring in My Hometown,* which depicts the father as a character who is complicit with the foreign colonizers.

6. *Seven Female Prisoners* focuses on a North Korean officer and his psychological dilemma before he defects to the South during the war. Although it is hardly a film that praises socialism or criticizes the South, its creators were prosecuted for not following the ideological mantra of the government, which firmly stipulated that "no film will positively represent any member of the People's Army."

7. Yi Man-hŭi was eventually released, without being found either guilty or innocent, and his sentence was suspended. The court took into consideration his rationale: Yi and his supporters insisted that his film is art, which deserves constitutional protection in accordance with the precept of freedom of expression.

8. The diminished significance of Chŏlla Province in popular culture throughout the postwar period and well into the '80s reflects the unfair treatment the region has received both politically and economically, despite its productive rice fields. Bruce Cumings writes, "The Chŏllas [of the southwest] had been left alone to feed rice to Japan in the colonial period, and they were left alone as the [Park Chung Hee] regime poured new investment into the southeast." Bruce Cumings, *Korea's Place in the Sun: A Modern History* (New York: Norton, 1997), 362.

9. The pilots in the Korean air force featured in *The Red Mufflers* (*Ppalgan mahura,* Shin Sang-ok, 1964) are ill-equipped and inexperienced. Yet they are spiritually elated as they risk their lives, not only because the mission is strategically important—to destroy the enemy's bridge—but more importantly because it cannot be accomplished by the Americans, despite their technological superiority.

10. Cumings, *Korea's Place in the Sun,* 238.

11. Cumings, in his superb research on the Korean War, has repeatedly asserted that the war had no single cause but rather many overlapping ones in Korea's modern history. See Bruce Cumings, *The Origins of the Korean War* (Princeton: Princeton University Press, 1981).

12. *The Taebaek Mountains* was supposed to have been made in 1992, before *Sopyonje.* However, it was canned after government officials told Im that it should be deferred until the inauguration of a civilian government. A director not noted for opposing the government, Im delayed the production of *The Taebaek Mountains* until 1994, one year after Kim Young-sam, the first civilian president since 1961, came into power.

13. Approximately U.S. $2,000,000 was spent on the production of *The Taebaek Mountains.*

14. This highly anticipated film did not do well in the box office nor did it excite foreign critics; indeed, it was shunned by foreign film festivals. Its failure to generate positive reaction from foreign critics can probably be attributed to its uncritical use of melodramatic conventions.

15. A famous historical figure who had a brother across the ideological barrier is Park Chung Hee, the notorious right-wing military president of South Korea (1961–79). Park's older brother, a socialist, was killed in an uprising that took place before the Korean War.

16. Given the historic summit between Kim Dae Jung and Kim Jong-Il in June 2000, it is to be hoped that tensions between the two Koreas will ease.

17. See Homi K. Bhabha, "The World and the Home," *Social Text* nos. 31–32 (1992): 141.

18. There are two moments in the film where women retaliate in self-defense against men who approach them physically. In this scene, Chuksandaek bites off Lim's ear, and later Oesŏdaek bites Sang-gu's tongue when he tries to rape her. In every public screening of *The Taebaek Mountains* I have attended, these two scenes elicit audience laughter. Women biting men's body parts apparently releases the tension and horror projected when women are attacked by men. However, the laughter also consigns the film to genre conventions familiar to popular audiences rather than opening it up to realist conventions. Built-up suspense is released through comical actions. The symbolic significance of ear and tongue perhaps deserves some mention as well. When Chuksandaek bites Lim's ear, this underscores both their inability to communicate and the desperate measures of protest she must apply before she receives appropriate attention from the authorities. While the ear "receives" communication however, the tongue emits words and rhetoric. Also, the tongue's metonymic signification as a sexual object allows Oesŏdaek's attack on Sang-gu to be read as a gesture to castrate him.

19. The film adaptation seems to have merged the two characters, Namyang-daek and Oesŏdaek, both of whom are raped by Sang-gu in the original novel. An even more intriguing development in the novel is that Namyangdaek also contracts the "unhomely," allowing her socialist husband Ha Tae-ch'i to co-opt his own mistress elsewhere in the diegesis and further spread the "disease."

20. Gayatri Chakravorty Spivak, "Can the Subaltern Speak?" in *Colonial Discourse and Post-Colonial Theory: A Reader,* ed. Patrick Williams and Laura Chrisman (New York: Columbia University Press, 1994), 93.

21. Rey Chow, *Ethics after Idealism: Theory-Culture-Ethnicity-Reading* (Bloomington: Indiana University Press, 1998), 129.

22. Ibid.

CHAPTER 9

# In Defense of Continuity: Discourses on Tradition and the Mother in *Festival*

*All that is solid melts into air, all that is holy is profaned.*
Karl Marx and Friedrich Engels, *The Communist Manifesto*
(Harmondsworth: Penguin Books, 1967), 83.

The process of modernization in South Korea was so enormously extensive, intense, and violent that it became the major constituent core of the nation's collective experience during the latter half of the twentieth century. Like other forms of cultural representation in South Korea, cinema confronted the profound upheavals caused by modernization both directly and indirectly, offering many forms of dramatization of the people's fears and pleasures, their anxieties and aspirations, during this unprecedentedly cataclysmic epochal shift.

Director Im Kwon-Taek has been a prominent figure in representing Korea's social, economic, and cultural transformation. Spanning from 1962 to the present, his career exactly overlaps with its most turbulent phase, and he has consciously and persistently addressed the issues surrounding modernization, particularly in his later works. His major themes have been the effect of modernization on traditional Korean culture and the role of traditional culture in modern society. Im has clearly expressed this concern for traditional Korean culture in several interviews—for example: "My personal desire has been to capture

223

elements of our traditional culture in my work. . . . The fear is, of course, that those aspects of Korean culture that are not favored by the terms of this new international and more aggressive culture may be absorbed, and in the end, disappear."[1]

Of the films in which Im addressed the issue of the survival of tradition within the sweeping modernization process, two relatively recent works are especially important: the phenomenally successful *Sopyonje* (*Sŏp'yŏnje*), made in 1993, and, three years later, *Festival* (*Ch'ukche*), based on novels by the renowned writer, Yi Ch'ŏng-jun. In the former, tradition is represented mainly by the traditional folk opera, *p'ansori*, while in the latter it is represented mainly by the rituals of a funeral. Though it resembles *Sopyonje* in its general thematics, *Festival* addresses the role of traditional culture in the present in a very complicated way, and its attitude to tradition is radically different. Whereas *Sopyonje* describes the bitter defeat of tradition in the recent past, *Festival* represents its victory in the present. Whereas in *Sopyonje* tradition appears to be unquestionably opposed to modernity, in *Festival* the relation between past and present is much more complex. *Sopyonje* simply laments the disappearance of traditional culture, but *Festival* addresses the question of its contemporary meaning, presenting it as an important source of continuity even as it simultaneously examines its discontinuity.

In this essay, I examine *Festival* in the context of other films about funerals, arguing that what I call its "tradition-discourse" posits the culture of the past in opposition to modernity, but that it also paradoxically attempts to restore premodernity in the modernizing present. The film is thus internally split to create a tragic nostalgia. This nostalgia is associated with and substantially mobilized by a cluster of metaphors assembled around the figure of the mother—what I call the film's "mother-discourse." Thus I read *Festival* as a dialectically masterful text that dramatizes an inherent ambivalence towards tradition in a modernizing society. To frame this reading, I begin with a preliminary discussion of the concepts of modernity and tradition and their relationship in the context of Korea's modernization.

Modernity as a historically specific order is in essence a relational concept based on a periodization; only when viewed in relation to traditional order does a post-traditional order emerge in its entirety. Likewise, modernization designates the transition from an agrarian order to an industrialized society. Anthony Giddens characterizes modernity mainly in terms of its dynamism, which is brought in by the industrialization of the economy and the rationalization of culture. Through its "disembedding mechanism," modernity reorganizes time and space, and by its "radical doubt" it creates circumstances of uncertainty and multiple choice. It is thus a much more open system, one in which new forms of risk are intrinsic.[2]

Conversely, tradition can be understood fully only in relation to modernity. According to Stephen Vlastos, the term has conventionally been used in two overlapping and somewhat contradictory senses. First, tradition is associated with the historical period preceding modernity; used in this way the concept aggregates and homogenizes premodern culture and posits a historical past against which the modern human condition can be measured. Unlike the pervasive riskiness and uncertainty of modernity, traditional society imparts feelings of belonging, "ontological security," and the "moral bindingness" of life through kinship, religion, custom, and ceremony. In this sense tradition is a temporal and evaluative frame that is discontinuous with, and stands in opposition to, modernity.[3] In the second usage, tradition represents a continuous transmission of the discrete cultural practices of the past. The core transmission of tradition is strongly normative, containing the intention and the effect of reproducing patterns of culture. Edward Shils notes that "It is this normative transmission which links the generations of the dead with the generations of the living."[4] In this conception, rather than representing culture left behind in the transition to modernity, tradition is that part of the past that remains vital in the present and works to prevent modern society from flying apart.[5]

Largely because of the intensity and comprehensiveness of the dislocation experienced in modernization, the Korean people have had an uneasy relationship with their past, and premodern culture has been the object of great ambivalence for them. On the one hand, it has been easy to associate tradition with ignorance, superstition, social hierarchy, and a fatalistic worldview; from this perspective, tradition was an obstacle to modernization and had to be removed as soon as possible. On the other hand, the overarching impact of the modernization process itself forced

Koreans to discard their premodern culture. The universalizing effects of modernization pushed large portions of tradition into oblivion or, at best, into the realm of collective memories. In this respect, tradition always involves a sense of loss and alienation.

This ambivalence is expressed in two opposing ways. In the negative sense, tradition is to be denounced and replaced with Western values and styles, and the linkage with the past must be severed. But as far as its social meaning is concerned, tradition must remain as the grounding on which our security and national identity are anchored. Tradition as a positive force must not be completely negated or erased. The past, however, is not easily divisible into two separate entities, one positive and one negative, and it should be considered as a whole. So for the Korean people, modernization as the transition from a traditional society to a Westernized one necessarily causes serious ambivalence. To be released from traditional confines is potentially a liberation and an emancipation that brings the freedom to form one's own life in new ways; but it also means a loss of security.[6] Given these circumstances, the question of tradition must be no less salient and sensitive for South Koreans than for other peoples, and certainly no less complex—as *Festival* makes clear.

*Festival* is the story of a traditional funeral, specifically the funeral of the mother of a famous novelist. Chun-sŏp, the novelist and main protagonist, receives a phone call in Seoul informing him that his mother, who has suffered from senile dementia for years, has died at last. He drives hurriedly to his remote hometown in Chŏlla Province, taking his wife and small daughter with him. The entire extended family congregates in the small town for the funeral—even Yong-sun, Chun-sŏp's illegitimate niece and the black sheep of the family, who ran off more than a decade ago. The preparations for and the performance of the funeral entail a series of elaborate rites that extend over several days. During this time, interactions among the family members, especially the hostility of most of them to Yong-sun, gradually bring to light a family history marked by misfortune and conflict. Tensions among family members rise, but despite these conflicts, the complicated rituals are all successfully completed, and through these festival-like rituals of death and mourning, Chun-sŏp's family comes to terms with each other. Interwoven with the main narrative of the funeral proceeding in the present are two additional temporal dimensions: key episodes in the family history and the progress of the mother's senility are shown in flashbacks, and a fairy tale involving an exchange of identity between Chun-sŏp's mother and his daughter without specific temporal relation to the main narrative.

*Festival* offers a dense text of traditional Korean culture. Through its multilayered narrative structure and elaborate mise-en-scène, it kaleidoscopically dramatizes traditional Korean views on life and human relations, as well as the traditional cultural heritage. The interpolated fairy tale that is masterfully knitted into Chun-sŏp's recollection of his mother is significant not only as an elaboration on the film's main narrative but as a rare formal experiment in Im's filmography, otherwise defined as essentially realist. On the other hand, the remainder of the film approaches the condition of documentary. Many scenes, particularly those depicting the conflicts during the funeral, are so nuanced and dependent on the context that they must be unintelligible to audiences unfamiliar with the arcane rituals of traditional Korean funerary culture. By alternating these temporal dimensions and narrative modes, and by staging complicated elements within single scenes, the film narrates two main thematic concerns: the contemporary role of traditional culture and, overlapping with it, a complex assessment of the role of the mother. In the film's portrayal of the funeral as a festival, the combination of these discourses eventually figures the family's reconciliation and re-unification.

The most impressive aspect of *Festival* is its detailed documentation of the traditional funeral, an emphasis introduced in the opening title sequence of the film, which depicts the main funeral procession. The body of the film depicts the complicated procedures and rituals, from the witnessing of the last moment of life to the burial of the coffin. For example, before shrouding the body, the family uses a wooden spoon to put rice and marbles in the dead mother's mouth. This procedure, called *panham,* is intended to let the deceased have access to them while traveling to heaven; in effect, it expresses a wish for her well-being after death. These rituals are now familiar to only a minority of Koreans, and Im's meticulous documentation is reminiscent of an ethnographic documentary. Rather than concealing his documentary interest in the ceremony the filmmaker insistently draws attention to it by inserting

subtitles explaining the name and meaning of each procedure, a strategy
that no doubt is meant to help young Korean audiences as well as
foreigners—both of whom are ignorant of the tradition—to understand
the social meaning of the formalities.[7]

This intent is a major key to reading the film's tradition-discourse.
The filmmaker invests his pedagogy about the funerary traditions with as
much importance and seriousness as his other thematic concerns. The
insistent transmission of these customs is meaningful in two respects.
First, as the subtitles explain, every formality has significant meanings
within the traditional value system, which is an amalgam of Confucianism, Buddhism, and shamanism. The conventions are presented not as
annoying inconveniences that should be discarded but as prayers for
the deceased's peace and for the descendants' happiness. For example,
the act of pallbearers breaking a gourd dipper at the threshold is meant
to prevent the ghost of the deceased from returning. Thus the ritual
formalities have their own meanings and rationality, of which modern
Koreans, like foreigners, are usually ignorant. Secondly, as enacted in
the film, the traditional rituals have the positive effect of integrating
antagonisms and disjunctions among the family members, and as such
they are inherently communal and carnivalesque. A communal chanting
for example, led by a drunken local relative of Chun-sŏp and meant to
appease the bereaved, in fact cheers up the heavy atmosphere and transforms the supposedly solemn ritual into a playful game (see figure 9.1).

The procedure even manages to bring reconciliation to some
mourners who had been engaged in a fight caused by a bout of gambling.
By mediating individuals into a community, it creates a community of
festivity. Tradition magically turns a ceremony of mourning for the deceased into a festival of reunion and harmony for the living.

In *Festival,* tradition is important not because it formalistically trans-
mits empty patterns of premodern culture into the future, but because
its meanings and functions are still viable in the present. Through its
elaborate documentation of every detail of the funeral rites, the film
invests tradition with great significance, indicating the filmmaker's desire to preserve it. But it claims that what matters in tradition is not its
formality but its underlying value, which is ultimately even more important. Yong-sun's unorthodox way of paying respect to the deceased

FIGURE 9.1.
*Festival:* Chanting during a traditional funeral ceremony

figuratively demonstrates this point. A scene in which she dresses in snow-white clothes, whose color is regarded as unfit for a funeral, and dedicates some unconventional offerings—including a lit cigarette, a bottle of imported whiskey, and a cup of coffee—to her father on his grave emphasizes her love for him, even at the expense of ritual incorrectness. Suggesting that her acts are more genuine than the others' following the traditional formality as dictated, the sequence modifies the primacy of traditional formality by allowing it a considerable range of flexibility. But although the film reveals an ambiguity toward the formal aspects of tradition, it primarily valorizes the meaning of tradition over mechanical observance of formalities.

In this aspect, Im's film is crucially different from *The Funeral* (*Ososhiki,* 1984), a Japanese film directed by Juzo Itami, which in some respects it resembles. In *The Funeral,* the sudden death of their father obliges his daughter and son-in-law to set in motion the elaborate three-day ritual of a traditional Japanese funeral. The couple becomes confused and embarrassed as they realize their total ignorance of traditional customs. As the funeral proceeds, they have to make decisions about matters of which they know nothing: in which direction is the deceased's head supposed to point, how much do they donate to a priest who directs the ceremony, and so on. All these traditions have been almost forgotten by modern Japanese, and eventually the couple has recourse to an instructional video, "The ABC of the Funeral." They become comfortable with the traditional only after watching the video, which thus has the same function as Im's film.

Despite the many similarities between the two films and their common topic of a traditional funeral, the tradition-discourse in *Festival* is radically different from its equivalent in *The Funeral*. By foregrounding the distance of modern Japanese life from tradition, *The Funeral* constructs the father's death as a moment of discontinuity and the traditional funeral as a dead ritual. Whereas *Festival* presents tradition as a necessary connection to those of us who are living here and now, the Japanese film treats tradition no more than empty rituals to be routinely followed. Since *The Funeral* does not provide any real reason to observe the complicated procedures, its characters' clinging to them makes them appear absurd and ridiculous. The ritualized patterns transmitted in *The Funeral* lack the organic connection to the past they have in *Festival;* they remain mere vestiges without present meaning. They are too detached from contemporary life to evoke any emotion toward it. The traditional funeral merely serves as a backdrop to satirize the modern Japanese lifestyle. Because this distance between the past and the present is not associated with a felt sense of loss, the characters' ignorance of tradition simply provides humor and satire without invoking the ambivalence that Koreans have about it.

However real the links with the premodern, precolonial ways of life and worldview that knowledge of tradition sustains, in *Festival* they are nevertheless threatened with obliteration, and the film's claim for the urgency of tradition is constructed in opposition to modernity. Therefore it does not and cannot make fun of contemporary people's ignorance of tradition; instead it tries to educate the audience about its spiritual meanings and possible social functions. The seriousness with which the film treats tradition manifests the filmmaker's fear of its obliteration, and its implicit assumption of the audience's ignorance of tradition is related to that fear. Unlike the characters in *The Funeral*, those in *Festival* still have traditional knowledge available to them: there is no confusion or dispute over the funeral procedures as they unfold. The procedures are not contested by any characters, and it is taken for granted that they are to be followed. In this, the film posits a contradictory position regarding tradition. That is to say, tradition is supposed to be alien to the audience but familiar to the characters, though the assumed audience and the characters are all Koreans in the here-and-now. This contradiction and the consequent suppression of the characters' possible ignorance of tradition in a way foreshadow the intrinsic contradiction of the film's tradition-discourse, as I will discuss below.

The discourse of tradition in *Festival* is enriched and given added resonance by the theme of maternity. In fact, the mother-discourse is if anything even more prominent than the tradition-discourse, constructed as it is in the main narrative, in Chun-sŏp's recollections, and in the fairy tale. During the ceremony initiated by her death, the family matriarch is repeatedly recollected and revived in multiple flashbacks. Since her powerful presence continues to be manifested even after death, the film might be regarded as an interaction between the family and their mother in both her living and dead forms. She is represented as a figure who embraces everything and nurtures everyone. As recalled by her family and other local residents, her existence was characterized by boundless benevolence, unstinting love for her family, and sympathy with the poor. It is discovered that even when she became senile, she continued her practice of making secret tours of Buddhist temples to collect charms for her children. During the Korean War, she was the only one who dared to bury enemies' corpses when others pretended to be indifferent to them out of fear. Noting that she would feed beggars as if they were members of her family whenever they asked for food, one of her daughters defines the mother as a paragon of virtue.

The value of the mother is most clearly presented in the fairy tale, written by Chun-sŏp and narrated by his daughter Ŭn-ji. It offers a crystallized view of the mother and family, expressed in a warm but slightly surreal ambience with unusual lighting and background music.

In the tale, a young girl, also called Ŭn-ji, lives with her grandmother, father, and mother. As she grows old, the grandmother physically diminishes and begins to behave like a child. When Ŭn-ji expresses wonderment at the grandmother's shrinking, Chun-sŏp explains that this phenomenon occurs as the grandmother passes on her wisdom and age to her descendants. Benefiting from this, Ŭn-ji grows, but the grandmother continues to shrivel, eventually passing away to be born again. In this fable, the mother (the grandmother from Ŭn-ji's point of view) is presented as a wholly selfless giver. Through unconditional benevolence to the younger woman, the mother becomes the basis of familial continuity and well-being. The tale carries strong connotations of renewal, in which each generation rediscovers and relives the modes of life of its forebears.

As the mother is presented as the anchor of the traditional family, the mother-discourse necessarily overlaps with the tradition-discourse. Completely embedded in the family structure, the mother is represented only in relationship to it; other aspects of her existence and subjectivity as a woman and a citizen are ignored. As the film glorifies and somewhat mythologizes the mother as the ultimate giver, the family also becomes a sacred entity, which the film represents as potentially a community of love and trust. The ideal type of Korean traditional family is grounded in the inseparable connection between the mother and her children, and it is maintained by mutual trust, which comes from the mother's endless love for them and their respect for her. The primacy of family is neither questioned nor contested. Instead it is presented as possessing a universal value.

Other characters in the film are also principally represented as primarily members of a family rather than as individuals. During the course of the funeral, each character, despite the prevalence of conflicts within the family, plays the role allocated to him or her by the traditional family system. As the eldest surviving son, Chun-sŏp is clearly the chief mourner, and his older brother's widow Oedong-taek, the first daughter-in-law, takes charge of all the preparations for the elaborate feasts for the mourners. Even Yong-sun, who holds a grudge against her stepmother Oedong-taek and other family members, does not negate the universal value of the family. She violates some of the norms of the traditional funeral but she wholeheartedly admits the value of the traditional familial system, as when she says, "I wished to take care of grandmother with my own hands." Despite her initial disruption of the family, Yong-sun ultimately reinforces its importance; the family as the fundamental community is foregrounded, and the individual is relatively subordinated.

With respect to its claim of the family's universal value, *Festival* forms a striking contrast to Louis Malle's *May Fools* (*Milou en mai,* 1989), a French film that also deals with the funeral of a mother. Set in a remote mansion in a rural region of France in May 1968, when members of a bourgeois family reunite for the funeral, this film strongly contests the universal value of the mother. The deceased's daughter Claire, who is so rebellious that she brings her lesbian lover to the house, recollects her mother as a tyrannical figure, who forced her to wash her hands all the time and practice the piano everyday whether she wanted to or not. Other family members do not respect the deceased any more than Claire does, and they are clearly no more distressed by her death. All they are interested in is the division of the property and the pursuit of their own sexual pleasures. Claire scuffles with her niece Camille over the mother's emerald ring, a sign that the bourgeois family relations now exist only at a monetary level. The younger son, Georges, is a foreign correspondent for *Le Monde;* while he focuses all his attention on news of the May 1968 political upheavals transmitted through a radio, his elder brother Milou woos Georges' young wife. When a local grave diggers' strike makes it impossible for them to go ahead with the funeral, everyone goes on a picnic, leaving a handyman with the responsibility of digging a grave on the estate—an act that would be unimaginable for Koreans. Overall, the death of the mother is pushed to the side, and individual desires pervade all social relations. There is no family of the kind that *Festival* posits as a natural and sacred institution, and the mother's death is only a pretext for displaying individual desires and fears. The mundaneness that typifies the characters of *May Fools* is wholly unlike the mood of *Festival,* where, from the beginning to the end, family members are so overwhelmed by the presence of the dead mother that they do not even allude to the division of her estate.[8]

In *Festival,* the mother's senile dementia adds another, enriching element to its mother-discourse. While the mother is reconstructed by others' recollections of her as sublimely self-sacrificing on behalf of her family when she is healthy, when she begins to suffer from dementia she becomes a burden to them—especially for Oedong-taek, who lives with her and takes care of her. Dressing up like a girl, the mother wanders and becomes lost in remote places outside the village; she also does irrational things, like washing already clean clothes, harvesting unripe persimmons, and setting a fire with her cigarettes. When Oedong-taek is working in the fields, she has to confine her mother-in-law in a room in order to prevent her from going astray. The problems caused by dementia also create tension between Oedong-taek and the other family members. Nevertheless, it is taken for granted that the family will care for the senile mother, because they recognize that her behavior results from her dementia. Her senility is represented not so much as a burden on the family but as another evidence of her love for them.

It is significant that while the mother retains her presence in *Festival* even after her death, the father figure is almost entirely absent. He is present only in stories about his profligacy and early death. Yong-sun's father, the deceased eldest son of the family, is similarly portrayed as a source of misfortune. Though as its patriarch he is supposed to support the whole family, he is an alcoholic hedonist, and eventually he commits suicide after losing the family fortune in an unsuccessful business venture. Thus both father and the eldest son, the central figures of the traditional Confucian concept of family, are absent or negative. This suggests that the film's negotiation with traditional culture does not produce an unequivocally strong or unqualified endorsement of it, and that the mother theme exceeds the requirements of traditional family relations.

Two decades earlier, Im provided a prototypical representation of the Korean father figure in a traditional upper-class family in *The Geneal-ogy* (*Chokpo*, 1978). Set in the 1940s of the Japanese colonial rule, the film concerns a patriarch who, in order not to dishonor his seven-hundred-year-old genealogy, adamantly refuses to change his family name to a Japanese one. Responsibility for preserving the imperiled family name falls entirely on his shoulders, and he finally commits suicide, unable to deal with the pressures imposed on him by the atrocious Japanese policy—an attempt to erase the Koreanness of the Korean people by thorough Japanization. In *The Genealogy*, the father figure's resistance to threats to familial continuity results in self-annihilation, ironically leaving the family with no hope. Unlike that father, the mother in *Festival* is a powerful source of family continuity as well as a personification of familial communality.

In *Festival* the intimate association of the mother with prelapsarian blessedness is no less symptomatic than the absence of the father figure. When the senile mother is asked why she wanders around in a young girl's dress, she answers that she wants to return home—a desire that is even more salient in the fairy tale. When Ŭn-ji wonders why the grandmother is behaving like a child, Chun-sŏp explains, "She wants to go back to her joyful childhood." In this way the old mother also represents the desire to return to a premodern period of security and continuity. Given the psychoanalytic explanation that the presence of the father initiates the child's oedipal trajectory (or the entry into the Symbolic Order, to use Lacan's terminology) and that the mother is associated with the original unity between the infant and the world, the strong presence of the mother, combined with the absence of the father, can be seen as a symptomatic manifestation of a deep-rooted desire to return to the pre-Symbolic world of original unity. The mother's impulse to regress to the "good old days" thus allegorizes the desire for ontological security. With a discourse that privileges the past over the present, *Festival* implicitly problematizes the present of modernity, which necessarily bears a negativity.

The mother is also represented as continuity through several false alarms of her immanent death. On one occasion, she awakens out of a coma, after family members have been told that her death is probable this time. When Chun-sŏp is about to depart for the mother's funeral, the history of these postponements leads Ŭn-ji to ask whether her grandmother has died "once again." Indeed, when they arrive at the hometown after a hurried drive, they find that the mother has come back to life. To everyone's astonishment, she regained consciousness three hours after her body had been wrapped in preparation for the funeral. The fact that her death is delayed several times suggests the possibility that she is still alive, even after her actual death.

Compared to both *The Funeral* and *May Fools,* both of which begin with the sudden death of a parent, this embarrassing repetition of death is distinctive in *Festival.* It is understandable enough, however, given the film's concern with tradition, which is inherently associated with continuity. The film constructs the mother as the ultimate sign of continuity, the anchor for the family in this ever-changing, modernizing society; it represents her death not as a moment of discontinuity but as an implied continuity. Both mother and tradition are alike in their ontological connection to continuity. The two main discourses of tradition and the mother are intimately connected and reinforce each other. In short, *Festival* weaves its celebration of continuity through both the powerful presence of the mother even after her death and the traditional ritual of funeral.

Though *May Fools* also combines a rural location and a mother's death and funeral, it does not countenance continuity. The mother's death reaffirms the disintegration of the family, and the funeral is a ritual that articulates the discontinuity between the deceased and the bereaved as well as the antagonism between individuals. Tradition as continuity is scarcely represented in *May Fools.* It is not even clear whether the mansion, the symbolic site of familial communality and continuity, is to be sold or retained. Tradition is represented only in minor incidents—as for example, when the elder son shows the traditional way of catching crawfish by putting his hands into the river and pulling them with their claws wrapped around his fingers.

*Festival* foregrounds the viability and utility of traditional values by combining the mother-discourse with the communality arguably intrinsic to traditional rituals. In order to narrate the integrating power of tradition and the mother, *Festival* initially poses a series of conflicts within the rural family home, which thus becomes a social microcosm. Oedong-taek criticizes Chun-sŏp's wife for not helping with the preparation of food for the mourners. Her complaints are not without reason, for without a husband she has led a life filled with grief, and she has had to care for the demented mother all by herself; but Chun-sŏp's wife, who comes from an urban family, is apparently not accustomed to such tasks. The complicating factor of sexual desire, which does not fit with the solemn ritual, is also present. For example, the man who is invited to chant for the funeral attempts to seduce Yong-sun. Even the hero's conjugal fidelity is suspect; it is suggested that Chun-sŏp had a sexual relationship with a magazine reporter, who admires him and who attends the funeral in order to write about it. Conflicts owing to money also occur. Several individuals become involved in a fight during an extended bout of gambling. A mourner who slept with a local prostitute gets in trouble when he is unable to pay her because he loses his money in gambling. And when the county governor comes to mourn, the local citizens use this opportunity to interrogate him about deficiencies in public services.

The character who primarily represents conflicts and disruptions within the family is Yong-sun. Her unexpected appearance—no one informed her of her grandmother's death—and her antagonistic attitude toward other family members create serious tensions, prompting revelations that her stepmother severely mistreated her and that when she ran off she took some money stolen from her stepsister. Along with these uncomfortable memories dredged up from the past, her gaudy looks—inappropriately lurid makeup, black sunglasses, and white clothes—and her bold behavior reinforce the repulsion the others feel toward her. In short, she is a black sheep who emblematizes all the conflicts among the family members.

As the title suggests, *Festival* represents a traditional funeral as a festival in which family conflicts are exposed and finally resolved. What turns such an inauspicious event into a festival is the presence of the dead mother, for this prevents all the conflicts from exploding into severe hostility. People who are bickering with each other stop their criticizing as soon as someone reminds them of the mother's death, the event which has brought them together. Even Yong-sun becomes willing to embrace reconciliation with the other members of the family after reading her uncle's fairy-tale book about the mother. Yet the mother's power to bring reconciliation to the family can be fully manifested only through engagement with tradition; the links between her funeral and the worldview of communality and continuity provide the site where maternal power operates. Centering on the universal theme of the mother, the film's discursive strategy makes persuasive its underlying theme of the importance of tradition; it also makes possible the final achievement of harmony. Completed by Yong-sun's acceptance into the group, this harmony is symbolized in the film's finale, when the entire family poses for a commemorative photograph (see figure 9.2).

However, it should be noted that *Festival*'s optimistic view that reconciliation can be reached is not unequivocal. First, reconciliation is attained only through the temporary suspension of modernity and the uncritical acceptance of a traditional worldview. This suspension takes place on an occasion which those who live in modern society seldom experience. It occurs by virtue of a combination of a rural location, the existence of a benevolent mother and her natural death, and a traditional funeral. Secondly, the unusual triumph of traditional values in *Festival* takes place through familial communality. The main conflict in the film, that between Yong-sun and other family members, is resolved when they come to realize anew that they all belong to the same family. The communality of family is the basis of its happy ending. Thirdly, the reconciliation in the film also owes a debt to the reemergence of a father figure. Chun-sŏp—a soft-spoken and unimposing, but thoughtful, figure—now becomes the new center of the family, not only with his prestige as a respected novelist but also with the image of continuity that he represents. Appropriately, he plays the father in his fairy tale that tells the truth of family—namely, the necessary and mutually beneficial connection between its older and younger members. As Yong-sun points out when denouncing him for exploiting the family's history for his work, the focus of his writing in the past has generally been his family. The accomplishment of reconciliation in the family, represented by the acceptance of Yong-sun, is actually initiated by Yong-sun's reading of his fairy tale.

This triumph, however, can only be short-lived in nature, because it is made possible through the existential situation of the death of the mother. It can last only during the funeral and within the hometown. After the funeral, family members and relatives will eventually disperse to their modernized spaces throughout the country. They will come to recognize that the harmonious community experienced during the funeral is an exception, that it no longer exists in their dreary reality. In fact, until the death of their benevolent mother, the scattered family has been physically and emotionally disparate. Had there been no funeral, such a

FIGURE 9.2.

*Festival:* Communal photograph of the reconciled family

reconciliation would not be possible. *Festival* offers no critical reflection on what initially tore the family apart and then led them to reconcile. It thus lacks the negating power of the possible oppositionality of tradition to modernity, which Im's *Sopyoje* prominently displays. In that regard the harmonious ending of *Festival* is temporary, superficial, and illusory. When a past tradition is presented as a practical centering point of our present lives, not as an oppositionality to modernity, it remains fictitious and powerless, despite its surface charm. This is why tradition is also the very source of ambivalence. It would be fair to say that the world *Festival* unfolds is nothing but a utopia, where modernization does not exert its overwhelming disembedding mechanisms, and where present lives and traditional values intermingle to form an organic whole.

*May Fools* also offers a utopian moment. When the family members and their friends go on a picnic, the group becomes intoxicated from the effects of wine, marijuana, and revolutionary fervor; for a while, they contemplate turning the estate into a utopian commune. The Edenic situation in *May Fools* is conceived by a subversive imagination that has its origins in the affirmation of human desire and individual preferences, and thus it opens toward an uncertain future. By contrast, the utopia suggested in *Festival* is a retrospective and closed one, made possible only on the basis of communal patriarchal values and the suppression of individual desires and differences, particularly female ones. It rests on a traditional order, whose symbolic ritual tries to reconstitute boundaries and habits that social change threatens to dissolve or problematize.

*Festival*'s optimistic view is rather exceptional in light of other Korean films that address the question of the significance of family in a modernizing society. A negative attitude is evident in *Green Fish* (*Ch'rok mulkogi*, 1997), a film loosely based on the gangster genre and released a year after *Festival*. *Green Fish* depicts the inevitable marginalization of traditional values in modern Korean society. Its narrative revolves around a young gangster named Mak-tong, the youngest son in his family and a criminal novice whose circumstances oblige him to commit a murder. Living in a suburb of Seoul, his family consists of the mother, four brothers, and a sister. As shown figuratively by their shabby house on the edge of an emerging modernized city, the family is apparently disintegrating; the eldest brother suffers from epilepsy; the second, a detective, is an alcoholic; the third leads a humble life as an egg peddler; and the sister works as a waitress in a tearoom. The father is absent and the mother works as a housemaid. The disintegration of the family is vividly illustrated in a family picnic sequence. Organized to celebrate Mak-tong's discharge from military service, the picnic is completely spoiled, both by a wrangle between the second brother and his wife over his excessive drinking and by the eldest's falling down in a fit. Mak-tong, who cherishes a wish to forestall the further disintegration of his family, becomes a gangster in hopes of making enough money to acquire a small family business. With sober realism, the film traces the inevitable failure of Mak-tong's quest, emphasizing the naïveté of his dream of a traditional harmonious communal life amid the reality of modernized Korean society. Contesting the aggressive, ruthless, and violent reality exemplified by the gang boss, he is doomed to failure. On orders from his boss he executes a rival gang leader, but ultimately he is himself brutally murdered by his boss. He sacrifices his life in his search for familial communality, which the film suggests is impossible in modernity. In contrast to *Festival*, *Green Fish* claims that Korean modernity leaves no space for a family that is anchored in traditional love and trust.

Although there are few explicit comments about modernity in *Festival*, the film implicitly constructs its own discourse about the phenomenon. It represents modernity as a necessary condition for reconciliation within the family, both with fragmentary celebrations of modernity and by the absence of its negative aspects. *Festival*'s consistent efforts to reauthorize tradition may indirectly allude to the destructive effects of modernization, but it does not address them directly. Rather, some scenes clearly depict the bright side of modernization, as instanced by widespread material affluence and considerable leisure time. The return of Chun-sŏp's family to the ancestral home, as they drive their own car along a highway made possible by modernization, demonstrates this point. The cellular phone Chun-sŏp uses in the car to inform his friends of his mother's death is another product of modern technology. That most of the mourners drive their own cars is a sign of Korea's material accomplishments. A neighbor says, "What a crowd of cars! If another funeral takes place, we'd have to broaden the road first." Even Yong-sun, who ran away because of mistreatment and poverty, now returns home with her own reasonably satisfactory automobile.

It is symptomatic that the main conflict in *Festival* is rooted in the past. The conflict between Yong-sun and the family, for example, is presented as a result of their past misfortune, specifically Yong-sun's father's dissipation, poverty, and suicide. Now that poverty, the fundamental cause of their misfortune, has been alleviated by the material affluence brought by modernization, a true reconciliation may occur within the family. Since *Festival* presents modernization as a necessary condition for a harmonious future and does not represent the negativity of modernization, the ambiguities of modernization are masked.

Nor does the film interrogate the discursive effect of modernization. It does not question why and how we Korean people have discarded our splendid traditional values and institutions, the very sources that provided us with the social meanings by which our people have lived. What matters in the film is only that we do not appreciate the deep meaning of tradition—as if to imply that the disappearance of tradition is due not to the totalizing effect of modernization or Westernization but rather to our negligence. With its negative aspects concealed, tradition becomes a mysterious abstraction to be preserved and celebrated. Furthermore, by claiming the possibility that observance of tradition can restore a community torn apart by modernization, the film suggests that traditional culture can coexist with Western customs and values. It thus ignores the fact that the issue of national cultural identity arises only in response to a challenge posed by the other. Any discourse of national cultural identity is always and from the outset oppositional—and thus not necessarily conducive to progressive positions.[9] By failing to capture the tension stemming from the oppositionality of traditional culture to modernization, *Festival*, despite its realistic rendering, remains a fantasy film. Repeating the rituals of authenticity, it unintentionally exposes the implicit danger in "encourag[ing] the practice of a 'traditional' culture separated from the social conditions by and for which cultural forms are shaped."[10]

It should also be noted that as it constructs a discourse of premodern communality and continuity at a deep level, *Festival* does not question the relevance of the traditional worldview underlying it. For example, the procedure of breaking the gourd dipper to prevent the ghost of the deceased from returning is apparently based on a traditional belief in the existence of the spirits of the dead. This belief is not questioned; it is implicitly presented as true. In particular, the film's failure to question the patriarchal character of Korean traditional culture reveals the limitation of its tradition-discourse. Although tradition is valorized because of its power to bring communal festivity, women are largely absent from the festivities, apart from their ancillary role in preparing and serving food. Because the traditional family system debars women from full participation, they are almost entirely excluded from the unrestricted exposure of human desires and subsequent conflicts that form the backdrop of the festival. Those who have fun while drinking and gambling are all male. By contrast, the women work to serve the predominantly male mourners. Because the festival in the film proves to be primarily for males, the exclusion of women becomes an internal contradiction that undermines the meaning of festival.[11] In this context, Yong-sun and Hye-rim, the female reporter, are exceptional women: rather than working on behalf of men, they devote their time to smoking and drinking together. Nevertheless, the potential threat to patriarchy introduced by the two is eventually tamed by Chun-sŏp. As his admirer, Hye-rim is, needless to say, subordinate to Chun-sŏp's authority from the beginning; and Yong-sun is reintegrated into patriarchy by her embrace of traditional family values. In this regard the film is a text concerned with the reemergence of patriarchal authority—represented by Chun-sŏp—which is in jeopardy in modern Korean society. Because it is based on the traditional patriarchy naturalizing women's subordination, the reconciliation remains fragile and implausible. The film betrays its inevitably patriarchal viewpoint through its failure to take note of the fact that the communal festivity depends on the sacrifice of women.

Here *Festival* exposes serious internal fissures. As discussed earlier, its discourses of mother and tradition implicitly but tenaciously attempt to sustain continuity and security threatened by modernization. Modernization and modernity are the sources of the sense of loss and uncertainty; they express a desire to return to the "good old days" that are imagined to have been replete with continuity and security. But by presenting modernization as a necessary precondition for harmonious

community in the present, the film suppresses its negative aspects. Similarly, the uncritical acceptance of patriarchy impairs the current relevance
of its tradition-discourse and exposes its structural limitations.

The film's obvious feature as a personal homage to maternity, cul-
minating in Chun-sŏp's dedication of his fairy tale book to the altar of
the dead mother, may shed light on these textual contradictions. Im
commented on *Festival* in an autobiographic memoir: "I have felt sorry
to my mother for not doing my *hyodo* with devotion. With *Festival* I
wanted to repay her for this feeling of guilt."[12] His remarks on *hyodo*
and the "feeling of guilt" suggest not only the traditional character of
the film's perspective based on kinship obligations but also the great intensity of his wish to repay his mother. His strong personal investment
in the film suggests that it may be seen as wish fulfillment. Given that
dreaming is the prototype of wish fulfillment in the Freudian schema, its
utopian feature takes on another meaning. Since dreaming as wish fulfillment implies the impossibility of fulfilling desire in the real world, the
world depicted in the film may be a dream unrealizable in the present:
a traditional world in which people live under maternal love, mutual
trust, traditional expectations, and paternal authority. Yet by and large
the overall experience of ordinary Koreans contradicts the film's support
for the positivity of traditional values in the here and now and its endorsement of the possibility of peaceful coexistence with Western values.

Consequently, *Festival* raises an important question: Can traditional
values be reestablished in settings that have become thoroughly post-
traditional? To this it responds without reservation: "Yes." Or, more
precisely, the film's answer is, "It should." Given the country's ambivalence toward tradition in a modernizing society as well as toward
modernity in general, the cultural continuity constructed in *Festival*
reveals a utopian or transcendent potential, which expresses the desire
for original communality and harmony. In particular, the absence of
the representation of modernization's negative aspects underscores the
underlying desire for escape from the risk lurking in the uncertainty of
modernity and for a return to a state of security, which traditional order
gave us. In this sense, *Festival* proves the relevance of Fredric Jameson's
celebrated thesis that "the works of mass culture cannot be ideological

without at one and the same time being implicitly or explicitly Utopian as well."[13]

As discussed at the beginning, tradition has a two-fold connotation: on the one hand, the aggregate of the disappearing or already disappeared premodern culture and values, and on the other, the current patterns or formalities passed down from the past. Yet the tradition-discourse of *Festival* forms a contradictory amalgamation of both; that is, tradition is presented here as simultaneously premodern and currently viable. In reality, what modernity allows to tradition are only its particular rituals and motifs, not the values that give them their meaning, which are necessarily in opposition to modernity. Modernity appropriates the formal elements of tradition for its own sake but divests them of their value. *Festival*'s attempt to revive tradition as a value system tenable in the here-and-now inevitably proves to be illusory, for the process of modernization that transforms the material basis of society requires a corresponding transformation of discursive practices—especially those that are gender-specific. Such a self-contradictory attempt to restore a traditional world in the context of modernity creates a sense of "tragic nostalgia": The present of modernity inevitably makes us look back to our traditional past, but such a nostalgic look provides us with no substantial solution. *Festival* unwittingly materializes this feeling, deepening our ambivalence toward modernity as well as toward tradition, and paradoxically proving the lasting relevance of Marx's observation that "it is as ridiculous to yearn for a return to the original fullness as it is to believe that with this complete emptiness history has come to a standstill."[14] Because of this ambivalence, we can neither unilaterally criticize the retrogressive character of *Festival* nor wholeheartedly endorse modernity.

## Notes

1. "Im Kwon-Taek: Between Blockbusters and Art Films," Harvard Asia Pacific Review (Summer 1997) [on-line], available at http://hcs.harvard.edu/~hapr.

2. Anthony Giddens and Christopher Pierson, *Conversations with Anthony Giddens: Making Sense of Modernity* (Stanford: Stanford University Press, 1998), 102. See also Anthony Giddens, *Modernity and Self-Identity* (Stanford: Stanford University Press, 1991), introduction and chs. 2, 5.

3. Stephen Vlastos, ed., *Mirror of Modernity: Invented Traditions of Modern Japan* (Berkeley: University of California Press, 1998), 2.

4. Edward Shils, *Tradition* (Chicago: University of Chicago Press, 1981), 24.

5. Vlastos, *Mirror of Modernity*, 2.

6. Johan Fornäs, *Cultural Theory and Late Modernity* (London: Sage, 1995), 43.

7. Although the cinematic version of *Festival* released in 1996 and the video with English subtitles have additional subtitles that explain both the terminology of funeral procedures and their significance, the Korean video version, I found, has only the terminology subtitles, with no explanatory contents.

8. According to Korean customs, mourners at a funeral house are encouraged, as a way to appease the sorrow of the deceased's family, to take part in such various mundane activities as drinking and gambling; by contrast, family members must remain solemn and austere.

9. Paul Willemen, "The Third Cinema Question: Notes and Reflections," *Question of Third Cinema,* ed. Jim Pines and Paul Willemen (London: BFI, 1989), 18.

10. Paul Willemen, "The National," *Fields of Vision,* ed. Leslie Devereaux and Roger Hillman (Berkeley: University of California Press, 1995), 22–23.

11. Many Korean women hate traditional ceremonies such as *chesa,* an annual religious service for deceased ancestors. While men perform the ceremonies and enjoy food and entertainment, women are generally responsible for preparing these and serving the men. *Yŏsŏng Minu-hoe,* a Korean women's organization, has recently pointed out this gendered practice as a major example of sexism in Korean society.

12. Im Kwon-Taek, "My Filmmaking, Yi Ch'ŏng-jun and *Festival*: The Story I Want to Leave," *The Joong-Ang Ilbo,* (http://gocinema.joongang.co.kr/news/199903/19990408042.html. [May 1999]). *Hyodo* is children's filial duty to their parents; heavily emphasized in Confucian ethics, it was formerly regarded as a foundational principle of human life in Korea, although its importance has become rarefied.

13. Fredric Jameson, *Signatures of The Visible* (New York: Routledge, 1992), 29.

14. Karl Marx, *Grundrisse* (London: Penguin, 1973), 162.

# CHAPTER 10

# An Interview with Im Kwon-Taek

*Interviewers:* During the last ten years, following the controversial popularity of *Sopyonje*, you emerged as the most prominent film director in Korea. There was the Munich retrospective of your films and now the retrospective here. How has this recognition affected your sensibility as a filmmaker?[1]

*Im Kwon-Taek:* Since the 1980s, I have been considering my films with these matters in mind. Before the mid-1970s, I produced films that pursued only cheap entertainment values. Then I became aware that I would not survive as a director if I continued to pursue mere entertainment, like American films do, because I realized that in every aspect—power, technology, and human resources— competing with American films was impossible. I began to think, "How can I survive as a film director?" At the time, I was also getting old. Realizing that my life is connected to my films, I had been thinking of myself critically: "How can I spend my whole life so degraded?" "What could I possibly lose from making serious films?" Since films can in some ways be connected to our lives, I realized that I could move beyond the lies, and deal truly with the serious issues of our lives. With this in mind, I made *The Deserted Widow* (*Chapch'o*) in 1973 that featured a woman whose life had incredible resilience despite the fact that she was constantly being stepped on like wild grass. This character was developed from my own experience of interacting with some Korean women around me, our mother figures, who had resilience in life. I could continue dealing with these issues in my films because after all there was the need that Korean films should travel abroad and be seen by foreigners.

*Interviewers:* When did this happen?

*Im Kwon-Taek:* Toward the end of the 1970s, around the time of *The Genealogy* and *The Hidden Hero,* these issues were identified. After all, it is true that Korean film packaging technology and production talents cannot match those of the United States, Europe, Japan, and other nations. But I reached the conclusion that if we could capture the look of Korea as a specific region, along with the people and culture that grow out of that regional condition, and send them outside, then people all over the world could have a strong sense of the unique characteristics of Korea. I also realized that films I wanted to send abroad required topics from the period in our history that I myself have experienced. I went to elementary school during the Japanese colonial period, at a time when the "name change order" was initiated.[2] I experienced the turbulent period that soon followed—the liberation, the left/right conflict, the Korean War, the military dictatorship, the military politics, the April 19th Revolution [of 1960]. All of these became the subjects of my films. After all, I grew up in an environment that obliged me to react to this period sensitively. During the postliberation period and the left/right conflict, our family participated in the leftist movement. As a child, I experienced the leftist movement and the subsequent oppression: the arrests like the unannounced break-in at night when the police took my father away.

*Interviewers:* Would you then say that the characters in *The Taebaek Mountains,* Yŏm Sang-jin and Sang-ku, are reflections of the people you knew in real life?

*Im Kwon-Taek:* Of course, those characters are based on the novel by Cho Chŏng-nae, but they were also people who could be easily seen within my circle of family and friends, and in incidents that happened around me. But there were also many people who had nothing to do with those tumultuous times. If you were living in an ordinary household and were not affiliated with the left, or if you were in the position of the assailants, then you could not have felt the same kind of pain as I did. In my case, my family members were leftists who were defeated during the Korean War. As you know, in South Korea, the rightists acquired power—and the setback was acutely felt. Although I was young, as a member of a family that suffered from oppression, these pains impacted me psychologically. When I began making my living as a film director, I felt the responsibility or obligation to go back to that historical period and deal with it in film. However, such films could not easily be made because we were restricted in the range of our choices for subject matter. Of course, today we are still living in a divided country with a dominant anticommunist ideology. Films dealing objectively with the issues of ideology should have been made earlier, but social conditions prohibited it. *The Taebaek Mountains,* made in 1994, was planned earlier, during the Roh Tae-woo regime immediately after the military dictatorship, but we received a formal notice stating, "We still cannot allow subjects that deal objectively with the issue of ideology." Thus, since the film was not made until the civilian government, it arrived belatedly. When the film was screened abroad, interest in the subject matter was already only lukewarm. The world was no longer engulfed in the cold war. Of course, it's still a reality in Korea, but where is there ideological conflict of this kind overseas?

*Interviewers: Gilsottum, Surrogate Mother, Come, Come, Come Upward,* and so on have all received awards and have been successful in the international film circuit. Has this international recognition changed you much?

*Im Kwon-Taek:* My films and I have been acknowledged to some degree. The people who live in the Far East, in the small cornered region called Korea, need to find their unique characteristics. If our culture fails us in this then our lives will be ignored and our existence not respected. In my films, I have attempted to feature the lives of Koreans, what we have lost, what we find tragic, the source of this tragedy, the barriers in our lives, why we have these barriers, and so on. If these feelings can possibly be displayed in the medium of film, then I find it tempting to do so and send this regional culture abroad to gain some kind of recognition for it.

*Interviewers:* As you travel more abroad and engage in international exchange, what kind of things do you hear and see that make you feel a need to reclaim your own national heritage?

*Im Kwon-Taek:* In the past, Korean films were completely ignored, but now when my films travel to Europe and other places, they are noticed. My films have been acknowledged to some extent in Europe for quite a while, even though this has just begun in the U.S. Since we cannot make films that are as entertaining as American films, for Korean cinema to survive, we have to make films based on our stories, the ones that no one else can tell. Their subject matter must be something that couldn't have been conceived unless you're a Korean.

*Interviewers:* When you were thinking about this in the late 1970s, did you know other directors, writers, or friends who were thinking the same way? Did any earlier Korean directors influence you?

*Im Kwon-Taek:* If others around me had been thinking the same things I had been thinking, I don't think I could have lasted this long as a director. Some others did try for a bit, but only I continued. I think my results were produced by the fact that I never gave up and just kept trying.

*Interviewers:* When you were working in the 1960s, were you ever influenced by the directors Shin Sang-ok and Yu Hyŏn-mok?[3]

*Im Kwon-Taek:* The world they pursued differed radically from mine. Remember this was only a few years after the war. I was a member of a leftist family and had no academic training. I shot five or six films a year. I could not think of myself as a man who could do positive things for society, a man with dreams and the means of realizing them. For me, there was no tomorrow: just eat, drink, and shoot. Since I was making only B-grade movies, if I did an adequate job and the film did well in the regional box office, the distributors requested another one. Whatever the production company required, I would do it. My life was not one of success and accomplishment. My life was completely different from either Yu Hyŏn-mok's or Sin Sang-ok's.

*Interviewers:* Since *Sopyonje*'s financial success and your foreign recognition, what is the production environment like? Does the production company support you financially in any way you want, or are there still pressures to place more emphasis on box-office results?

*Im Kwon-Taek:* Right now, I find the subject matter, propose it to the company, and the production company consents. This process began in the 1980s and has been intact for nearly fifteen years. In the past, I only did projects that were assigned to me. Now I control my own work. Yet, since I know the Korean film market too well, having been around since the 1960s, I never propose projects that would require a budget that exceeds the capabilities of our current film production. I only consider topics that our production environment can afford. Fortunately, films like *The General's Son* did well financially. You may ask why, at an old age, I did such a film that would make money but not be well received by the critics. But

I did it as a compromise, in order to find production freedom for the next picture. Now, *Sopyonje* is an ironic project. In preparing the film, I made sure that the producer understood that this film would never make a cent. The producer was prepared to absorb the loss since he made a lot of money with the previous *The General's Son* series. He said that we would send *Sopyonje* out to the film festivals and publicize our remarkable traditional culture, of which *p'ansori* is a big part. That was the objective, and we did not anticipate it being such a big financial success. Since this success, the producer agrees to anything I say, hoping for another tremendous event.

*Interviewers:* So even though *The Taebaek Mountains,* which immediately followed *Sopyonje,* required the biggest production budget up to that time, the producer readily consented?

*Im Kwon-Taek:* Yes.

*Interviewers:* Traveling abroad, you have met many directors from East Asia, and seen many of their films. What do you think of them? How do you feel about Chen Kaige, Zhang Yi-mou, and Hou Hsiao-hsien?

*Im Kwon-Taek:* In the past, apart from the accomplished Japanese films, East Asian films were not listed among the great films. But now Chinese films are receiving much attention globally and do well financially. As a fellow Asian, I feel gratitude toward the Chinese filmmakers. I don't see all of their films, but I also feel that their successful films are perhaps excessively packaged to accommodate the interest of the West.

*Interviewers:* Do you also warn yourself about these dangers?

*Im Kwon-Taek:* I always have to caution myself. People here in the West often tell me: "There are things in your film that I could never understand, even if I was reborn." But I don't like to make films that are processed for them to consume too easily. Since this is a period when many people in the West are interested in Asian culture and have ample opportunity to see more Asian films, I think they will eventually understand things that they don't understand now. In any case, I present stories of the people of Korea without much packaging, whether it works or not. I can't make films that match their interest, and even if I tried I'm not sure that it would work.

*Interviewers:* Is there a common ground where the desires of the Korean spectators overlap with the expectations of Western film festivals?

*Im Kwon-Taek:* Most of my films that were regarded highly in the West did not do well financially in Korea. For instance, *Mandala* took in around 100,000 box office receipts in Seoul in its opening run. That was okay, but *Gilsottum* was also 100,000. *Surrogate Mother* was about 40,000. *The Hidden Hero* was ridiculously low, between 2,000 and 4,000. Foreign evaluations and the domestic box-office receipts don't correspond well. This disparity became more acute when actress Kang Su-yŏn, the star of *Surrogate Mother*, won an award in Venice, and the film was rereleased. But not many people went to see the film even then.

*Interviewers:* You mentioned earlier that *The Taebaek Mountains*, for instance, could not be made during the Roh Tae Woo administration, and its release only was possible during the civilian government. I think Korea is still in a transitional period from an authoritarian period to a democratic one. Just recently, film censorship was found unconstitutional. In times like these, what political issues influence your film production?

*Im Kwon-Taek:* Even when *The Taebaek Mountains* was being made during the civilian rule, our film production was constantly under rightist surveillance. The intelligence agency and the police did not openly prohibit the film's production, but they always let us know that we were being watched. Every time we woke up in the morning, we would see the police cars in front of our camp, having spent the whole night there. After the film was completed, it proved to be unsatisfying for both left-oriented people and right-oriented people, all of whom questioned its ending. I spent my youth as a member of a leftist family, and I've asked myself why I've had to live a painful and repressed life, and what the origin of my sufferings was. The competition among the superpowers in the war was one answer. Ideology is another. The nation was not prepared for either communism or the democratic system. Capital was not yet systematic, and not capable of either large-scale accumulation or exploitation of the workers. But the sudden liberation from the colonial period and from the Chosŏn-period feudalism allowed communism to fall suddenly into our laps. But the people hadn't demanded it after identifying the contradictions in the previous system. Communist ideology just fell upon us, and if its objective is to allow people to live as people, why did it involve so much sacrifice from us? The guerrilla war in the mountains was so hideous that we were torn apart and have become bitter enemies. But people who pursue ideological goals can never be derailed. Even in capitalist countries, it's the same. If there are any barriers blocking the objectives of capitalism, they must be eliminated, and victims are produced. Humans cannot be sacrificed, even to attain an ideologically ideal world. I made *Fly High, Run Far* from such a position, that people should not be used as tools in the name of ideology. When I was little, some of my younger cousins participated in the guerilla movement; they were made to kill people using bamboo spears and later bragged about it.

*Interviewers:* In *Fly High, Run Far* and *Gilsottum* you demonstrate sympathy toward the peasants and lower class. Then doesn't this sympathy, if interpreted ideologically, suggest that you may be closer to the left than the right?

*Im Kwon-Taek:* Now communism has revealed its contradictions, even though some people still believe the socialist paradigm is ideal. Most people now are placing their faith in democracy. Whether this promises a new future, I am not so sure, but at least democracy involves self-determination rather than having others determine choices for you. We have to create a framework in which humans respect humans. The religion of Tonghak [the Eastern Learning], as shown in my film *Fly High, Run Far*, accepts all beings as god and respects them all. Isn't this democratic, I wonder? This is what I argue, not a simple leftist-orientation.

Emphasizing the need we have to respect each other preoccupies my thoughts. That's why in *The Taebaek Mountains* I cannot accept either side. I have also been criticized heavily for *Fly High, Run Far*. Critics interrogated the extent of my focus on the life of Ch'oe Hae-wŏl [the leader of the Tonhak religion], not on the Peasant Uprising itself. But it was never my point to deal with the rebellion. Rather I saw the utility of Tonghak as the antithesis of Western thought, of Christianity. Tonghak as a religion was based on democratic principles, claiming that humans are heaven themselves. That is a very significant principle for our times, yet our ancestors had already foregrounded this democratic religion over 100 years ago. Of course, it is true that the Peasant Uprising, along with the corrupt bureaucracy and the effect of foreign influences, is significant. But I thought the religious spirit of Tonghak was far more important. And that was scandalous for the critics.

*Interviewers:* As Korea became industrialized, there were many interesting novels and essays about contemporary working-class life. Why have you not featured them much in your films?

*Im Kwon-Taek:* Conglomerates like Hyundai enjoy great government privileges while eating away at the wages of the workers. If you focus on the exploited workers, then the employers become the target of criticism. But I had opportunities to travel abroad during the difficult period, and I saw that Hyundai products were publicizing Korea, facilitating national growth, and making great contributions to the whole country. Our conglomerates are now targets of much criticism. But looking from the outside, their contribution to Korea cannot be underestimated. We were in a period of an anomaly that had to be overcome. But which side should I have been on? I thought that this subject could be better handled by younger colleagues since it was rather ambiguous for me.

*Interviewers:* What is the position from which you go back to Korean history? By making historical films, do you tell stories of our society today? Or do you make them to preserve the history we are forgetting?

*Im Kwon-Taek:* Films could serve the function of preservation, I guess. Could we talk about this using *Surrogate Mother*? Why do we need such representations today? For example, I am the first son in the family, but there is a conflict between my mother and me, because my mother thinks that I won't pay attention to the ancestor worshipping rituals when she passes away. Even though I am responsible while she is alive, my going around making movies and giving them more attention than our ancestors is a potential crisis. Our lifestyle today is such that we can't possibly give as much care as they did in the old days, but my mother still insists I give more. So we still face very traditional questions, and even now there are incredible efforts to have a male child, creating scandals with the doctors and so on. We create massive movements all over the nation around New Year's Day and Autumn Harvest Day, when an estimated twenty million people return to their original homes, to meet their ancestors and to perform the rituals according to the Confucian framework. There is nothing in Confucianism that stipulates itself as a religion except its emphasis on self-restraint and education—and filial piety. The requirement that the descendants guard the parents' graves for three years without doing much else is a religious concept. Three years to demonstrate filial gratitude, that's a scary thing about our national identity. And it's not simply the powers above that force us to place so much emphasis on worshiping ancestors. When people die, they become gods to us, and we think that if we obey them well, we will be blessed. There is no way for us to say, "It's over when we are dead." The ones who live and the ones who die cannot easily be separated. This is why our nation goes through massive migration

[during the holidays] and prefers male children. How could we not
think that we need a film like *Surrogate Mother*?

*Interviewers:* Do you then think that there are problems with our
national feudal traditions?

*Im Kwon-Taek:* I think there are many problems. I made *Surrogate
Mother* in that belief. I thought that the story of one woman being
unjustly sacrificed to bear a son could be used as an element of
resistance. But, three years after the film, I told a foreign critic that
the film might have been a mistake because I had criticized the
process of acquiring a son in exchange for the human sacrifice of
a surrogate. I changed my position since the film. Why is that the
case? In Korea, we intermix Buddhism with Shamanism and so on,
but I had judged other people's religious principles by my own
logic. How could I arrogantly make a film and make precipitous
statements when the nation itself already has that kind of complex
religious mentality? Similarly in *Festival*, I attempted to display how
comical our funeral process is.

*Interviewers:* The fact that it is complicated and cumbersome?

*Im Kwon-Taek:* It's not that it's cumbersome but that it lacks any logic
and is full of contradictions. Traditional Korean religion is made up
of Shamanism, Confucianism, Buddhism, and some Taoism. The
Confucian philosophy insists that when people die, spirit and flesh
become divided. Flesh returns to nature when the body decomposes
in the grave, and the spirit lives with us for four generations. But
in Buddhism, when people die, a messenger comes and Yama, the
king of Hell, then determines whether you belong in hell or nirvana.
Shamanism is different again. The function of Shamans is to heal
the sick and send the bad spirits of the dead to heaven, so that they
don't haunt the living people. Whether they go to heaven or not
is beside the point. But in our religion, as you can see in *Festival*
when a character climbs up the roof, he calls out, asking the spirit to
come back and live again. This must be Confucian since according

to Shamanism, spirits should not come back. Then there's a part that concerns Buddhism. For the three messengers who have come to take away the dead, we must prepare three rice bowls, three pairs of shoes—I guess heaven is that far away—and traveling money. But if the dead is taken away, that should be the end of it. But no, they break the rice bowls, preventing the return of the dead spirit. This is Shamanism. Then, after the burial, they carry the ancestor tablet back home. According to Buddhism, the spirit that should have been sent away is carried back into the house. And finally, breaking the gourd while carrying away the dead body is a Shamanist act, to ban the dead from returning home. Nothing works logically here.

*Interviewers:* Because the three religions are mixed together?

*Im Kwon-Taek:* Every possible good deed for the dead is done, whether or not it makes sense. I am not being critical, but I am dealing with the subject with the mentality that if we are really concerned with the funeral, then perhaps there could be a change in the social consensus. I think if we use the film to get a "close-up" on the contradictory elements, we could change things that need repair.

*Interviewers:* There have been some criticisms of *Sopyonje*. From feminist perspectives some people have pointed out that Yu-bong's blinding of Song-hwa is legitimized and the film ends too ambivalently. What do you think?

*Im Kwon-Taek:* I am aware of that concern. I argue that you should not see *Sopyonje* as a film that exploits women. The reason I made a film about *p'ansori* was because our culture was being toppled by Western culture. Since the Japanese colonial period, our culture has been delegated to the lower class and often regarded as trash. Even I—who since 1978 or 1979 had been thinking of making a film about *p'ansori*—would switch to other channels when it was on television, searching for something more entertaining. To demonstrate that our beautiful and moving *p'ansori* is as great as—if not superior to—any other music, was my first objective. Then the question is how to interpret the characters, especially Yu-bong. When our life becomes economically sound and prosperous, our values change, and when life is hard, then our objectives also change. For Yu-bong, training his voice to achieve excellence is the most important objective in his life, and if that's not possible, he wants to do it through someone else. From the perspective of Yu-bong, looking at his child Song-hwa, he thinks that even for her the greatest value in life must be singing a great song. He thinks that whatever the sacrifice, if Song-hwa can acquire an extraordinary voice, then she will be happy. Of course, this is stubbornness and egotism, especially since it entails the abuse of a human being in pursuing its objective, and he is an egotistical bastard. After Song-hwa's brother runs away, he is worried that she might also run away. Therefore he decides to believe the myth that the *han* entailed in losing one's sight allows one to acquire a great voice. He doesn't know whether this is true or not, but his worry that she may run away and his greed as a man force him to trap her, and so Yu-bong is not a great person. In my films, sometimes there are saints like Ch'oe Hae-wŏl and Ch'oe Si-hyŏng in *Fly High, Run Far,* but most are ordinary people who make us wonder if we would have done the same thing. Yu-bong's not an ideal figure, and I don't want it to be thought that because he blinded her, men are superior. Human beings are full of contradictions and ironies. Sound was also another thing to consider. In the section where she sings the part of Simch'ŏng, who goes around begging for rice in the shabby house, the poverty delivered through the song and the images only makes the song more convincing. In *Sopyonje,* the most important objective was visually to complement the beauty of the singing and transfer it to the audience clearly.

*Interviewers:* You have made two films that have explicitly dealt with Buddhism: *Mandala* and *Come, Come, Come Upward.* What attracted you to this religion?

*Im Kwon-Taek:* I shot *Mandala* thinking how beautiful it is to live with intensity. In filming it, I found a little more about the worldview of the monks, which led me to the next project, *Come, Come, Come Upward*.[4] The Buddhism Korea accepted was the Mahayana sect, whose objective is to bring ordinary people to enlightenment. Many monks, however, do not follow the precepts of Mahayana Buddhism and communicate it to ordinary people. They live as Hinayana hermits in the mountains. If reality is painful for most people, then it is necessary to share ordinary people's pain and struggle by following Mahayana Buddhism. I made *Come, Come, Come Upward* to ask how the monks could separate themselves from ordinary life and follow Hinayana Buddhist ways.

*Interviewers:* You stressed earlier that it is necessary to search for Korea's unique style. How do you imagine this unique Korean style? When you prepare for the film set and composition, what kind of model do you have in mind?

*Im Kwon-Taek:* Overall, I think, it is achieved by placing our life and emotions in the film frame. It's changed now, but Koreans differ from Westerners in not being too oriented toward movement. Our world is not one of action but of emotions. For instance, when happiness, anger, sadness, or joy are experienced, we do not express our emotions explicitly like Westerners do. Initially, Koreans live in a world of inner emotions rather than one based on physical movement. Within the frame, we focus on human emotions, but something that is totally dramatic is already a distortion. In *Festival* and others of my films, there are spaces that are vacant. That space is filled by the audiences who watch my films. For instance, in our Eastern philosophy, emptiness is as such [pointing at a glass of water on the table]. It's no use if the glass is full, but if it is empty it's more useful. In American cinema, everything is filled so perfectly, and so much force of movement is exerted.

*Interviewers:* Could I ask you a question on cinematography? I think Chŏng Il-sŏng especially demonstrates the use of diverse styles.

*Im Kwon-Taek:* For me, it doesn't matter who actually shoots the film. After all, when we make films, we first decide on what kind of story to tell, complete the continuity script, and plan the images, so it's all predetermined. It's not as if the cinematographer could choose to do this or that otherwise. Of course, there may be differences between the director's opinions and the cinematographer's, but in my case that is rare. There might be a compromise about whether to use 50mm lens or 85mm lens, but nothing else can be changed by the cinematographer, especially if the script is perfectly ready.

*Interviewers:* Film historians are interested in what has influenced you. When you were young, were there particular styles that inspired you?

*Im Kwon-Taek:* Growing up, I wasn't in the environment where I could watch many movies. I only began working in the film industry in order to survive during the postwar period. Once working in film, naturally I watched all the films that were imported. And I think that influences were there, but mostly I learned the craft directly from the production set.

*Interviewers:* From *Farewell to the River Tuman* in 1962 to *Festival* this year, you have been in filmmaking for a long time. Could you tell us about the changes in your career?

*Im Kwon-Taek:* There have been some changes. For instance, I criticized myself for my excessive production of low-budget films, so then I produced more art-oriented films. I think that at one point the part of me that had pursued entertainment values had become so completely dominant that I had to purge myself, or undergo a process of emptying out, since it was influencing even the serious work I was doing. That process took me ten years, with *The Hidden Hero* marking the pinnacle; and even for me, that film was uninteresting. So next I decided that I could not make films that lacked flesh and blood, ones that would be completely neglected by the spectators, so I gave myself a little more freedom from my self-restraint. Then, during the next stage, I tried to engage the social climate. Now, getting older and looking back, I realize that life looks different as you age, and it may be that I have made films that reflect the changes that come with age.

*Interviewers:* Is there one of your films that is most characteristic of you?

*Im Kwon-Taek:* I usually think I have no representative film. Once one of my films is in the can, I can't bring myself to watch it again. It's so painful, since I only notice the things that didn't work. But at one point everyone thought that *Mandala* was my representative work, so I said that must be so. When someone else talked about *Gilsottum* the same way, I agreed again. But with *Sopyonje,* it's a different story. I don't think *Sopyonje* is especially excellent, but an extraordinary number of spectators found it interesting, and the culture shock was so great that I considered *Sopyonje* to be my representative film, regardless of its quality. From *Sopyonje* onward, I focused more on the social contribution my films could make. Then with *Festival,* I began to think that my representative film could only be my latest.

*Interviewers:* The critic Chung Sung-Ill once stated that each one of your films realizes a new look, a new style. What do you think?

*Im Kwon-Taek:* I always think that I have to go beyond the framework that I had. But it's not that easy. It's always painful and I don't know whether it always works.

*Interviewers:* I know that you have only recently seen Mizoguchi's films, yet in the West you are always asked about your relationship to Mizoguchi. Couldn't we say that it's not Im Kwon-Taek who has been influenced by Mizoguchi, but Mizoguchi who has been influenced by Im Kwon-Taek?

*Im Kwon-Taek:* How can that be? Mizoguchi came first!

*Interviewers:* Well, it was suggested during the conference that Mizoguchi was influenced by Japanese art, which was transmitted through Korea, so the aesthetic style of Mizoguchi is unthinkable without the influence of Korean art. Then, couldn't it be said that you are his "sŏnbae," his senior?

*Im Kwon-Taek:* It only makes sense if it's Korea that is the influence, but not Im Kwon-Taek. But beyond that, couldn't we claim that there is common Eastern sensibility? It's true that when I saw Mizoguchi's films, I was surprised to find similarities in them with images that I had envisioned. I was delighted, and the films didn't turn me off. It was like finding an old friend, feeling that our tastes are so similar. It needs to be pointed out that he made those remarkable films in the 1950s.

*Interviewers:* What films did you watch?

*Im Kwon-Taek:* I saw *Life of Oharu* (*Saikaku ichidai onna*) and *The Tale of the Late Chrysanthemums* (*Ugetsu Monogatari*). Watching these films, I realized that the Mizoguchi angles and the overall flow of his films embody the rigidity of the samurai spirit. I don't make films that carry that feeling, so that would undoubtedly be a difference between us.

*Interviewers:* In *The General's Son,* I felt the rigidity of samurai spirit a little bit.

*Im Kwon-Taek:* I really didn't want to make *The General's Son.* But I was really tied up until I finished *Come, Come, Come Upward.* I felt the pressure to win an award at one of those damn festivals, but things were not exactly working out that way. Time kept passing by. Then producer Yi T'ae-wŏn [of Taehung Production] suggested that I rest a year or two, but meantime he proposed *The General's Son* project. At the time, no one had remembered that I was an action film director in the 1960s.

*Interviewers:* Could you still remember in the 1980s how action films worked?

*Im Kwon-Taek:* At the time, there hadn't been many Korean action films. After I received that proposal, I thought it made sense to rest a bit, but I also wanted to explore how the 1960s action director had changed with age and with the shift to greater production budgets. I was a little scared, thinking that I could perhaps only make the 1960s kind of action dramas. To compensate for what I feared might be a haggard 1960s style, I decided to make the film with completely new actors rather than using the well-known action film actors. When I finished making *The General's Son,* I thought that perhaps I had more talent for entertaining action dramas like it than for serious films.

*Interviewers:* Speaking of action films, here we talk a lot about John Ford. Do you remember watching John Ford movies?

*Im Kwon-Taek:* I saw many of his films. At the time, I saw every film that was imported, and his were the most entertaining. I also liked how in his case the enormity of the epic narrative and landscapes drives the whole movie.

*Interviewers:* Do you find that the gigantic scale of Ford's landscapes influenced some of your films like *Mandala?*

*Im Kwon-Taek:* I think that I have been more heavily influenced by American than by European films. I don't know whether there are similarities between our lives and Italians', but I found Fellini's *La Strada* quite interesting. But the influences of the American cinema are so huge and unremitting that I thought that the only way I could survive and think of myself as a true director was by escaping them. But how to escape, and how to make new films, I didn't know.

*Interviewers:* There's a popular saying in Korea now that the profit generated by *Jurassic Park* exceeds the profit made from exporting Hyundai cars.

*Im Kwon-Taek:* I don't think *Jurassic Park* just fell from the skies one day. In order to make the film, large investments had to have been made over time, and I guess it's good that it generated that much profit with special effects. But that world is so different from the one that I pursue. I saw *Jurassic Park* only on video. These days I don't watch many films. I saw *ET*, but I could not really get into it since it creates a world that is too removed from our lives and reality. But with *Schindler's List*, I was really surprised to find that the same director could also be so good and serious.

*Interviewers:* Lastly, how would you define your world?

*Im Kwon-Taek:* I don't know whether I have a world of my own. Getting old, I don't have anything else I can do other than make movies. I will make movies—I don't know how many—until I die. Since film as a medium needs to help people to make better lives, one needs to find a way to feature the way to live a better life in film, and record better lives on film. I think cinema should contribute to making society brighter and healthier. So displaying on film what we have suffered from, the problems that need to be thought about and solved, those are the kinds of films I would like to make.

# Notes

1. Im was interviewed in Los Angeles at the University of Southern California on November 3, 1996, by Hyun-Ock Im, David E. James, and Kyung Hyun Kim.

2. This is the name change promulgation (*ch'angssi kaemyŏng*) ordered by the Japanese colonial government in 1939, requiring that all Korean names be changed to Japanese.

3. Shin Sang-ok and Yu Hyŏn-mok are two of the most representative directors of the Golden Age of Korean cinema, which began in 1955 and lasted until 1974. See chapter 1 in this volume for more information about this period.

4. *Piguni,* another Buddhist film proposed by Im Kwon-Taek—starring Kim Chi-mi in the title role and scheduled to be produced in 1983—was aborted when its casting of a female in the role of a Buddhist monk generated intense protests.

# Korea: Political and Cultural Events, 1876 to 2000

| Sociopolitical History | | Film History | |
|---|---|---|---|
| 1876 | Kanghwa Treaty | | |
| 1894–95 | Tonghak Uprising | | |
| 1895 | Sino-Japanese War; Shimonoseki Treaty | | |
| | | 1899 | First films shot and screened in Korea by Burton Holmes |
| | | 1903 | First public film screening announced in a newpaper (*Hwangsŏng sinmun*) |
| | | 1903 | Tongdaemun Motion Picture Studio (Tongdaemun hwaldong sajinso), the first motion picture theater in Korea, opens |
| 1905 | Russo-Japanese War; under Taft-Katsura Agreement, Korea becomes a protectorate of Japan | | |
| | | 1907 | Tansŏngsa opens, later renovated in 1918 as a theater devoted to film exhibition |

|       |                                        | 1909 | Recorded on film: King Kojong surveying downtown Seoul and Prince Yŏngch'inwang studying in Japan |
|-------|----------------------------------------|------|
| 1910  | Korea formally annexed by Japan        |      | |
| 1919  | March 1st Movement                     | 1919 | *Just Revenge* (*Ŭirijŏk kut'u*, prod. by Kim To-san and Pak Sŭng-p'il), the first *shinp'a* (*shimp*a) theater/film, opens in Tansŏngsa |
| 1922  | Yi Kwang-su's "A Treatise on National Reconstruction" published | 1923 | *National Boundary* (*Kukkyŏng*, prod. by Kim To-san), the first film entirely made by Koreans |
| 1925  | Peace Preservation Law                 | 1926 | Na Un-gyu directs *Arirang* |
|       |                                        | 1926 | Japanese colonial government announces the Motion Picture Censorship Guidelines |
| 1927  | The founding of Sin'ganhoe (New Korea Society) | | |
|       |                                        | 1930 | Film department established within KAPF (Korean Proletariat Artists' Federation); Seoul Kino and Pyongyang Kino, other leftist collectives, begin producing films |
| 1931  | Seizure of Manchuria by the Japanese Kwangtung army | | |
|       |                                        | 1935 | First Korean talkie, *The Story of Chunhyang*, appears |
|       |                                        | 1937 | Na Un-gyu dies |
| 1938  | Mass army recruitment of Koreans       |      | |
| 1939  | Promulgation of the Name Order, requiring Koreans to change their names to Japanese forms | 1939 | Release of *Military Train* (*Kunyong yŏlch'a*), first Korean film to openly support the Japanese war effort |
|       |                                        | 1940 | Korean Film Decree requires all Korean films to endorse the Japanese imperial system and its military actions |
| 1945  | Liberation of Korea                    |      | |
| 1945–48 | U.S. Military Government Rule         |      | |

1950    Outbreak of the Korean War
1953    Cease-fire signed by North
        Korea and the U.S.


1960    April 19th Revolution
1961    Military coup d'état, led by
        Park Chung Hee

1965    Normalization of diplo-
        matic relations between
        South Korea and Japan
1965    South Korea enters the
        Vietnam War
1970    Chŏn T'ae-il, a labor union
        martyr, immolates himself
1971    New Village (*Saemaŭl*)
        Movement launched
1972    Yushin Constitution
        approved
1975    Ban announced on any
        criticism of the president or
        of the Yushin Constitution
1979    Park Chung Hee assassinated
1980    Second military coup d'état,
        led by Chun Doo Hwan
1980    Kwangju Massacre: popular
        uprising for democracy
        quelled violently, estimated
        2,000 civilians killed

1946    U.S. Military Government
        in Korea announces a
        new Motion Picture Law,
        allowing film censorship to
        continue
1955    *Story of Chunhyang* and
        *Madame Freedom* released,
        ushering in "the Golden Age
        of Korean Cinema"
1962    First Motion Picture Law
        established by the South
        Korean government

1973    Fourth Amendment of the
        Motion Picture Law passes,
        centralizing the Korean film
        industry and ending the era
        of "the Golden Age"

1982    Seoul Film Collective, a
        student underground film
        organization, established;
        members include Park
        Kwang-su and Chang Sŏn-u,
        key figures of "the New
        Korean Cinema"
1986    Sixth Amendment of the
        Motion Picture Law passed
        by Congress, allowing the
        U.S. to directly distribute its
        films in Korea

|      |      |      |      |
|------|------|------|------|

1986    *P'arangsae* (*Bluebird*)
        Incident: trial of two
1987  June Uprising, demanding           filmmakers of an 8mm
      direct election of president       documentary protest film
                                         in court for violating the
                                         Motion Picture Law
1988  Seoul Olympics          1988  First Hollywood film
                                    distributed by an American
                                    company opens in Korea
                              1990  *Night Before the Strike,* a
1992  Kim Young-sam elected as        labor underground film, is
      the new president               released, causing a sensation
                              1993  *Sopyonje* sets new box-office
                                    record
1996  Ex-military presidents Chun   1996  Korean court rules that the
      Doo Hwan and Roh Tae-               current censorship practice is
      woo charged with Kwangju            unconstitutional
      massacre, coup d'état, and    1996  First international film
      corruption; both found              festival held in Pusan with
      guilty                              great fanfare
1997  International Monetary Fund
      bails out Korean economy;
      Kim Dae Jung, the first
      opposition leader, elected to
      office
1997  Censorship ruled
      unconstitutional; Korean     1999  *Shiri* (dir. Kang Che-gyu)
      Public Performance Ethics          sets a new box-office record
      Committee (censorship
      board) is renamed
2000  First summit between North
      Korea and South Korea held
      in Pyongyang

APPENDIX 2

# Im Kwon-Taek: Filmography

| | | |
|---|---|---|
| 1962 | Farewell to the Duman River | Tumangang a chal ikkǒra |
| | Old Man in the Combat Zone | Chǒnjaeng kwa noin |
| 1963 | Actors Disguised as Women | Namja nǔn an p'allyǒ |
| | A Wife Turned to Stone | Mangbusǒk |
| | The Throne Memorial Drum | Sinmungo |
| 1964 | The Prince's Revolt | Tanjangnok |
| | The End of Desire | Yongmang ǔi kyǒlsan |
| | Father of Ten Daughters | Sipchamae sǒnsaeng |
| | The Latecomer | Tangol chigaksaeng |
| | The Ten-Year Rule | Simnyǒn sedo |
| | Queen Yonghwa's Avenger | Yǒnghwa mama |
| 1965 | Death of an Informer | Pitsok e chida |
| | A Bogus Nobleman | Wang kwa sangno |
| 1966 | Schoolmistress on the Battlefield | Chǒnjaeng kwa yǒgyosa |
| | Miss Ok and the Divided Court | Pǒpch'ang ǔl ullin ogi |
| | I Am a King | Na nǔn wang ida |
| | A Triangle in Noble Families | Nilliri |
| 1967 | The Feudal Tenant | Ch'ǒngsa ch'orong |
| | Swordsmen | P'ungun ǔi kǒmgaek |
| | A Wife Retrieved | Manghyang ch'ǒlli |

| 1968 | The Vamp Chang Huibin | Yohwa Chang Hŭibin |
|------|----------------------|---------------------|
|      | A Man Called the Wind | Param kwa kat'ŭn sanai |
|      | The Walking Woman | Mongnyŏ |
|      | Return from the Sea | Toraon oensonjabi |
| 1969 | Escape from Shanghai | Sanghae t'alch'ul |
|      | Full Moon Night | Siboya |
|      | Three Generations of Men | Sanai Samdae |
|      | Thunder Sword | Noegŏm |
|      | Eagle of the Wilderness | Hwangya ŭi toksuri |
|      | Would You Help Me? | Sinse chom chijaguyo |
|      | Best Friends and Their Wives | Pinari nŭn Komoryŏng |
| 1970 | Swords under the Moon | Wŏlha ŭi kŏm |
|      | One-eyed Mr. Park | Aekkunun Pak |
|      | Unmarried Mother | Isŭlmannŭn paegilhong |
|      | A Vagabond's Story | Pinaerinŭn sŏnch'angga |
|      | A Woman Pursued | Kŭ yŏja rŭl tchoch'ara |
|      | Hidden Investigator | Pamch'a ro on sanai |
|      | The Flying Sword | Pigŏm |
|      | A Snapshot and a Murder | Songnunssŏp i kin yŏja |
| 1971 | Snowing on Grudge Street | Wŏnhan ŭi kŏri e nun i naerinda |
|      | The 30-Year Showdown | Samsimnyŏn manŭi taegyŏl |
|      | Revenge of Two Sons | Wŏnhan ŭi tu kkopch'u |
|      | In Search of the Secret Agent | Na rŭl tŏ isang koerop'iji mara |
|      | Swordswoman | Yogŏm |
|      | A Stepmother's Heartache | Tultchae ŏmŏni |
|      | Gangsters of Myongdong | Myŏngdong samgukchi |
| 1972 | Cruelty on the Streets of Myongdong | Myŏngdong chanhoksa |
|      | Arrivals and Departures | Toraon cha wa ttŏnaya hal cha |
|      | Seize the Precious Sword | Samguktaehyŏp |
| 1973 | Five Hostesses for the Resistance | Kisaeng O Paek'wa |
|      | Pursuit of the Bandits | Tae ch'ugyŏk |
|      | The Deserted Widow | Chapch'o |
|      | The Testimony | Chŭngŏn |
| 1974 | Wives on Parade | Anaedŭl ŭi haengjin |
|      | I'll Never Cry Again | Ulji anŭri |
|      | The Hidden Princess | Yŏnhwa |
|      | The Hidden Princess Part II | (Sok) Yŏnhwa |
| 1975 | Who and Why | Wae kŭraettŭnga |
|      | Yesterday, Today and Tomorrow | ŏje onŭl kŭrigo naeil |

| | | |
|---|---|---|
| 1976 | A Bygone Romance | Wangsimni |
| | Overcome by Misfortunes | Maenbal ŭi nunkkil |
| | Commando on the Nakdong River | Naktonggang ŭn hŭrŭnŭnga |
| | The Industrious Wife | Anae |
| 1977 | The Virtuous Woman | Ongnye gi |
| | Madam Kye in the Imjin War | Imjinnan kwa Kye Wŏl-hyang |
| 1978 | The Evergreen Tree | Sangnoksu |
| | The Little Adventurer | Chŏ p'ado wi e ŏmma ŏlgŭri |
| | The Genealogy | Chokpo |
| 1979 | Near Yet Far Away | Kakkapkodo mŏn gil |
| | Again Tomorrow | Naeil tto naeil |
| | The Divine Bow | Singung |
| | The Hidden Hero | Kippal ŏmnŭn kisu |
| 1980 | The Wealthy Woman | Pokpuin |
| | Pursuit of Death | Tchakk'o |
| 1981 | High School Tears | Usang ŭi nunmul |
| | Mandala | Mandara |
| 1982 | Abenko Green Beret | Abengo kongsu gundan |
| | The Polluted Ones | Oyŏmdoen chasiktŭl |
| | In the Bosom of a Butterfly | Nabi p'um esŏ urŏtta |
| | Village in the Mist | Angae maŭl |
| 1983 | Daughter of the Flames | Pul ŭi ttal |
| 1984 | The Eternal Flow | Hŭrŭnŭn kangmul ŭl ŏtchi magŭrya |
| 1985 | Gilsottum | Kilsottŭm |
| 1986 | Ticket | T'ik'et |
| | Surrogate Mother | Ssibaji |
| 1987 | Diary of King Yonsan | Yŏnsan ilgi |
| 1988 | Adada | Adada |
| 1989 | Come, Come, Come Upward | Aje aje para aje |
| 1990 | The General's Son | Changun ŭi adŭl |
| 1991 | The General's Son II | Changun ŭi adŭl II |
| | Fly High, Run Far: Kaebyŏk | Kaebyŏk |
| 1992 | The General's Son III | Changun ŭi adŭl III |
| 1993 | Sopyonje | Sŏp'yŏnje |
| 1994 | The Taebaek Mountains | T'aebaek sanmaek |
| 1996 | Festival | Ch'ukche |
| 1997 | Chang the Prostitute | Nonŭn kyejip, ch'ang |
| 2000 | Chunhyang | Ch'unhyang dyŏn |

# Selected English Language Bibliography of Korean Cinema

## Books and Articles

Armes, Roy. "The Newly Industrializing Countries." In *Third World Film Making and the West*, 154–56. Berkeley: University of California Press, 1987.

Bae, Chang-ho. "Seoul in Korean Cinema: A Brief Survey." *East-West Film Journal* 3, no. 1 (December 1988): 97–104.

Berry, Chris. "My Queer Korea: Identity, Space and the 1998 Seoul Queer Film and Video Festival." *Intersections* 2 (May 1999) [on-line journal]. Available from http://www.she.murdoch.edu.au/hum/as/intersections/

Ehrlich, Linda C. "Why Has Bodhi-Dharma Left for the East?" (film review). *Film Quarterly* 48, no. 1 (Fall 1994): 27–32.

Kim, Kyung Hyun. "The Fractured Cinema of North Korea: The Discourse of the Nation in *Sea of Blood*." In *In Pursuit of Contemporary East Asian Culture*, 85–106. Edited by Xiaobing Tang and Stephen Snyder. Boulder, Colo.: Westview Press, 1996.

Kim, So-Young. " 'Cine-Mania' or Cinephilia: Film Festivals and the Identity Question." *UTS Review* 4, no. 2 (1998): 174–87.

Kim, So-Young, and Chris Berry. " 'Suri suri masuri': The Magic of the Korean Horror Film: a Conversation." *Postcolonial Studies* 3, no. 1 (2000): 53–60.

Lee, Young-Il. *The History of Korean Cinema: Main Current of Korean Cinema*. Translated by Richard Lynn Greever. Seoul: Motion Picture Promotion Corporation, 1988.

Lent, John A. "South Korea." *The Asian Film Industry*, 122–45. Austin: University of Texas Press, 1990.

———. "Lousy Films Had to Come First." *Asian Cinema* 7, no. 2 (winter 1995): 86–92.

Leong, Toh Hai. "Postwar Korean Cinema: Fractured Memories and Identity." *Kinema* (fall 1996) [on-line journal]. Available from http://www.arts.uwaterloo.ca/FINE/juhde/kfall96.htm

Pok, Hwang-mo. "On Korean Documentary Film." *Documentary Box*. Yamagata City, Japan: Yamagata Documentary International Film Festival, 1999.

Rayns, Tony. "Cinephile Nation." *Sight and Sound* 8, no. 1 (January 1998): 24–27.

———. "Korea's New Wavers." *Sight and Sound* 4, no. 11 (November 1994): 22–25.

———. "Sexual Outlaws." *Sight and Sound* 10, no. 2 (February 2000): 26–28.

Rist, Peter. "An Introduction to Korean Cinema." *Offscreen* (1998) [on-line journal]. Available from http://www.horschamp.qc.ca/offscreen

Segers, Frank. "Korea Movies." *Hollywood Reporter*, April 18, 2000, 14–16.

Standish, Isolde. "Korean Cinema and the New Realism: Text and Context." In *Colonialism and Nationalism in Asian Cinema*, 65–89. Edited by Wimal Dissanayake. Bloomington: Indiana University Press, 1994,

Totaro Donato. "Sopyonje." *Offscreen* (May 3, 1999) [on-line journal]. Available from http://www.horschamp.qc.ca/offscreen

Wilson, Rob. "Filming 'New Seoul': Melodramatic Constructions of the Subject in *Spinning Wheel* and *First Son*." *East-West Film Journal* 5, no. 1 (January 1991): 107–17.

———. "Melodramas of Korean National Identity: From *Mandala* to *Black Republic*." In *Colonialism and Nationalism in Asian Cinema*, 90–104. Edited by Wimal Dissanayake. Bloomington: Indiana University Press, 1994.

## Film Festival Catalogs and Special Journal Volumes

Choi, Chungmoo, ed. *Post-Colonial Classics of Korean Cinema*. Irvine: Korean Film Festival Committee at the University of California, Irvine, 1997.

James, David E., and Hyun-Ock Im., eds. *Im Kwon-Taek: The Heart of Korean Cinema Film Festival*. Los Angeles: University of Southern California, 1996.

SELECTED BIBLIOGRAPHY 277

*Koreana* (special cinema issue) 3, no. 4 (1989). Seoul: Ministry of Culture and Information.

*Korean Culture* (special cinema issue) 17, no. 3 (Fall 1996). Los Angeles: Korean Cultural Center of the Korean Consulate General.

Lee, Yong-kwan, and Sang-yong Lee, eds. *Yu Hyun-Mok: The Pathfinder of Korean Realism.* Pusan: Fourth Pusan International Film Festival, 1999.

————, eds. *Kim Ki-young: Cinema of Diabolical Desire and Reason.* Pusan: Second International Film Festival, 1997.

Rayns, Tony. *Seoul Stirring: 5 Korean Directors.* London: Institute of Contemporary Arts, 1994.

Yi, Hyo-in, and Yi Chŏng-ha, eds. *Korean New Wave: Retrospectives from 1980 to 1995.* Pusan: First International Film Festival, 1996.

## Ph.D. Dissertations

Joo, Jinsook. "Constraints on Korean National Film: The Intersection of History, Politics and Economics in Cultural Production." University of Texas at Austin, 1990.

Kim, Hoonsoon. "An Orientation Toward Tradition in Contemporary Korean Film Narrative and Structure: A Study of a Western Medium Produced in a Non-Western Culture." Temple University, 1991.

Kim, Kyung Hyun. "The New Korean Cinema: Framing the Shifting Boundaries of History, Class, and Gender." University of Southern California, 1998.

## Korean Film Websites

Chonju International Film Festival. A festival focusing on digital and alternative cinema; inaugurated in 2000. Available from http://www.ciff.org/

The House of Kim Ki-young. Maintained by the Department of Cinema Studies at the Korean National University of Arts (KNUA). Dedicated to the study of the works of the late director Kim Ki-young. Available from http://www.knua.ac.kr/cinema/KKY/Open-Home/home%202.htm

Korean Film Commission. A governmental agency that promotes Korean films internationally. Available from http://www.kofic.or.kr/

The Korean Film Database. Maintained by the Korean Film Archive. Provides useful database resources in both English and Korean. Available from http://www.Koreafilm.or.kr

The Korean Film Page. Maintained by Darcy Parquet. Annual reviews, useful resources, and various links to Korean film organizations. Available from http://www.koreanfilm.org

Puchon International Fantastic Film Festival. Devoted to screening aesthetically
    diverse films; inaugurated in 1997. Available from http://www.pifan.or.kr/
Pusan International Film Festival. Korea's largest film festival, with a special
    focus on Asian cinema; inaugurated in 1996.
    Available from http://www.piff.org/

# Contributors

*Eunsun Cho* is a graduate student in the School of Cinema-Television at the University of Southern California. Her main interests are images of women in Korean cinema, the cinematic representation of Korean modernity, and the intercultural circulation of visual images and discourses.

*Cho Hae Joang* has a Ph. D. from UCLA and is a professor in the Department of Sociology at Yonsei University in Seoul. She has written numerous books, and her recent publications include a three-volume study of postcolonialism in South Korea, *T'al Sikminji Sidea-eu Keul Ilkgi-wha Salm Ilkgi* (*Reading Text and Reading Life in a Post-Colonial Age*), (Seoul: Ddo Hana-eu Munwha Publishers, 1992 and 1994).

*Chungmoo Choi* is director of Critical Theory Emphasis and associate professor at the University of California, Irvine. She teaches critical theory, cultural studies, and Korean culture and literature. She writes about postcoloniality and feminist issues in Korea. Her book *Frost in May: Decolonization and Culture in Korea* is forthcoming from Duke University Press. With Elaine H. Kim, she coedited *Dangerous Women: Gender and Korean Nationalism* (New York: Routledge, 1998) and also the catalogue for the exhibition "Post-Colonial Classics of Korean Cinema."

*Mison Hahn* teaches Korean language in the Department of East Asian Languages and Literatures, University of California, Irvine.

*David E. James* teaches in the School of Cinema-Television at the University of Southern California. His most recent book is *Power Misses: Essays Across (Un)Popular Culture* (London: Verso Books, 1996).

*Kyung Hyun Kim* is an assistant professor in the Department of East Asian Languages and Literatures at the University of California, Irvine. He is currently writing a book on Korean cinema and masculinity. He has also curated film exhibitions at the UCLA Film and Television Archive, the UCI Film and Video Center, the Korean Cultural Center at Los Angeles, and the Korean American Museum.

*Han Ju Kwak* is a graduate student at the School of Cinema-Television, University of Southern California. His main interest is cinematic representation in a sociohistorical context, particularly in contemporary Korea. He edited a book on cult film and co-translated Francois Truffaut's *Hitchcock* into Korean.

*Julian Stringer* lectures in the Institute of Film Studies at the University of Nottingham, England, and sits on the editorial board of *Scope: An Online Journal of Film Studies*. He is currently working on a study of the cultural politics of international film festivals.

*Yi Hyoin* lectures on film theory and Korean film history at several universities in Korea, including Kyung Hee University. His publications include *Hanguk yŏnghwa yŏksa kangŭi 1* (*Korean Film History Lectures*) (Seoul: Yiron kwa silch'ŏn, 1992) and *Yŏnghwa mihak kwa pip'yŏng ipmun* (*Introduction to Film Aesthetics and Criticism*) (Seoul: Hanyang University Press, 1999). He also writes film reviews for *Hangyoreh,* a progressive daily in Korea.

*Yuh Ji-Yeon* is an assistant professor of history at Northwestern University. Her research interests include Asian migration and diaspora. She is currently revising a manuscript about Korean military brides in the United States and working on a comparative study of Korean immigrants in China, Japan, and the United States.

# Index

Berlin Wall, 12
Berman, Marshall, 114
Berry, Chris, 157, 158
Bhabha, Homi K., concept of
"unhomely," 205, 206, 210
Bodhisattva, 71
Bodhisattva of Compassion, 65
Brocka, Lino, 36
Buddhism: dialectical logic, 47;
Korean, 60; and Korean cinema,
60–77, 81 n. 26; Mahayana, 60,
65. *See also* Són Buddhism

Cannes Film Festival, 15
Carter, Jimmy, 41 n. 9
Catholicism, 184
Celibacy, 61, 79 n. 17
Censorship, 12, 45 n. 33, 69, 121–22
Ceramics, 55
*Chaebols,* 14
*Chang, the Prostitute (Nonǔn kyejip,
Ch'ang)* (Im Kwon-Taek), 37–38,
39
Chang Kil-su: *Silver Stallion (Ǔnma
nǔn oji annǔnda),* 190, 198, 200,
201, 215, 219
Changsan'gonmae, 45 n. 33
Chang-sǒng, 24
Chang Sǒn-u, 36; *A Petal (Kkotnip),*
189
Chang Sǒn-u: *Road to the Racetrack
(Kyǒngmajang kanǔn kil),*
190
Chatterjee, Partha, 130, 170; *The
Nation and Its Fragments:
Colonial and Postcolonial
Histories,* 166
Cheil Jedang, 14
Chen Kaige, 158, 178, 252; *Yellow
Earth (Huang tudi),* 158

*Chilsu and Mansu* (Park Kwang-su),
23
Chinese Civil War, 21
Chinese films: ethnographic, 160;
Fifth Generation, 159; first film
made, 52; global attention, 252;
opera as stylistic resource, 52;
self-exoticism, 160
Cho, Fran, 81 n. 26
Cho Chǒng-nae: *Land of Exile
(Yuhyǒng ǔi ttang),* 197–98, 202,
249
Ch'oe Che-u, 184–85, 187, 190
Ch'oe Ha-rim, 125
Ch'oe Myǒng-hǔi: *The Soul Fire
(Honbul),* 117
Ch'oe Si-hyǒng, 185–86, 187, 188, 190,
191
Ch'oe ǔn-hǔi, 32
Chogye Order, 61, 79 n. 17
Cho Hǔi-mun, 40 n. 4
Choi, Chungmoo, 91, 170–71, 181 n.
14; *Dangerous Women,* 199
Chǒlla Province, 220 n. 2; in Korean
War films of 1990s, 200; as "land
of exile," 24; *p'ansori* in, 155 n.
20, 174; unfair treatment of, 221
n. 8
Chǒng Ch'ang-hwa, 25
Chǒng Chi-yǒng, 189
Chǒng Chi-yǒng: *The Southern Army
(Nambugun),* 189, 190, 199, 200,
201
Chǒng chung tong, 66
Chǒng Il-sǒng, 15, 65, 72, 80 n. 22,
260
Ch'ǒng-jun, 148
Chong Son, 80 n. 22
Chǒn Pong-jun, 188, 190, 191, 193, 195
n. 6

Red Sorghum (Hong gaoliang)
   (Zhang Yimou), 158
Reinhardt, Ad, 81 n. 26
Reproduction technology, 130
Rhee, Syng-man, 79 n. 16
Riefenstahl, Leni, 130
Road to the Racetrack (Kyŏngmajang
   kanŭn kil) (Chang Sŏn-u), 190
Robinson, Michael, 172
Rocha, Glauber, 36, 37, 45 n. 35
Roh Tae-woo, 79 n. 16, 195 n. 2, 249,
   253
Rosaldo, Renato, 127

Sadaejuŭi, 137, 154 n. 4
Said, Edward: Orientalism, 127
Samsara, 65
Samsung, 14
Samulnori (Kim Tŏk-su), 154 n. 5
Sangha, 71
Sato, Tadao, 77 n. 6
Schindler's List, 265
Schwartzenegger, Arnold, 34
Scientism, 113
Sea of Blood (P'ibada), 117
Sembene, Ousmane, 36, 37
Semiotic, 105 n. 8
Seung Sahn, 83 n. 29
Seven Female Prisoners (7 in ŭi
   yŏp'oro) (Yi Man-hŭi), 44 n. 27,
   199, 221 n. 6
The Seven Samurai, 148
Sexuality, and landscape, 68–69
Sexual transgression, 198–99, 206,
   210–15
Shamanism, 186, 228, 258
Shils, Edward, 225
Shin Hae-ch'ŏl, 152, 156 n. 26
Shinp'a (shimpa), 21, 41 n. 7, 112, 131
   n. 2
Shin Sang-ok, 24, 26, 27, 28, 32,

122, 137, 251, 265 n. 3; The Red
   Mufflers (Ppalgan mahura), 221
   n. 9
Shiri (Kang Che-gyu), 14–15, 16, 42
   n. 17, 42 n. 19, 51
Silhak, 184, 195 n. 3
Silla, 66
Silla unification, 60
Silverman, Kaja, 93
Silver Stallion (ŭnma nŭn oji
   annŭnda) (Chang Kil-su), 190,
   198, 200, 201, 215, 219
Sino-Japanese War, 195 n. 6
Sin Yun-bok, 78 n. 11, 80 n. 22; Women
   on Tano Day, 56–57
Small-film movement (chagŭn yŏngwa
   undong), 49
Sobaek Mountains, 24
Social critique films, 34
Socialist modernism, 51
Socialist realism, 51
Sŏhak, 195 n. 3
Solanas, Fernando, 45 n. 35
Sŏl Chinyŏng, 132 n. 12
Sŏn Buddhism, 71, 79 n. 15; dominant
   force in Korean Buddhism,
   60; lack of social engagement,
   64; meditational practice, 65;
   mountain/city binary, 66;
   opposition of natural world and
   sexuality, 61
Sŏnch'ŏn kaebyŏk, 185
The Son of Man (Saram ŭi adŭl) (Yu
   Hyŏn-mok), 32
Sopyonje (Sŏp'yŏnje) (Im Kwon-Taek),
   31, 52, 85, 183; as allegory of
   postcolonial nation, 113–21;
   as antinomian text, 181 n.
   14; bridging of local and
   international markets, 13–14;

*Surrogate Mother (Ssibaji)* (*continued*)
of woman, 58, 85; criticism of
Confucian patriarchy, 99; female
subject and parturition of
language, 96–103; fetishization
of woman, 98–99; nature
anthropomorphized into female
body, 97–98; orientalism, 151;
parturition, treatment of, 101–3;
reception in Korea, 253; still
photos, 97; as story of women's
*han*, 96; as study of working-class
exploitation, 69; woman as
symbol of working class, 59
*Swan Song (Juexiang)*, 179
Symbolic, 92–93, 105 n. 8

*The Taeback Mountains (T'aebaek
sanmaek)* (Im Kwon-Taek), 37,
183, 186, 188, 249; concept of
"unhomely," 205–6, 208–12, 219;
controversies surrounding, 23,
189, 190; erosion of boundaries
between public and private
spheres, 213; melodrama, 203–4;
and need to restore patriarchical
authority, 200–201; phallocentric
liberalism, 218–19; production
of, 221 n. 21, 253–54; sex as
destructive and deceptive
element, 198–99; sibling
animosity, 206–8; significance of
nighttime, 204–5; still photos,
203, 206, 207, 210; transgressive
sex, 206, 210–15; two versions of
family in, 215–16; women's guilt
for sexual transgression, 212–13;
women's retaliation, 222 n. 18
*T'aep'yŏngso*, 149, 155 n. 22
*T'alch'um* (mask dance), 100–103, 154
n. 5

*Tale of Ch'unhyang*, 56, 114, 118, 120,
153 n. 1
*Tale of Simch'ŏng*, 110–11, 120, 153 n. 1
*The Tale of the Late Chrysanthemums
(Ugetsu Monogatari)*, 263
*Tangun Ch'ŏnbukyŏng (The Celestial
Text of Tangun)*, 186
Tangun thought, 186
Taoism, 186, 193–94
Tarkovsky, Andrei, 36
Taussig, Michael, 130
Television, popularity of, 43 n. 22, 137
*The Testimony (Chŭngŏn)* (Im
Kwon-Taek), 122
*That Winter So Warm (Kŭ hae
kyŏul ŭn ttattŭthaetne)* (Pae
Ch'ang-ho), 199
Third Cinemas, 45 n. 35, 51
Third World cinema, 36
*Ticket (T'ik'et)* (Im Kwon-Taek), 37,
59–60, 179; brutalized heroines,
58; study of working-class
exploitation, 69
Toenjang, 154 n. 8
*To Live* (Zhang Yimou), 219–20
*Tong-a-Ilbo*, 37
Tonghak, 184–86, 190; central
principle of, 194; humanism, 192
Tonghak Peasant War, 190, 191, 195 n.
6, 255
Tongmulwŏn, 152
*Tongp'yŏnje*, 111, 155 n. 20, 174
*To the Starry Island (Kŭ sŏm e gago
sipta)* (Park Kwang-su), 49, 159,
200, 201–2
Tourism, 129, 130
Tradition: Im Kwon-Taek on, 256–57;
and loss and alienation, 226; and
mother, integrating power of,
236–38; relation to modernity,

225–26, 240; South Korean
attempt to revive, 149, 174–75
Tsui Hark: *Asia the Invincible*, 42 n.
19; *Once Upon a Time in China*,
42 n. 19
*Tǔgǔm*, 155 n. 10
Tǔlgukhwa, 152, 156 n. 26
*Two Stage Sisters*, 52

"Underground Village" (Kang
Kyǒng-ae), 116
United States: protest of Korean
screen quota, 44 n. 30; troops in
South Korea, 41 n. 9
University of Southern California, Im
retrospective, 9, 17 n. 1
Urbanization, 57
*Uri munhwa ch'atki* ("Searching for
our culture"), 152, 154 n. 5

Vietnam, 51
*Vinaya Pitaka*, 61
Vlastos, Stephen, 225

Whitney, James: *Yantra*, 81 n. 26
*Who and Why (Wae kǔraettǒnga)* (Im
Kwon-Taek), 28
*Why Has Bodhi-Dharma Left for
the East? (Dalma ga tongtchok
kǔro kan kkadakǔn)*, 79 n. 18,
151
*Wings (Nalgae)* (Yi Sang), 117
*The Wives on Parade (Anaedǔl ǔi
haengjin)* (Im Kwon-Taek), 122
*Woman Demon Human (Rengui
qing)*, 52, 179
Women: destructiveness of aesthetic
sublimation for, 88–90;
fetishization of, 98–99; as
ghosts, 106 n. 20; guilt for
sexual transgression, 212–13;

*han*, 88–89, 172; institutionalized
subordination to husband's
families, 88; landscape and, 56,
58, 59, 85–86, 90–91, 96–97;
retaliation, 222 n. 18; as symbols
of oppression of working class,
59; use of to represent violation
of nation, 58; victimized, 58, 85,
107–9, 216
*Women on Tano Day* (Sin Yun-bok),
56–57; still photo, 56–57
"Women's time," 106 n. 22
Wong Kar-Wai, 108
Wǒn-hyo, 66
Working class, use of women to
symbolize, 59
*Written on the Wind*, 204

Yanagi Soetsu (Yanagi Muneyoshi),
124–25, 126, 128, 132 n. 13;
"Thinking about the Korean
People," 125
Yanagita Kunio, 124
*Yanghang*, 184
*Yantra* (Whitney, James), 81 n. 26
*Yellow Earth (Huang tudi)* (Chen
Kaige), 158
Yi Ch'ang-dong: *Green Fish (Ch'orok
mulgogi)*, 159, 240–41
Yi Chang-ho, 28, 43 n. 23
Yi Chǒng-ha, 44 n. 28
Yi Ch'ǒng-jun, 148, 224
Yi In-won, 165
Yi Kwang-mo: *Spring in My
Hometown (Arǔmdaun sijǒl)*,
198, 201, 219, 221 n. 5
Yi Man-hǔi, 32, 199, 221 n. 7; *Seven
Female Prisoners (7 in ǔi yǒp'oro)*,
44 n. 27, 199, 221 n. 6
Yi P'il-je, 190
Yi Sang: *Wings (Nalgae)*, 117